THE RUSSIAN CIVIL WAR

Also by A. B. Murphy

ASPECTIVAL USAGE IN RUSSIAN
INTRODUCTION AND COMMENTARY TO SHOLOKHOV'S
  TIKHIY DON
MIKHAIL ZOSHCHENKO: A Literary Project

Also by G. R. Swain

EASTERN EUROPE SINCE 1945 (*co-author*)
THE ORIGINS OF THE RUSSIAN CIVIL WAR
RUSSIAN SOCIAL DEMOCRACY AND THE LEGAL LABOUR
  MOVEMENT, 1906–14

The Russian Civil War

Documents from the Soviet Archives

Edited by

V. P. Butt
Senior Scientific Collaborator
Institute of Russian History
Russian Academy of Sciences

A. B. Murphy
Professor Emeritus of Russian
University of Ulster

N. A. Myshov
Senior Scientific Collaborator and Chief Archivist
Russian State Military Archive

and

G. R. Swain
Professor of History
University of the West of England

First published in Great Britain 1996 by
MACMILLAN PRESS LTD
Houndmills, Basingstoke, Hampshire RG21 6XS
and London
Companies and representatives
throughout the world

A catalogue record for this book is available
from the British Library.

ISBN 0-333-59318-9 hardcover
ISBN 0-333-59319-7 paperback

First published in the United States of America 1996 by
ST. MARTIN'S PRESS, INC.,
Scholarly and Reference Division,
175 Fifth Avenue,
New York, N.Y. 10010

ISBN 0-312-16337-1

Library of Congress Cataloging-in-Publication Data
The Russian civil war : documents from the Soviet archives / edited by
V. P. Butt . . . [et al.].
 p. cm.
Includes bibliographical references and index.
ISBN 0-312-16337-1 (cloth)
1. Soviet Union—History—Revolution, 1917-1921—Sources.
I. Butt, V. P.
DK265.A5372   1996
947.084'1—dc20   96-19904
                                                                    CIP

Selection, editorial matter and translation © V. P. Butt, A. B. Murphy,
N. A. Myshov and G. R. Swain 1996

All rights reserved. No reproduction, copy or transmission of
this publication may be made without written permission.

No paragraph of this publication may be reproduced, copied or
transmitted save with written permission or in accordance with
the provisions of the Copyright, Designs and Patents Act 1988,
or under the terms of any licence permitting limited copying
issued by the Copyright Licensing Agency, 90 Tottenham Court
Road, London W1P 9HE.

Any person who does any unauthorised act in relation to this
publication may be liable to criminal prosecution and civil
claims for damages.

10 9 8 7 6 5 4 3 2 1
05 04 03 02 01 00 99 98 97 96

Printed in Great Britain by
The Ipswich Book Company Ltd
Ipswich, Suffolk

Contents

Introduction vii

Glossary of Russian Terms xvi

1 The Directory 1
2 The Don Rebellion 45
3 The Kaleidoscope of War 82
4 The Labour Armies of the Soviet Republic 124
5 The Final Curtain 175

Index 207

Introduction

For historians of Russia interested in the twentieth century it was until recently traditional to include in the preface to any book a disclaimer about the problems caused by the closure of the Soviet archives. For historians of the Russian Civil War such comments were *de rigueur*. Thus over twenty-five years ago John Bradley wrote in *The Civil War in Russia, 1917–20* (Batsford, 1975) that the Soviet Government's policy concerning the Russian archives meant 'nothing fresh and revealing can be expected from that source' (p. 7), while as late as 1990 Bruce Lincoln could bemoan in his *Red Victory* (Simon & Schuster, 1990) that 'parts of Russia's Civil War story will almost certainly never be told for the documents remain locked away in the Soviet archives' (p. 13). That has all changed. The opening of the Soviet archives in the years since Mikhail Gorbachev's term as President of the Soviet Union, and the subsequent collapse of the Soviet Union itself, have enabled scholars to gain new perspectives on the Russian Civil War.

The Civil War was a rather strange episode in the historiography of twentieth-century Russia. It saw an unlikely degree of agreement between Western and Soviet scholars on its origins and the reasons for the Bolshevik triumph. Whereas on most aspects of Russian history in the twentieth century Western and Soviet scholars took diametrically opposite views on how to interpret events, the Civil War period witnessed something quite different. Western and Soviet scholars were pretty much at one.

Take, for example, Bruce Lincoln's *Red Victory*. He writes in the preface (p. 12):

The Bolsheviks' desperate struggle to survive during the Russian Civil War shaped the Soviet system of government and dictated its future course. Only by placing all human and natural resources within reach at the service of a government that spoke in the name of the people but acted in the interest of the Communist Party did Lenin and his comrades defeat their enemies. These included soldiers from fourteen countries, the armed forces of nearly a dozen national groups that struggled to establish independent governments upon the lands that once had been part of the Russian Empire, and a half-dozen White armies that formed on Russia's frontiers between 1918 and 1920. To comprehend the Soviet Union of today, it is important to understand how the Bolsheviks triumphed against such crushing odds and how that struggle shaped their vision of the future.

Apart from the reference to the Communist Party, few Soviet scholars would have been unhappy with such a summary.

Of course, there have been differences of interpretation. Evan Mawdsley has done much in his definitive study, *The Russian Civil War* (Allen & Unwin, 1987), to qualify the received wisdom on a number of issues. In particular he had debunked the myth of the fourteen interventionist powers (foreign intervention was half-hearted and ineffective); he had made clear that the Red Army won not simply as a result of its military skill, but because it was far bigger than the White armies; and he had reminded us that, more than the Reds winning the Civil War, the Whites lost it since they represented nothing but the old pre-revolutionary ruling elite. But, with the honourable exception of Mawdsley, the differences between historians tend to be nuances within the same broad approach. For most, the Civil War was a heroic period in Russian history, before things started to go wrong, as it were. The Civil War took place before the emergence of Stalin as leader of the Russian Communist Party and saw Trotsky playing the leading role on the Bolshevik side in both building the Red Army and marshalling it towards victory. Progressive opinion in the West and Soviet propaganda could therefore be at one.

Among the points on which Western and Soviet scholars were agreed were the following. One, that the 'democratic' phase of the Civil War, over the summer of 1918, was a meaningless interlude; the only group capable of defeating the Bolsheviks were the White generals. The Bolsheviks' democratic opponents, if referred to at all, were depicted as ineffectual idealists who could talk but not fight. The true Civil War was fought between the Bolsheviks, who represented progress, and reactionary White generals, who were supported in their attempt to restore the old regime by the rampant imperialist ambitions of almost every conceivable European and world power. Another point of agreement was that the Bolsheviks, partly through their exceptional propaganda but also through their progressive social policies, succeeded in winning the hearts and minds of the bulk of the Russian population. And finally, it was agreed that, if a little brutally, Trotsky succeeded in turning the Red Army from a rabble to an incomparable fighting force.

All historians agree that, to paraphrase Bruce Lincoln, Russia's Civil War experience determined the framework within which the Russian people thought and governed throughout the Soviet period; what the newly released documents on the Civil War reveal is that the events of 1918–22 reflected struggles and tensions in Russian society far more complex than the simple Red–White struggle of 'progress' versus 'reaction', and foreshadow all the horrors of the Stalin period. They remind us first that many of the Whites were not 'White' at all, and that the Civil War began as a war between the Bolsheviks and their socialist opponents – the 'peasant' socialist SRs (Socialist Revolutionaries) – who did not simply talk but created the People's Army which at times had the Red Army on the run and always held its own. They show how the antipathy towards peasant socialism led the Bolsheviks to be suspicious of Russia's entire rural population, making it tremendously difficult to adopt a social policy in the countryside which could win even lukewarm support.

They show how this failing was linked to the Bolsheviks' essentially urban ideology, and how that ideology was central to Bolshevism. The first attempt at post-war reconstruction took place according to the dictates of Bolshevik ideology, and the firm conviction that world revolution was only a matter of months away. They show a regime founded on terror, and which relied on terror throughout the war. They show that while the Red Army was able to defeat the Whites, it was not the disciplined army of Bolshevik propaganda. Desertion, low morale and poor supplies dogged it at every level; and the much vaunted commissar system of political education scarcely operated. Finally, they show us the limitations and otherworldliness of the Bolsheviks' White opponents.

THE COURSE OF THE WAR

The Russian Civil War began the moment the Bolsheviks seized power on the night of 24–25 October 1917. Within a week forces loyal to Kerensky's Provisional Government tried to wrest power from the Bolsheviks at the Battle of Pulkovo Heights on the outskirts of Petrograd. Few, however, were keen for a fight and Lenin's promise to hold elections to the Constituent Assembly and form a coalition administration with the Left SRs was sufficient to restore relative calm. In the run-up to the opening of the Constituent Assembly the only forces committed to war were the future White generals, those associated with General Lavr Kornilov's attempt to seize power from Kerensky in August 1917; by December 1917 these had gathered on the river Don, but by February 1918 they were in full retreat to a safe area in the distant Kuban. These first armed incidents, however, did point to the two very different groups which were prepared to take up arms against the Bolshevik regime. Kerensky's supporters were SRs, fellow socialists committed to Russia's democratic revolution of February 1917; the White generals on the Don had no time for democracy, and while not all of them wanted to restore the Tsar's autocratic monarchy, all wanted a dictatorial regime of some sort.

Over the summer of 1918 it was the Bolsheviks' democratic opponents who were the first to take up arms. As democrats, the SRs were committed to the Constituent Assembly. Although infuriated by the Bolshevik decision to close the Assembly down after just one session on 5 January 1918, the SRs did not respond at once for they had reason to believe it might be recalled in the not-too-distant future. By the middle of May 1918, however, they had concluded that the recall of the Constituent Assembly was highly unlikely and decided to prepare for an armed insurrection to overthrow the Bolsheviks by force. Hardly had those preparations begun than the Allied Czechoslovak Legion, for its own reasons, turned against the Bolsheviks and rallied to the SR cause; in a matter of days in June 1918 the Bolsheviks lost control of most of the Volga basin and Siberia, and the Civil War proper had begun.

This stage of the Civil War was a war between socialists. The SRs established their own version of socialism in the areas they controlled and created a People's Army to defend it; the Bolsheviks defended their version of socialism with their Red Army. In August 1918 it looked as if the People's Army would triumph, particularly when Kazan fell on 8 August 1918. The Bolsheviks, however, lived to fight another day. Despite signing the Brest-Litovsk Treaty with Germany in March 1918, relations with Germany had remained so tense that the bulk of the Red Army had continued to be stationed in the west in case the Germans were tempted to overthrow the Bolshevik regime. However, on 10 August 1918 Lenin initialled a trade treaty with Germany and, confident that his relations with the Germans were now good, he moved as many troops as he possibly could to attack the People's Army and recapture Kazan in early September 1918. The People's Army was only just beginning to stage a comeback in November 1918 when the nature of the Civil War was changed forever.

On 18 November 1918 Admiral Kolchak seized power from the democratic administration established by Lenin's socialist opponents and established a military dictatorship in Siberia; from then on the Civil War would be a war between Red Bolsheviks and White Generals, a war between progress and reaction. At approximately the same time, the ending of the First World War meant that Allied intervention in the Civil War could be channelled through the Black Sea rather than arriving in Russia through the Arctic north or Far East. Thus when fighting resumed in the spring of 1919 it was the southern Russian front, where General Denikin had emerged as the dominant figure, which would be important in a way that it had never been in 1918.

The year 1919 saw the most dramatic of the fighting. It began with

Introductionxi

Kolchak's advance from Siberia in March, retaking Ufa and advancing to within less than a hundred miles of the Volga; but a Red counter-offensive started in April and by June Ufa had again changed hands. Although Kolchak staged a counter-offensive in September 1919, this failed; and by November 1919 his capital at Omsk had fallen to the Bolsheviks. At the very moment Kolchak began to retreat, Denikin began to make a dramatic advance from the south. The main focus of the Red Army had been the battle against Kolchak in the east, and the secondary campaign against Denikin had not been going well in the spring of 1919; repeated efforts in March, April and May 1919 had not resulted in the Bolsheviks extending their position on the Donets river. Then, in the most dramatic counter-attack, Denikin broke out and advanced within three weeks to Kharkov and beyond; on 30 June Tsaritsyn fell. As Denikin's troops advanced up the Volga, he made desperate efforts to co-ordinate activity with the retreating forces of Kolchak.

Denikin's failure to effect any substantive liaison with Kolchak saved the day for the Bolsheviks, but it was a close call. Their first counter-offensive of 15 August was unsuccessful, and although Denikin's advance had been temporarily stopped, he was able to launch a further offensive in September which captured Kursk and Orel, only 120 miles from the arsenal town of Tula and 250 miles from Moscow. At the same moment General Iudenich launched an assault on Petrograd from Estonia, and by 21 October 1919 he had reached the suburbs. In October 1919 the days of Lenin's regime really did seem to be numbered. However, the tide did turn. On 20 October 1919, the Red Army retook Orel; Trotsky's inspired counter-attack meant that by mid-November Iudenich was back in Estonia; and on 24 October 1919 the Red Cavalry of General Budyenny recaptured Voronezh and forced Denikin's army to begin an ever more desperate retreat until it was back beyond the Don in the first week of 1920.

By the spring of 1920 both Kolchak and Denikin had been defeated and the Civil War seemed over. Then, at the end of April 1920, the Polish Army invaded Russia and the two countries were embroiled in a war that was to last until an armistice was signed on 12 October. The fighting enabled the remnants of Denikin's forces to evacuate the Kuban and regroup in the Crimea, from which General Wrangel launched a new assault on the Bolshevik regime in June 1920. While the Polish war was still going on the Bolsheviks could do little but try to confine Wrangel's activities to the region immediately north of the Crimean peninsula and prevent any link-up between Wrangel and the Poles; this they did successfully, for the two armies were never less than 250 miles apart. Even before the Polish War was over the Red Army began to concentrate on Wrangel, though the decisive fighting occurred at the end of October and during the first fortnight of November; Wrangel set sail from Sevastapol into exile on 14 November 1920.

The Crimea was not the last White refuge in Russia. Although the British, French and American interventionist forces had abandoned the cause by the end of 1919, this was not the case for the Japanese. After the overthrow of Kolchak and the Red advance into Siberia, the Bolsheviks attempted to assuage Japanese *amour-propre* by establishing not a Bolshevik regime in eastern Siberia but a nominally independent Far Eastern Republic. The Japanese at first went along with this, but when it became clear that the Far Eastern Republic would actually be under Soviet control, they decided to cling on to Russia's Maritime Province, establishing a White administration there and turning it into a last haven for the supporters of Kolchak. It was not until October 1922 that the Japanese, under diplomatic pressure from the USA, agreed to evacuate the Maritime Province and thus Russia's last White administration, that of General Diterikhs, collapsed.

Fittingly, the year 1922 also saw the end of the democratic strand to the Civil War, of which little had been heard since the coup staged by Kolchak in November 1918. The SRs were involved in the events surrounding the arrest of Kolchak over the winter of 1919–20, and some played a role in the Far Eastern Republic; still others were involved in the wave of peasant disturbances that permeated every stage of the Civil War and culminated, after the Red victory, in the Tambov insurrection of spring 1921. In February 1922 the remnants of the SR Party leadership were arrested, and put on trial in June; it marked the end of the political careers of the Bolsheviks' democratic opponents, those who in the summer of 1918 had established both Komuch and the Directory as alternative socialist administrations to that of the Bolsheviks.

THE DOCUMENTS

Any selection of documents from a topic as vast as the Russian Civil War is essentially arbitrary. In this collection we have deliberately sought out documents which highlight the complexities of the struggle, often exploring episodes which are relatively unknown for the light they shed on what was a multi-faceted struggle which left deep wounds on the Russian and non-Russian peoples of what became the Soviet Union. So the Red versus White struggle has been virtually ignored and more difficult issues addressed. If this means that some of the documents need extensive contextualisation, then that has been done, for there is no way around it; the Civil War was complex, not a simple Red versus White struggle, and any selection from the newly opened archives is bound to reflect that fact. Chapter 1 relates to the democratic phase of the Civil War, the period when the Bolsheviks were fighting their fellow socialists. As the reader will realise, much of the time these socialists were less worried by the activities of the Bolsheviks than by the activities of the anti-democrtic groups of generals waiting in the wings with whom they were forced to co-operate and whom they feared, justifiably, might turn against them. While traditional historiography has not taken seriously the attempt by Russia's moderate socialists to build a democratic administration, the Directory, around the economic power of the Siberian co-operatives, these documents serve to advance the counter view.

The second chapter centres on the Don rebellion of spring 1919. Denikin's dramatic advance and near victory over the Bolsheviks was less a product of his military success than the Bolsheviks' political failure. As would happen repeatedly until Lenin adopted the New Economic Policy (NEP) in March 1921, the Bolsheviks were stumped when it came to understanding peasant aspirations. Hamstrung by Lenin's false analogy between urban class struggle and social stratification in the village, the Bolsheviks were always trying to identify poor peasants, with whom the working class could ally themselves against rich peasants, and thus antagonising the peasants *en masse*. The most acute example of this, but far from the only example, was the attempt to apply class politics among the Don cossacks; this led to such a widespread rebellion in the late spring of 1919 that Denikin could effectively leapfrog from the Don to Tsaritsyn and beyond in June 1919. The Don rebellion paved the way for Denikin's near victory.

Chapter 3 is a mixed bag designed to highlight several of the issues of 1919 which are rarely fully explored in the propaganda vision of the war. First, there is the question of the 'Greens': the Bolsheviks found it very difficult to work with autonomous radical organisations, but had to if the Whites were to be defeated; this was particularly important in the ultimate defeat of Denikin. Second, there is the question of morale: of course the propaganda vision of the Red Army as a body of highly motivated and politically conscious fighters for freedom was always suspect, but the documents now available show how far this was from the truth. Third, there is the question of terror, which applied at every level; just as the highest serving officers could find themselves charged with political crimes, so could the rank and file soldier. Fourth, there is desertion, an enormous problem on both sides in the war, but affecting the Reds just as much as the Whites. Finally, there is the day-to-day struggle of ordinary people to survive, which is too vast a topic for a collection like this but a few random documents give a flavour of some of the issues.

The fourth chapter is devoted to another little-studied episode, the campaign to form Labour Armies in the spring of 1920. These documents tell us much about the persisting importance of ideology, about how the Bolsheviks envisaged the forward march of socialism developing in those few weeks before the Polish War broke out and the Wrangel campaign condemned the Civil War to last another debilitating year. By the time that campaign was over, the country was on its knees and facing the three-pronged crisis of the Petrograd strikes of February 1921, the Kronshtadt rebellion of March 1921, and the Tambov peasant insurrection which lasted throughout the spring; faced with such popular unrest Lenin had no choice but to introduce NEP in March 1921 and put the socialist experiment on hold. But the Labour Army episode shows us what might have happened if the Civil War had been over in 1919, how socialism might have been constructed, and foreshadows many of the issues raised later in the decade when Stalin began to move the country away from NEP and towards socialist planning.

Chapter 5 considers the final White campaign led by General Diterikhs in the Maritime Province in October 1922. It is another neglected area, but the true value of the documents is perhaps in the poignancy of Diterikhs' agonised question: why did we lose? No one fought the Bolsheviks longer than Diterikhs, and no one had clearer motives for continuing to fight. Yet when we read his self-justification, we can see how divorced he was from the world of most Russian workers and peasants.

ARCHIVES AND AUTHORS

The documents in this collection are taken from five archives: the State Archive of the Russian Federation (GARF), the Russian State Archive of Economics (RGAE), the Russian State Military Archive (RGVA), the Russian Central Depository for Documents relating to Contemporary History (RTsKhIDNI), and the State Archive of the Rostov Region (GARO). Not all documents are given in full, but all are referenced by their *fond*, *opis*, and *ed. khr.* numbers in accordance with the usual Russian practice; unless the files are so small that there could be no confusion, the *list*, or folio, numbers are also given.

Dr V.P. Butt was in essence the originator of this project, having worked for many years in the Soviet and then Russian Academy of Sciences; he

Introduction

was until its disbandment co-ordinator of the group writing the official history of the Russian Civil War. Professor A.B. Murphy taught Russian at the University of Ulster and was attracted to the study of the Civil War through Mikhail Sholokhov's epic novel *The Quiet Don*; his study of the Don rebellion was published in *Revolutionary Russia*, no.2 (1993), pp. 315–50. Dr N.A. Myshov is a scientific researcher with the Russian Academy of Sciences, attached to the History of the Russian Civil War project. Dr G.R. Swain teaches history at the University of the West of England, Bristol, and has published *The Origins of the Russian Civil War* (Longman, 1996) a study of the democratic phase of the Civil War in 1918. The documents were assembled by all four authors and translated by Professor Murphy; the introduction and commentaries on individual documents were written by Dr Swain. The authors would like to thank the British Academy for the financial support given to Professor Murphy as part of this project.

Glossary of Russian Terms

All-Russian Council of the National Economy The council appointed by the Bolshevik Government to run the economy
ataman An elected leader of cossacks
black hundreds Right-wing thugs who in Tsarist times were responsible for organising pogroms against the Jews
C-in-C Commander-in-Chief
Cadet A member of the liberal Constitutional Democratic Party
Cheka The Extraordinary Commission or Secret Police
commissars People responsible for the political training and reliability of the Red Army
Committees of the Poor Committees established by the Bolsheviks to mobilise poor peasants
comrades' courts The lowest level of court, responsible for both political and criminal misdemeanours
Council of People's Commissars The Bolshevik Government
desyatin Unit of measurement, equivalent to 1.09 hectares
Donburo Communist Party executive for the Don region
Duma The representative assembly with limited constitutional powers tolerated by the Tsar from 1906 to 1914
dzhigit Mounted tribesman
GHQ General Headquarters, the Bolshevik supreme command
Komuch Committee of the Constituent Assembly, given the task of reconvening the assembly after its dissolution by the Bolsheviks
kulak Rich peasant
oblast A region smaller than a province
Orgburo The chief administrative body for the Communist Party
pood Unit of measurement, equivalent to 16.38 kg
pravitel Archaic word for political 'ruler'
People's Commissariat A Ministry in the Bolshevik Government
Politburo Ruling body of the Communist Party
RKP(b) Russian Communist Party (bolsheviks), full title of the Communist Party
RSFSR Russian Soviet Federal Socialist Republic
RVS Revolutionary Military Council – these existed at every level, from the chief RVS of the Republic to regional RVSs
Special Section The Red Army section responsible for political reliability

Glossary of Russian Terms xvii

stanitsa Cossack term for village
troika A committee of three people
verst Unit of measurement, equivalent to 1067 metres
voisko A cossack administrative unit
volost A local district
zemstvo An elected assembly of local, regional or provincial government

1 The Directory

THE SETTING

The documents in this chapter deal with events on the Volga, in the Urals and in Siberia during the summer and autumn of 1918. In this first phase of the civil war, often forgotten, the fighting which took place was not between the Bolsheviks and reactionary White Generals and their Allied interventionist supporters, but between the Bolsheviks and their fellow socialists, the SRs.

When Lenin and the Bolsheviks seized power in October 1917 they agreed that the long-promised elections to the Constituent Assembly, Russia's first freely elected parliament, could go ahead. The elections, held in November 1917, produced an assembly dominated by the SRs; Lenin and his allies promptly dissolved the Constituent Assembly after a single session on 5 January 1918. The SRs' response to the dissolution was at first cautious; while they did not accept it, they had good reason to believe that Lenin's government would not stay in power long and that peaceful political activity might force both Lenin's resignation and the consequent recall of the Constituent Assembly.

The SRs' hopes for Lenin's early political demise rested on the near universal hostility to the peace treaty which the Bolsheviks had signed with Germany at the start of March 1918, the Treaty of Brest Litovsk. This treaty, endorsed by the Fourth Congress of Soviets but not the Constituent Assembly, involved such loss of territory and created such a sense of national humiliation, within the Bolshevik Party as much as outside it, that Lenin could only persuade his supporters to endorse it by promising that the peace would be a mere 'breathing space' before war against Germany was resumed. That the 'breathing space' would be of short duration was the near unanimous view of leading Bolsheviks; and Trotsky, the Commissar of War, busied himself in preparing for a secret deal with Britain and France when the fighting resumed. For the SRs, then, the most patriotic of socialists, pushing Lenin's government to a resumption of hostilities was seen as both a national duty higher than the issue of the Constituent Assembly, and a way of encouraging divisions between pro- and anti-peace Bolshevik elements, making a political crisis and the eventual recall of the Assembly more likely.

What gave the SRs even more cause for optimism was their success, in alliance with the Mensheviks, in mobilising working-class and peasant opinion to their cause. In Petrograd, during the spring of 1918, they were able to establish a rival to the Petrograd Soviet, capable of mobilising the labour force and weakening the Bolsheviks' grip on the city; the Assembly of Petrograd Factory Delegates could soon both threaten and deliver disciplined political strikes. At the same time, the spring and early summer saw SRs and Mensheviks winning provincial soviet elections throughout the country. By working through the soviets and mass organisations such as the Assembly of Petrograd Factory Delegates, the SRs were confident they could weaken Lenin's authority still further, get a new congress of soviets to annul the Treaty of Brest Litovsk, and then recall the Constituent Assembly.

What transformed the situation was the close-fought decision of the Bolshevik Party Central Committee to extend the 'breathing space' with Germany and drop Trotsky's idea of a new alliance with Britain and France. By early May 1918 plans for an Anglo-Russian alliance were well advanced, but at the very moment when the British Cabinet instructed General Poole to sail for the northern Russian ports of Murmansk and Archangel with supplies and a small expeditionary force to help Trotsky in the renewed fighting with Germany, Lenin succeeded in persuading his closest comrades to abandon the idea of an Anglo-Russian alliance. It was a bitterly fought debate in the Central Committee, lasting several days. What made the issue singularly acute was the fact that, a few days earlier, the German Army (which under the terms of the Brest-Litovsk Treaty had occupied the Ukraine) overthrew the democratic government there and imposed a reactionary dictatorship. Many leading Bolsheviks, including Stalin, feared that the German Army might be tempted to repeat the manoeuvre in Moscow. Lenin, however, was convinced that the Germans could be bought off by offering a bribe to its imperialist minded businessmen; and Lenin got his way. On 13 May 1918 the Bolshevik Central Committee decided to reject the proposed Anglo-Russian alliance and turn the Brest-Litovsk 'breathing space' into something more stable by seeking an economic treaty with Germany. At the same time the Bolsheviks moved to dissolve by force those soviets which were in the hands of the SR and Menshevik parties.

For the SRs, the Bolshevik decision of 13 May 1918 was a clear sign not only that Lenin was determined to pursue a pro-German policy at whatever cost, but also that he was determined to do so by establishing a dictatorial regime; as a consequence there could no longer be any hope of peacefully transforming Russia's political life in such a way that might make possible the recall of the Constituent Assembly. As a result in mid-May the SRs resolved to prepare to overthrow the Bolsheviks by force.

Leading members retreated to the party's heartland on the Volga, where they had won most seats in both the Constituent Assembly elections and the provincial soviet elections, and began to prepare for what was initially billed as a peasant insurrection in the autumn. The insurrection was brought forward in time dramatically by the arrival near Samara of Czechoslovak forces led by a certain Colonel Cecek.

The Czechoslovak Legion had been formed, before the overthrow of the Tsar in February 1917, from Austro-Hungarian prisoners of war, and was to have played a crucial role in the proposed Anglo-Russian alliance. With the signing of the Treaty of Brest Litovsk, the Czechoslovak Legion could see no point in remaining on the Eastern Front and had decided to make the long and arduous journey across Siberia and America to the Western Front; as a result they were by May 1918 spread out along the Russian railway network from Penza in the west to Vladivostok in the east. Since, however, there were no spare Allied forces on the Western Front which could be moved to the Eastern Front to help the Bolsheviks annul the Treaty of Brest Litovsk and re-open the war with Germany, as Trostky's plan had envisaged, the British Cabinet had instructed its emissary, General Poole, to take charge of all those Czechoslovak forces which had travelled no further east than Omsk and use them in his planned collaboration with Trotsky.

The Bolshevik decision of 13 May 1918 left these plans in chaos. The Czechoslovak Legion was informed that the Allies wanted those units west of Omsk to rendezvous with Poole, but was also painfully aware that the Allies were no longer welcome in Moscow and suspected that if they did proceed to rendezvous with Poole they would be walking into a trap. So they decided to mutiny, ignoring the order to contact Poole and reverting to the initial plan of leaving Russia via Vladivostok, forcing a passage there if necessary. This decision, which for the most westerly Czechoslovak unit based in Penza meant forcing a passage through the Volga town of Samara, transformed the SRs' insurrectionary ambitions. If they could ally themselves with the Czechoslovaks, and use their forces to help SR militia units seize strategic towns on the Volga, then the insurrection could begin at once.

Thus when on 8 June 1918 Czechoslovak forces entered Samara they did so in co-operation with the local SR insurrectionary committee and, somewhat reluctantly, agreed to help the SRs control the town, using it as a base for a new Russian government loyal to both the Constituent Assembly and the Allies. The SR insurrectionary committee was composed of people elected to the Constituent Assembly, and they agreed at once to form a Committee of Members of the Constituent Assembly (Komuch), which would act as a sort of proto-parliament controlling a temporary executive authority until the Constituent Assembly itself could be summoned. The documents in this first section relate to Komuch and its attempt to gain universal acceptance of the idea that Russia's interim anti-Bolshevik administration should be loyal to the Constituent Assembly.

DOCUMENT 1.1

The problem for the Komuch administration, which carefully avoided calling itself a government and appointed departmental directors rather than ministers, was that it had not only been in Samara that anti-Bolshevik forces had sought to make effective use of the Czechoslovak mutiny. In Omsk, in Siberia, an anti-Bolshevik administration had been formed; but the leading members of that administration were former members of the SR Party, whose experience of office in Kerensky's Provisional Government during 1917 had left them jaundiced about both political parties and democratic politics. They wanted to keep their distance from the Komuch administration set up by the SRs and decided to do so by insisting that the Komuch administration was simply a regional administration for the Volga region which, although made up of Constituent Assembly members, could have no pretensions about representing all of Russia.

This document, which from its content can be dated at approximately 12 July 1918, is a letter from Komuch to the French consul in Samara who was travelling to Chelyabinsk for a meeting which the Allies hoped might bring about some sort of understanding between the rival administrations in Samara and Omsk; at the very least it could agree to some sort of congress being held of anti-Bolshevik forces. The letter provides a very clear picture of Komuch's point of view. The SRs, while keen on devolving as much power as possible to regional government and self-government for Russia's nationalities in a Federal Russia, were equally insistent that Russia was a unitary state: it followed logically from this that while governments like that in Siberia could have certain powers, state power belonged to Komuch because Komuch was the home of the Constituent Assembly.

The letter clearly shows the depth of distrust between the two sides. The comparison between the Siberian Government and that of the pro-German Krasnov on the Don and the pro-German Skorapadskii in the Ukraine was designed to infuriate the pro-Ally Siberian Government. The Siberian Government's unilateral decision to assert its control over the territory forming the border between the two states was one source of tension, as was the attempt to exclude the Komuch representative from the communication network. The reference to Colonel Guinet, a French military representative, hints at tension with the Allies, and probably concerned the conflicting views of Komuch, which saw its priority as consolidating its position in Samara, and the Allies, who hoped a rapid advance northward might somehow be co-ordinated with Poole descending southward from Archangel.

GARF, f. 667, op. 1, ed. khr. 27, l. 1

Much-esteemed Citizen Janneau

Learning of your visit to Chelyabinsk and knowing your attitude to the tasks set by Komuch, I am turning to you with the request that, in your talks in Chelyabinsk, you support us in clearing up some questions which very much concern the Committee [Komuch].

First of all, Komuch considers Russia to be a united whole, which, on the basis of a democratic republic, needs to establish a system of internal order and administration which allows for national and regional self-administration; decisively opposed to the Brest-Litovsk peace, Komuch is preparing an army which will clear the enemy out of Russia. Komuch considers itself a democratic organisation, empowered by popular election to unite and organise Russia.

It considers the scope of all regional governments, the Siberian Government, the Urals Government and others, to be exclusively regional and temporary.

Komuch denies the state sovereignty of these governments, just as it denies the sovereignty of Krasnov, Skoropadskii and other traitors to Russia; for that reason Komuch considers that Russia needs to be united not on the basis of a union of states (Siberia, the Urals, etc.) but only on the basis of uniting the forces of a single united Russia – and certainly not disintegrating into new states, leaving Great Russia in tatters.

Komuch will not recognise such tattered statelets, and considers the Constituent Assembly as the only organ of state power. And of course, the Constituent Assembly, just like the committee of its members [Komuch], can only engage in democratic politics and dissociates itself from every attempt at restoration in the regions.

In the view of Komuch, only democratic forces can inspire the people to struggle for their motherland and to struggle for world freedom in the battle against German militarism. Any form of reaction or restoration can only weaken our national cause and will bring no aid to the Allies. For Komuch, the reactionaries are just as much enemies, just as much traitors, as the Bolsheviks – they are chips off the same block and any hesitation in recognising this is harmful, even criminal. Only Komuch stands clearly and firmly for nationalism and democracy.

On the basis of these views, Komuch is ready to establish the unity Russia needs with the governments of the various regions of Russia, a unity which the Congress of Members of the Constituent Assembly has proposed to the parties, and governments must have the task of forming a united All-Russian Government responsible to the Constituent Assembly until it can be re-elected.

Komuch cannot leave Samara, since that would mean wrecking all its work and would be interpreted by the population as flight, at a moment when fighting is taking place just a few dozen miles away. It can only send a delegation, which means depriving members of the Constituent Assembly of a vote in decisions of historic importance. For this reason Komuch categorically demands that any congress be held in Samara, which the Urals and Orenburg Governments are quite willing to accept.

We ask you to use your influence so that the congress is held in Samara, **which whatever happens Komuch will not leave**.

Komuch is made up of more than 30 people, all members of the Constituent Assembly, and firmly in support of its policies.

In Omsk the Komuch Representative Brushvit has been prevented from communicating with us by wire.

As to the Siberian Government seizing all Siberian territory, Komuch has protested to the Siberian Government and does not recognise these seizures, which simply raise tension and hinder the unity Russia needs.

Try to convince the Siberian Government of the inappropriateness of seizing territory in this way and of the need to return it to our administration.

Respectfully yours

Komuch President

Departmental Director for Foreign Affairs

Might I remind you of our conversation about the unpleasant telegram signed by Colonel Guinet.

DOCUMENT 1.2

On 15 July 1918 a meeting was held in Chelyabinsk between the Siberian Government and Komuch, and this document is the record of those talks kept by Komuch. I.A. Mikhailov was not only the Minister of Finance in the Siberian Government, but its leading figure and a *bête noire* for the SRs. Mikhailov had been an SR economist and leading economic adviser to Kerensky, before despairing of the politics of compromise and moving dramatically to the Right. The document clearly shows that no progress was made at this first round of talks, but gives a very clear picture of the SR position. Critics noted that, for all the talk of forming a coalition administration, Komuch was exclusively an SR concern until the Menshevik I.M. Maiskii joined as Departmental Director for Labour in August 1918.

GARF, f. 749, op. 1, ed. khr. 41, ll. 1-3

Notes of a meeting held between representatives of Komuch and the Siberian Government in Chelyabinsk, 15 July 1918

I.M. Brushvit (Komuch) chaired the session.
At the suggestion of I. Mikhailov, Minister of Finance in the Siberian Government, it was decided to clarify the powers of the two delegations. In the name of the Siberian Government Mikhailov made clear that they had been delegated only to make contact with the authorities in Samara to co-ordinate practical tasks and not to discuss the possibility of forming or constructing an All-Russian Government.
I.M. Brushvit suggested that the session should be for information only, and that, first of all, they should consider Komuch's project for establishing a new central authority.
That project consists of the following:

1. the supreme state authority in the country should recognise the All-Russian Constituent Assembly, elected on the basis of universal, direct, equal and secret voting;
2. until the Assembly can be summoned, authority should rest with the Committee of the Constituent Assembly [Komuch], made up of all its legally elected members, excluding the Bolsheviks and Left SRs who overthrew the power of the Assembly and are struggling to prevent it being summoned;
3. the basic law (the country's constitution) and other broad issues which can only concern the Constituent Assembly itself, are excluded from the concerns of Komuch and will be postponed until the Assembly has been summoned.
4. Komuch considers its immediate tasks to be:

(a) strengthening the authority of the Constituent Assembly and guaranteeing its summoning at the earliest opportunity;

(b) re-establishing the unity of Russia and its national resurrection;
(c) forming a popular army to struggle for Russia's independence as a united whole;
(d) restoring democratic local self-government and the normal functioning of all representative institutions;
(e) restoring the economy and transport system and taking immediate measures to restore production;
(f) restoring friendly relations with the Allied Powers in the struggle against Germany and restoring the front; as a consequence the Treaty of Brest Litovsk will not be recognised, since it violates the principles of Russia's self-determination.

Since the Bolshevik movement is the source of Russia's dislocation and the final destruction of her as a state, Komuch also includes as one of its basic tasks the merciless struggle against Bolshevism by forming armed forces and arming the people themselves.
5. To carry out these aims, Komuch will form (on the basis of a coalition) a central organ of All-Russian government whose duty will be to carry our all executive functions and attract to its side all the classes and peoples of Russia.
6. Legislative power will belong to Komuch, which will direct the activity of the government.
7. War, finance and foreign relations will be the exclusive concern of the All-Russian central government.
8. Devolution of other administrative concerns will be decided on by the All-Russian central government and sanctioned by Komuch.
9. Komuch will take over its executive state powers when its membership reaches thirty.

DOCUMENT 1.3

This telegram introduces a third player to this game and requires some contextualisation. After the Bolshevik decision of 13 May 1918 to abandon the idea of an Anglo-Russian alliance, the British decided to break their links with the Bolshevik Party and establish a new relationship with the anti-Bolshevik parties. Unbeknown to the SR activists in Samara, Right-wing SRs in Moscow had formed an alliance with the small Popular Socialist Party and some members of the liberal Cadet Party to form an umbrella grouping called the Union for the Regeneration of Russia (URR). It was with this organisation that the British agent Bruce Lockhart established contact in June 1918, and this organisation which was called upon by the Allies to organise a series of anti-Bolshevik insurrections in July 1918 which, if successful, would have enabled General Poole to land in Archangel and descend rapidly south along the railway and river network to the Volga to make contact with the Czechoslovaks and possibly even the White insurgents on the Don. When the Allies found the Komuch administration in Samara at odds with the Siberian Government in Omsk, they were tempted to refuse to recognise either, and to force the two to come to terms by recognising a third Urals Government. Their opportunity came with the liberation of Ekaterinburg by the Czechoslovaks – in the aftermath of the execution of the Tsar and his family – and the arrival of a URR emissary, L.A. Krol. This report from the SR activist Bogolyubov shows how worried the SRs were at developments in Ekaterinburg. Their immediate fear was that Krol's URR regime would be undemocratic and thus close to that established by Mikhailov in Siberia; in the author's view the evidence for this already happening was clear and as a result the existence of the Urals Government should not be recognised. The suggestion that the Czechoslovaks could be relied on to help Komuch soon became an almost instinctive reaction for Komuch supporters. Argunov, Pavlov and Granny Breshkovskaya were all leading members of the URR who were rallying to Krol's side.

GARF, f. 667, op. 1, ed. khr. 33, ll. 1–5

Telegram to the Komuch President Volskii or to Vedenyapin [Departmental Director for Foreign Affairs]

Chelyabinsk, 11.08.18

A very dangerous situation has been created in Ekaterinburg. There is no rule of law, and a military dictatorship with clearly reactionary tendencies has been established; on top of that only officer brigades are being formed. It is also worrying that, concerned by the Bolshevik traditions of the Urals workers, the garrison commander has ensured that local government does not reflect the interests of the working population. In a word, the situation is developing, in particular for an industrial area where the peaceful resolution of labour issues and the rapid restoration of heavy industry is pressing.

At the same time the attempt by the Siberian Government to become involved, and the request by the Urals Government leader, the Finance Minister Krol, for confirmation by the Siberian Government coincides with their decision to boycott Komuch. Krol rejected my proposal made at one meeting that he should immediately end the military dictatorship and introduce a proper legal order by delineating the sphere of military affairs and political affairs, and at the same time restoring heavy industry by resolving the labour question, and moving towards the establishment of the People's Army. After that, I, and many others got a clear understanding of Krol's position. At the same time the SR organisation here is weak, and the Social Democrats and Popular Socialists, who are joining the government, are even weaker.

My instructions were to find out what was going on and put right all unsatisfactory arrangements, acting in close contact with the Czechoslovaks – who are unhappy with the present state of affairs and might end the adventure, acting on the basis of information given to comrade Blinkin before his departure and on the basis of Order 35 of Komuch. After I have sorted things out in Ekaterinburg, I am going to Perm, so as to get there on time and prevent the same sort of unsatisfactory situation developing there, since the whole mess in Ekaterinburg can be put down to our representatives getting here late.

The way out of the situation in Ekaterinburg is to:

1. postpone the decision on formally establishing a Urals Government until the congress of members of the Constituent Assembly; for now to recognise Komuch as the authority in the region, appointing as garrison commander in the name of Komuch a Czechoslovak officer who would delineate military and civil affairs;
2. call a conference of workers, engineers and others involved in heavy industry to discuss restoring production and regulating employee-employer relations through local self-government.

Indicate by telegraph to the Ekaterinburg SR organisation what the Central Committee considers to be its line. At present Argunov, Pavlov and Granny Breshkovskaya are in Chelyabinsk; they intend today to come to Ekaterinburg. I too am going there today with [General] Voitsekhovskii [of the Czechoslovak forces] to try and find out the situation, but am delayed by fierce fighting with Hungarian and German forces, in which the Czechoslovaks were brilliant and victorious. This meant I could not leave, and was unable to make telegraph contact with comrade Blinkin, whose departure I consider premature.

Bogolyubov

Telegraph Ekaterinburg, the Palais Royale Hotel

DOCUMENT 1.4

At one level the intervention by the URR was very successful. Despite the frosty atmosphere at the first session of talks in Chelyabinsk on 15 July 1918 (document 1.2), pressure from both the Allies and the URR brought Komuch and the Siberian Government together and it was agreed to hold a further meeting in Chelyabinsk to be attended by all three protagonists and other interested parties; that Chelyabinsk State Conference agreed to call a further conference in Ufa which would set itself the task of establishing a single anti-Bolshevik government for the whole of Russia. At the Ufa State Conference, 8–13 September 1918, an agreement was reached (called the Ufa Accord) which went a long way to meeting the desires of Komuch, but which equally left its members dissatisfied with much of its interpretation and implementation.

The Ufa Accord recognised the formation of a five-member Directory comprising three members of the URR and two representatives of the Siberian Government, which was empowered to appoint an All-Russian Provisional Government. This government would be responsible to the Constituent Assembly, if a quorate session of that body could be convened in Siberia by early 1919; but until then the Directory would have no democratic check on its activities. All the existing regional governments would be dissolved and turned into organs of local government, while the members of the Constituent Assembly would dissolve their committee (Komuch) and form themselves into a congress charged with assembling the quorate Constituent Assembly session.

These extracts from 'conversations on the wire' concern the row that developed between Komuch – by October 1918 officially the regional administration for Ufa and the Urals but never using that name – and the Directory or All-Russian Provisional Government in Omsk.

At first Komuch was happy to go along with the dissolution of the regional governments in favour of the Directory; this had been the SR stance all along. At first, then, its worries were practical and financial, particularly exploring the borderline between local and state expenditure. As time passed it became clear that the Ufa authorities suspected that their old enemy I.A. Mikhailov, Finance Minister in the Siberian Government, was withholding funds from political motives.

Between 10 October and 3 November 1918 a dramatic incident had taken place concerning the implementation of the Ufa Accord; this concerned the so-called Administrative Council of the Siberian Government. At the end of August 1918 Mikhailov had decided that the day-to-day work of the Siberian Government was too much for the small number of actual ministers and had established under his own presidency an Administrative Council; what made this bureaucratic re-organisation significant was the concurrent decision that the Administrative Council could rule on the government's behalf in certain circumstances, and that it had to be consulted on all new government appointments. When the Directory was formed in October 1918, and moved its headquarters to the capital of the Siberian Government, Omsk, Mikhailov insisted that if the Directory wanted to make use of this administrative apparatus it too would have to accept the self-same terms, notably the insistence that all ministerial appointments were to be made in consultation with it. With great reluctance the Directorate agreed to this, but to many this seemed a betrayal of the Ufa Accord for, while the Siberian Government was indeed dissolved and transferred into the local administration for Siberia, the Directorate was beholden to the Administrative Council of the old Siberian Government. As a result the remnants of the Komuch administration in Ufa refused to dissolve and demanded to be allowed to continue in existence. The degree of retained authority suggested in the final extract was very limited and might have formed the basis for a compromise.

What gave the attitude of the Ufa authorities added piquancy was the fact that they had had some success in stopping the Bolsheviks' dramatic advance by forming volunteer battalions of people ready to fight in the name of the Constituent Assembly. Yet these volunteer units contradicted the spirit of the Ufa Accord, which had called for the merger of the Komuch People's Army and the Omsk Siberian Army into one depoliticised and centralised regular conscripted army. The apparent violation of the Ufa Accord concerning the dissolution of the Siberian Government put a question mark over other aspects of the Accord, in particular the promise to convene a quorate session of the Assembly in the near future.

GARF, *f.* 144, *op.* 1, *ed. khr.* 22, *ll.* 1–46 [extracts]

Conversations on the wire

13.10.18

A conversation on the wire between the Council of Departmental Directors and the Directory in Omsk; Znamenskii for Ufa, Zenzinov for Omsk.

Znamenskii: Tell Zenzinov [a Directory member] that the Council of Departmental Directors has been liquidated in its old form and a temporary administration of four established, comprising Filippovskii, Vedenyapin, Nesterov and Klimushkin, who have divided up responsibility among themselves. The most pressing need is financial. From the War Department, the Railway Department and other departments there are requests for money running into millions of roubles which we are not in a position to meet. In the bank we have 14 million paper roubles, and all that could be spent tomorrow; there will be a fearful protest in the sphere of finance if we do not take extreme measures. We want to ask the Provisional All-Russian Government for permission to issue in its name about 100 million roubles.

As well as that, we need to know as quickly as possible when the question of who will administer Samara, Ufa and Orenburg provinces will be decided. Will it be the next couple of days...?

It is essential that the Government take extreme measures to support the Ufa State Bank. The expenditure we are undertaking is not in local needs, but for the most part on matters of state interest. If we have no money at our disposal, then the army will end up without supplies and the railway workers might stage an uprising. The War Department is demanding 35 million and the railways about 10 million...

[Zenzinov replies giving the legalistic answer that since the formation of the Directory, these are the concerns of its executive ministries, in particular the Ministry of Communication and the Ministry of War, headed by Admiral Kolchak.]

Znamenskii: The Council of Departmental Directors has informed the Urals Government by telegraph, and General Galkin as well, that they should send all their requests for money direct to the Provisional All-Russian Government [and not, as in the past, to the Council]. But the Council of Departmental Directors is also fully aware that these are just formalities. The real situation is clear. We need to pay salaries to our railway workers and civil servants... If we do not pay the railway workers, as General Syrovoy [of the Czechoslovak forces] is also demanding, a railway strike is inevitable. I hope the government understands what this means.

3.11.18

Conversation on the wire between the Council of Departmental Directors in Ufa, and the Directory in Omsk; Filippovskii for Ufa, General Boldyrev for Omsk.

[Boldyrev informs Ufa that their expenditure of 200 million roubles cannot be endorsed; but a one-off payment of 40 million has been agreed.]

Filippovskii: We were promised 20 million roubles, but they were not sent, then 15 million which did not come... The Council of Departmental Directors must state that it has done all in its power to fulfil the obligations it took on at the Ufa Conference to support the authority of the Provisional All-Russian Government. But to our great regret, the various promises made on the part of the Provisional All-Russian Government have put us in the most difficult position, and for all our desire to support it, we cannot take responsibility for the terrible consequences of this financial catastrophe. The palliatives of which you speak are not going to save the situation.

Boldyrev: Tomorrow I shall personally contact the Minister of Finance [Mikhailov] and demand a clear explanation of how you are being supplied with money...

Filippovskii: Bit by bit work to rules are beginning everywhere, but particularly on the railways...

4.11.18

A conversation on the wire between Vedenyapin, former Departmental Director for Foreign Affairs in the Council of Departmental Directors, in Ufa, and Volskii, President of Komuch, in Ekaterinburg.

Vedenyapin: The decision of the Provisional All-Russian Government, apparently, to wind up all the regional governments, has in fact turned the Siberian Government into the All-Russian Government and destroyed the Council of Departmental Directors, liquidating its territory on which democratic forces could operate freely. There is every reason to believe that the destruction of the Council of Departmental Directors will be followed by the liquidation of the Congress of Members of the Constituent Assembly and then the Constituent Assembly itself.

At the present moment joint action by the Czechoslovak command and ourselves has restored the front. In reality, besides the Czechoslovaks, at the front it is only Kappel's volunteers, the Constituent Assembly Battalion, Fortunatov's Brigade, the Russo-Czechoslovak Regiment and Makhin's units which can really be relied on, and liquidating the Council of Departmental Directors will dislocate all those forces. And the participation of these forces has really raised the morale of the Czechoslovak forces, so if they are removed from the front it will have a devastating effect on Czechoslovak morale also and could end up by liquidating the front. As well as those units listed above, a broad-based campaign is under way to strengthen them with more volunteers; these democratic units promise to form a solid force with which to fight the Soviet forces...

5.11.18
Conversation over the wire between Vedenyapin in Ufa and Zenzinov in Omsk.

Vedenyapin: After the fall of Samara the army collapsed and almost fell apart. This forced the Central Committee [of the SR Party] to call all members of the Party to arms and this we managed to do, together with the Czechoslovak command; in spite of Boldyrev's orders we created volunteer units which are holding the front. In our units officers have agreed not to wear epaulettes and other symbols of the old army. Together with the Czechoslovaks we have undertaken a broad campaign to form volunteer units, and a few days ago they were sent to the front, with the task of retaking Samara. Spirits have risen noticeably, and our comrades are carrying out this task, so long as you do not carry out this change which will destroy everything.

In the Party there is a certain mood of ignoring the struggle, of total distrust of the Provisional All-Russian Government, which began as soon as it linked its fate to the Siberian Government and Mikhailov in particular...

For this region an exception must be made, and the Council of Departmental Directors should be kept intact. Did you know that the Bolsheviks were offering the Czechoslovaks free passage across Russia to Austria; this has weakened morale, and if our units also leave the front then it will be impossible to keep the Czechoslovaks there...

[Zenzinov explains that the decision has been made; after angry exchanges the conversation moves on to other matters.]

Vedenyapin: I think you have put Znamenskii [officially the Directory's representative in Ufa] in an impossible position. You ignore him. He learns of your instructions only from the press and the threatening orders of the Minister of Finance [Mikhailov], in which it is stated that our civil servants will be taken to court if they do not fulfil Mikhailov's orders.

Zenzinov: I know nothing of these orders from Mikhailov. Please send them to me...

12.11.18

Conversation over the wire between Vedenyapin in Ufa and Zenzinov in Omsk.

Vedenyapin: The Council of Departmental Directors considers that what is happening in Omsk is a new agreement between the Siberian Government and the Provisional All-Russian Government. It considers that this agreement has moved far away from the Ufa Accord. We, as true defenders of the Ufa Accord and loyal supporters of the Provisional All-Russian Government, consider that our dissolution is only possible on the following conditions:

1. the Provisional All-Russian Government and its Council of Executive Ministers, in some way or other, explain its attitude towards the Constituent Assembly and confirm that it will resign once the Assembly has gathered;
2. a law is passed guaranteeing personal inviolability to all members of the Constituent Assembly;
3. the programme of the Ufa Accord remains unchanged.

As far as our dissolution is concerned, the situation at the front must be considered, and the real influence of the volunteer units; some form of self-administration in the Urals area must be retained ... There must be at least one small corner of territory where democracy can be allowed to breathe deeply.

[Zenzinov responds that the Provisional All-Russian Government is loyal to the Ufa Accord, and that the other regional governments have all surrendered their authority.]

15.11.18

Conversation on the wire between Vedenyapin in Ufa, and Federovich in Ekaterinburg.

Vedenyapin: We are insisting on the type of broad self-administration for the Urals. We are thinking on approximately these lines: we will suggest three candidates for the post of Chief Representative, who will have various assistants carrying out such things as internal affairs, production, education, state property and the 'contacts office', i.e., working in Bolshevik areas. The personality of the person will not concern us; we will only insist that the person appointed to the post is a member of Komuch. So far nothing has been said about this in public ...

DOCUMENT 1.5

On 18 November 1918 Admiral A.V. Kolchak, who had been appointed Minister of War by the Directory, carried out a coup, deposed the Directory, and ended any pretence that the Constituent Assembly might be called and that the anti-Bolshevik forces might be fighting in the name of democracy. This document is Komuch's final appeal to the Czechoslovaks, who had helped them come to power and supported them on many occasions before. But with the armistice on the Western Front on 11 November 1918 and the creation of the new Czechoslovak Republic, the Czechoslovaks had no desire to remain embroiled in Russia's affairs. They had become increasingly frustrated with the squabbling between Ufa and Omsk and decided to stand aside from Russian politics at this crucial moment.

GARF, f. 144, op. 1, ed. khr. 20, ll. 1–3

Appeal from the Komuch Council Departmental Directors to the Czechoslovak National Council

(Copy to the President of the Czechoslovak Republic, President Masaryk)

23 November 1918

I. At the Ufa State Conference, in presence of official representatives from the Allies and the Czechoslovak National Council and with their active participation, an agreement was reached by those taking part, both representatives of regional governments, political parties and mass organisations. As a result of that agreement a Provisional All-Russian Government was chosen, a clear programme of its activities worked out, and it was agreed to make it responsible to the existing Constituent Assembly [elected in January 1918 and dispersed by the Bolsheviks]. The Provisional All-Russian Government carried out its duties to the letter, and was recognised as having Supreme Authority not only by those regional governments which participated in the Ufa Conference, but also those which did not take part, like the Northern Government and the Amur and Caucasian-Caspian Government which decided to wind up their activities to help the Provisional All-Russian Government fulfil its task of resurrecting a united Russia.

The executive ministers of the Provisional All-Russian Government, led by Vologodskii and Kolchak, have, by carrying out their coup, destroyed the agreement referred to above and wrecked the work of uniting the various regions of Russia; Vologodskii in particular broke the promise he had only just made to implement the conditions laid out in the agreement.

The following questions therefore arise:

1. What is the attitude of the National Council to the coup [by Kolchak]?
2. How does the National Council intend to react, actively or passively, to the breaking of an agreement concluded with its participation?
3. How will the National Council react if the dictator Kolchak, with his own forces or in collaboration with some other government force or sympathiser like General Dutov [who controlled an independent band of Cossacks in Siberia], tries by force to control regions other than Siberia?
4. Does the Czechoslovak National Council think that it is possible, even necessary, for Czechoslovak troops to take an active part in the military campaign to put down the Kolchak–Vologodskii rebellion and to restore the legitimate Provisional All-Russian Government and the legal order based on the above-mentioned agreement?

II. Until a united All-Russian authority which corresponds to the will and decisions of the regions has been restored, the authority of the former regional governments must be revived, and they must take charge both of the civilian administration and military forces necessary for the defence of that region from outside attack. In particular, in this territory the Council of Departmental Directors of the former Committee and now Congress of Members of the Constituent Assembly [Komuch] must retain authority, with executive power resting on the Council of Departmental Administration and the People's Army, created by the Committee, and other armed groups at the Council's disposal, acting, of course, in close contact, complete agreement and under the overall command of the Czechoslovak and other Allied forces and forces in other regions. In particular the armed units of the Constituent Assembly (created specially for the preservation and defence of the Constituent Assembly, and until its recall the Congress of Members of the Constituent Assembly) must remain under the direct control of the Congress of Members of the Constituent Assembly, and can be used for other military purposes only with the agreement of the latter.

1. Is the National Council in agreement with such a resolution of the question of local power in the regions until the restoration of an All-Russian authority?
2. If not, how would the National Council intend to establish regional power at the current moment, and the relationship between civilian and military authorities?

III. General Voitsekhovskii [of the Czechoslovak forces], in conversation with M.A. Vedenyapin, a member of the Council of Departmental Directors, stated on the orders of General Syrovoy [of the Czechoslovak forces] sent from Chelyabinsk, that they should have Supreme Command in this territory controlling the army, and that the Council of Departmental Directors should concern itself only with administration. Is this the view of the National Council? If not, then the National Council should respond to the situation created by General Syrovoy's statement concerning the power of the Council of Administrative Directors.

IV. The Council of Departmental Directors has good reason to believe that [the Siberian cossack] General Dutov is ready actively to support the Kolchak–Vologodskii rebellion. They are aware that after the Omsk coup Kolchak has held positive talks with Dutov over the wire, and as a result the Council of Departmental Directors decided not to allow the wire to be used for further talks, aimed at fanning and strengthening the rebellion. This decision was over-ruled within two hours by General Syrovoy, and Kolchak was able to carry on his plotting with Dutov. As a result of this intervention, the conversation between Dutov and Kolchak clearly shows (a copy of this is attached) that Dutov intends actively to support the Omsk coup. He can easily do this by moving his forces against those of the Congress of Members of the Constituent Assembly and the Council of Departmental Directors via Sterlitamak where we have no military forces. At the same time General Syrovoy, acting in the name of the National Council, has hindered every attempt by the Council of Departmental Directors to call on the population to defend our trampled order by confiscating the newspaper *The People* on the grounds that it was exciting the population.

1. Does the National Council consider these orders correct and helpful?
2. Does it accept responsibility for these orders, which have enabled the rebellion to spread and weakened the already difficult position of the Council of Departmental Directors?
3. If not, how does the National Council intend to respond?

In conclusion, the Council of Departmental Directors must point out that the rebellion begun in Omsk – headed by people who not only have no popular support among the democratically minded population, and who are, on the contrary, compromised by their clearly reactionary views – that rebellion can rely only on naked military force, and then only on the force of certain military formations, mostly the reactionary officer class.

This rebellion will undoubtedly be firmly opposed by democratic forces, by the railwaymen, the post and telegraph workers and mass strikes by workers, some organised, some wild-cat; there will also be insurrections.

Besides this, and this is particularly dangerous, when news of the coup reaches the army, it will suffer rapid dislocation: there will be a series of insurrections and the anti-Bolshevik front will be destroyed. Our democratic forces are, perhaps, still not sufficiently developed and are weakly organised, but then our revolution did not pass without trace, and no force can possibly compel our country to return to the old authoritarian regime. Any adventure like that in Omsk can only lead to further collapse in the life of the country and will prolong its suffering. In particular, the adventure will lead to the collapse not only of the people's forces of the Council of Departmental Directors, but also of the Siberian and cossack forces, for only a minority of them are reactionary, and the majority are without any doubt committed to democracy.

The Council of Departmental Directors asks that these questions be taken into consideration, and reminds you that Russian democracy cannot struggle against the Bolsheviks with a clear conscience if it becomes convinced that the result of that struggle will be the formation of an anti-people government. The Council of Departmental Directors is firmly convinced that its honestly democratic position is shared by the President of the Czechoslovak Republic, Professor Masaryk, and for that reason sees its friend and ally as the Czechoslovak National Council.

The Council of Departmental Directors

DOCUMENT 1.6

Komuch was a socialist administration, as was the Directory to which it eventually gave birth. The SRs who ran it wanted to turn the clock back to pre-October 1917, before the Bolshevik seizure of power, but no further. The gains of the February Revolution were to remain intact, and capital and labour were to find a happy *modus vivendi*. To make this clear the following declaration was issued.

GARF, f. 749, op. 1, ed. khr. 3, l. 4

Declaration by Komuch

Soviet power has been overturned and Bolshevism utterly defeated on all the territory controlled today by Komuch; despite this, however, there are quite a few people who dream about the return of Soviet power. These people, acting together with the dregs of society, are arousing the workers and peasants against the new order, using its organisational and political failings. They tell them that workers are again to be subject to capital, that the peasants will deprived of their land and handed over to the landlords.

Komuch, which considers such agitation to be a provocation, asserts that there are no grounds for such allegations, and to put an end to such vindictive accusations states the following:

1. Land belongs irretrievably to the people and Komuch will prevent any attempt to restore it to the landlords. All trading in agricultural land and forests is banned, and any secret or fictitious transactions are null and void. Those guilty of breaking this law will be brought to book.
2. The existing laws which protect workers will remain operative, until they are revised in due course.
3. The Labour Office, which from today takes over from the Commissariat of Labour, will ensure that labour legislation is implemented, and will refer to the courts any incidents of labour legislation being ignored.
4. Workers and peasants are called on to defend their rights only by legal means, so as to avoid anarchy and collapse.
5. Any dismissal of workers or closing down of production which is not justified on grounds of production, or is made in agreement with other employers to pressurise workers or the government, is banned and the firmest measures will be taken against perpetrators.
6. Factories can only be closed with the agreement of the responsible organ of state, the National Council of the People's Economy of the Economic Council.
7. The Labour Office will undertake to establish corresponding organisations to protect labour in all provincial towns, and through them all districts.
8. Trade unions retain all their existing rights until legislation concerning them is revised. Both workers and employees will send representatives to any committees concerned with such a revision.
9. Collective contracts between employers and trade unions should remain in force until they are changed by agreement, or the legislation concerning them is revised.

At the same time the needs of trade and industry have to be borne in mind, since the Bolsheviks have wrecked the economy. So, wanting to support the best representatives of the trade and industrial classes, who sincerely want to resurrect the motherland and restore normal economic life, Komuch also considers it its duty to declare the following:

1. Employers have the right to expect from workers intensive and good quality work throughout the working day, and according to agreements recognised in law can dismiss those who fail to live up to those expectations, so long as due legal process is observed.
2. Employers can dismiss those workers surplus to requirements, so long as all legal processes are observed.

Signed: Komuch President V. Volskii, and its members N. Shelov, I. Nesterov, P. Belozerov, I. Brushvit, I. Klimushkin and V. Abramov.

DOCUMENT 1.7

Balancing the interests of capital and labour was not always easily done. As this short extract from the minutes of a meeting of Komuch's Financial Council make clear, Komuch and the representatives of the private banks found it hard to find a common cause.

GARF, f. 749, op. 1, ed. khr. 28, l. 10 [extracts]

Protocols of the Financial Council

15 July 1918

Item 10. The request from the Samara Committee of Representatives of Commercial Banks concerning outstanding obligations.

[The bankers' representatives propose collating a full list of outstanding liabilities.]

A.K. Ershov [for Komuch]: The point is that under Bolshevik control the banks made all sorts of mistakes in this regard, which it is quite impossible to put right at the present time, let alone the 20–30 incidents raised by your representatives today.

L.A. De Sevo [for the banks] points to the need that some of the issues brought forward by the local banks really do need addressing, and since they all have elements in common they have been brought to the Financial Council. He protests at the insinuations of Ershov, and points out that the sort of picture being painted by Ershov is quite inappropriate; he accuses Ershov of being prejudiced against banking in general.

A.K. Ershov expresses surprise at L.A. De Sevo's protest, and the suggestion that the application being discussed is critical of the activity

The Directory

of private banks; in Ershov's view the application is not critical enough of the activity of private banks in Samara, since they pay no heed to the critical financial situation, are unwilling to restore current deposit accounts of clients and in this way are guilty of perpetuating the financial crisis. Ershov considers that it is not only his official duty but his duty as a citizen to protest in the firmest possible way at the, in his view, scandalous activity of the local private banks...

DOCUMENT 1.8

On 2 August 1918 General Poole landed a small force in Archangel. If all had gone according to plan, the URR, which had staged a successful insurrection in Archangel to help Poole's entry to the city, would have staged a series of insurrections in Yaroslavl and other towns on the upper Volga, and General Poole and his mission could have descended by Russia's rail and river network and been in the Komuch capital, Samara, within days. That is what prompted the British representative in Samara, Mr Cunningham, to request accommodation for the British Military Mission from the Komuch authorities.

The documents are self-explanatory, and show much about the housing crisis in Samara. By the time the police authorities had cleared the building for Cunningham, it had become clear that General Poole's advance had stalled, and Samara itself was facing imminent attack by the Bolsheviks.

GARF, f. 667, op. 1, ed. khr. 8, ll. 2–8

Correspondence with England's representative

From the Departmental Director for Foreign Affairs

To the Departmental Director for Internal Affairs

8.8.18

The Departmental Director for Foreign Affairs asks you, in connection with a request from Mr Cunningham of the English Mission in Samara, to take the necessary measures to find accommodation for the English Military Mission when it arrives in Samara.

30.8.18 Very urgent

To the Mayor

In confirmation of the proposal of the Department of Foreign Affairs that the representative of the English Military Mission in Samara Mr Cunningham be given the Shadrin house, or one similar if this first does not become available, and in view of your reply that the specified Shadrin house would not be available, the Department of Foreign Affairs asks you to take energetic measures to suggest suitable accommodation in the quickest possible time to Mr Cunningham for the English Military Mission which is to arrive in the next few days.

Departmental Director

Secretary

13.9.18 Very urgent

To the Regional Police Commandant

The Department of Foreign Affairs has proposed to the Mayor, by way of the Department of Internal Affairs, that, as a matter of urgency, suitable accommodation needs to be found for the representative of the English Military Mission, Mr Cunningham.

The Mayor gave Mr Cunningham a mandate to take possession of the Shadrin house, no.9 Kazan Street, and the owner readily agreed. However, those living in the house – Mr Savrimovich, Mr Kvitko, who is in the army, and Mr Belenskii – have until now, despite being given by the Mayor mandates for new accommodation, not left.

Reporting all this, and in view of the fact that it is very awkward that the official representative of an Allied power cannot find a flat, the Department of Foreign Affairs asks you to take urgent measures to occupy the flat already allocated by the Mayor to Mr Cunningham.

13.9.18 Very urgent

To the Director of the Department of State Security

[Mr Cunningham's story is summarised.]

Bearing in mind the accommodation crisis, and agreeing with the difficulty of the situation from one point of view, the Department considers that from the other point of view it is extremely embarrassing that for a whole month the local authorities could do nothing to find accommodation for an official representative of an allied power. Considering the Mayor powerless, the Department asks you to take immediate measures.

20.9.18

From the Department of State Security

To the Departmental Director for Foreign Affairs

To inform you that the representative of the English Military Mission Mr Cunningham has been provided with his accommodation, as requested.

DOCUMENT 1.9

The great hope of the Directory was that, if recognised by the Allies – and they justifiably had every anticipation that this would happen in the near future, despite Mr Cunningham's discomfiture (Document 1.8) – the economic power of Siberia could be used to support an army capable of defeating the Bolsheviks. To this purpose its first task was to take determined measures to unite the economy, army and Allies.

The Higher Supply Council for the Allied Armies was formed at the Chelyabinsk meeting on 16 July 1918, the day after the unsuccessful session described in Document 2. On it sat representatives of Komuch, the Siberian Government, the Czechoslovak forces, and the French military mission. Its functions were limited at first, but it began to operate effectively immediately after the Ufa State Conference and was based in Ufa from 20 September until 30 September, when it moved to Omsk.

On 4 October 1918 its powers were dramatically broadened. It was given ultimate authority on all questions of army supply until the Directory had concluded its task of government formation and established a permanent supply organisation; all relevant offices and factories were brought under its control. The decision to issue the bulletins reproduced here was no doubt linked in some way to this re-organisation and the appointment of Admiral Kolchak as Minister of War on 16 October 1918; General Knox of the British Military Mission also arrived in Omsk at this time. General Boldyrev, the Directory's only military figure, had the task of forming a single army out of the Komuch People's Army and the Omsk Siberian Army. The Higher Council on the Supply of the Allied Armies was dissolved after Kolchak's coup by a ministerial statement of

26 November and a joint government supreme command decree on 16 December 1918.

The documents produced here are economic bulletins issued during the Directory, which give a unique insight into the scale of economic activity in Siberia in the autumn of 1918. To British readers old enough to have read Sir Bernard Pares, *My Russian Memoirs* (Jonathan Cape, 1931), in which he describes a 10-month long visit to the area in 1919, the picture of vibrant economic life, largely carried on through agricultural co-operatives, will come as no surprise; but to Soviet scholars brought up on decades of anti-Directory propaganda, and to most Western students brought up on a rather similar diet, these rather stark economic notes have a stunning impact. The last of these bulletins was issued on 11 November 1918, just prior to Kolchak's coup on 18 November. Bulletin No.1 is given in full, and followed by extracts from other extant copies. Note in particular the reality of the co-operative ideal under the rule of the moderate socialist Directory.

RGVA, f. 39459, op. 1, ed. khr. 48, ll. 63–82 [extracts]

Bulletins of the Statistical Economic Section of the Central Military-Industrial Committee

Higher Supply Council for the Allied Armies operating in the territory of the Russian State.

Omsk, corner of Tobolsk and Aleksandrovsk Streets, 21, tel. 2–71.

Edited by Head of Section, V.G. Laskin

From the Statistical Economic Section

One of the tasks of the Statistical Economic Section is to note and collate press information on the day-to-day course of economic life. Information collected in this way can be extremely valuable for those who have practical charge of building up and managing our industrial and commercial life and in particular for those who work in the Military-Industrial Committee. In order to make the said material as widely available as possible to those concerned, the Section, with the agreement of the Secretariat of the Committee, is preparing to publish 3 or 4 times a week Bulletins with a survey of national economic life.

Commercial and Industrial News, No.1, 16 October 1918

Finance, Trade and Industry:

1. It has been decided to locate the management of the Russo-Asiatic Bank in Shanghai.
2. [The central organisation of consumer co-operatives founded in 1916] Zakupsbyt has decided to press for a branch of the Moscow Narodnyi Bank to be opened.
3. An article in *Trudovaya Sibir* indicates that German seizure of Russian harbours bodes ill for the future of Siberian dairy produce, since most Siberian butter was formerly exported.
4. In Vladivostok there has gradually been a huge build-up of all sorts of imported goods. The *Komuch Courier*, 18 September, contains a list of all these goods.
5. The Council of the Joint Trade and Industry Organisations has handed the Minister of Trade and Industry a report on measures against speculation.
6. To combat speculation in the Far East a post has been established with special powers at the Deputy Minister level.
7. Zakupsbyt intends to open agencies in England and America.
8. Attached to the Council of Congresses of Representatives of Trade and Industry, a special Far Eastern Office has been established for distributing goods purchased in the Far East.
9. Among the townspeople of Omsk, Centrosibir bonds were sold out to a total value of 100 000 roubles.
10. Investments made by Centrosibir have amounted to one million roubles.
11. From 1 October 1917 to 1 August 1918 the volume turnover of butter realised by the 23 offices of the Siberian co-operative creamery amounted to 63 834 324 roubles.
12. The Ministry of Finance has asked the town and *zemstvo* local authorities, the joint stock committees, etc., to supply information regarding the quantity of spare raw materials which would be suitable for export.
13. The State Bank of Siberia has been authorised to issue Treasury exchange notes of 1, 3, 5 and 10 roubles to an overall total of 50 million roubles. High denomination currency notes to the same value will be withdrawn from circulation.
14. From 1 August the public has been supplied with vodka to a value of 1 385 475 roubles by the Omsk Wine and Spirit Store and 61 560 roubles by the Kurgan Store.
15. Soyuzbank is requesting the State Bank (for the latter) to renew its operations for granting credits for loans to be made against deliveries of grain.

16. From 1 September duty will be charged on leaf tobacco at 22 roubles per *pood* [1 *pood* = 16.38kg].
17. The Ministry of Food has asked the Irkutsk Joint Stock Trade and Industry Congress to indicate those firms and persons who can be entrusted with buying goods in the East.
18. Prices for goods in the Far East remain quite low, due to the higher exchange rate for the rouble.
19. In Omsk a Joint Stock Siberian Trade and Industry Company has started operating with a basic capital of 5 million roubles.

Communications:

20. The Ministry of Transport is gathering materials for rail-building in Siberia, concentrating in particular on building rail links Tomsk–Yeniseysk and Krasnoufimsk–Tomsk.
21. The Ministry of Transport [MPS] has resolved to issue its own newspaper, *Vestnik MPS*.
22. The construction of a broad gauge railway is envisaged from Nikolayevsk to one of the stations on the Samara–Zlatoust line, as is also the repair of the narrow gauge section Yershovo–Nikolayevsk and the branch line Krotovka–Surgut.
23. It is proposed to found a special directorate for rail, road and waterways in the Uralsk *Oblast* [region].
24. It has been decided to make the following grants: to the Kolchuginsk line 15 million roubles for construction and 2 million roubles for running costs, to the Altay line 3 million roubles, to the Troitsky line 2 million roubles, to the North Uralsk line 1 million roubles.
25. The Ministry of Transport is considering the question of building the rail link Baikal–Bodaybo and making a safe haven on Lake Baikal.
26. In Vladivostok there are up to 100 000 wagons which America sent to Russia.
27. The rail line from Kostroma to the north Ural lines forms a continuous track to Tomsk. In the spring of next year work will commence on building a station in Ishim.
28. The question has been raised about releasing 350 000 roubles for research and work on constructing a harbour at the mouth of the Yenisey River.

Agriculture:

29. The Yakutsk Provincial Land Directorate has proposed to the Irkutsk Directorate to make joint purchases of agricultural machines and equipment.

The Directory

30. It has been proposed that a Department of Agronomy should be established in the University of Irkutsk.
31. The Ministry of Internal Affairs has ordered its agricultural sections to take steps to prevent the peasants seizing large agricultural holdings, a process which is still continuing in certain places.

Food supplies:

32. The right to buy and distribute salt from the Iletsk workings has been granted to the Mid-Volga Union of Co-operative Societies.
33. Huge stocks of sugar have been built up in Harbin, which were intended for Western Siberia.
34. Maximum prices have been fixed in Chita: wheat, 9 roubles 30 kopecks; rye, 8 roubles 25 kopecks; oats, 6 roubles per pood.
35. All commercial and co-operative organisations distributing grain to the public are forbidden to add more than 5 per cent mark-up on the basic prices.
36. The overall demand for kerosene in Siberia is calculated at 3 million poods. Only 250 000 poods have been allocated, i.e., 12 per cent of the quantity required.
37. It has been resolved in Samara to form a trust of co-operatives, towns, *zemstvos* and other bodies concerned with the processing of meat.
38. Co-operative societies and commercial unions who are concerned with the processing of grain in Irkutsk Province and Yakutsk *Oblast* are obliged to make applications in writing to obtain certificates authorising them to purchase. Anyone not observing this decree is liable to be punished by having their purchased stocks confiscated.
39. Irkutsk meat traders are seeking to export cattle from Mongolia.

Industry:

40. Factories in Kyshtym and Verkhne-Isetsk are proposing to produce brass.
41. In Samara Province many private factories nationalised by the Soviet Government are being returned to their former owners.
42. It has been resolved to requisition 172 500 poods of dye extract for the needs of the leather industry in Irkutsk Province.
43. The commission on growing, collecting and studying medicinal plants in Irkutsk has received from the province's *zemstvo* management a subsidy of 800 roubles for the completion of its work in the experimental field.

44. The Usole saltworks in the trans-Baikal area continue to work well, in spite of Bolshevik agitation, and are turning out 110–130 thousand poods of salt per month. The stocks at the works amount to 250 000 poods of salt.

Business of the co-operatives:

45. The regulations of the All-Siberian Council of co-operative congresses have been confirmed and a Council of 19 persons has been elected with its offices in Omsk.
46. Zakupsbyt has granted 100 000 roubles in aid to the Omsk Agricultural Institute.
47. The Ekaterinburg Central Board of co-operative unions has bought a leather factory from the Shadrinsk merchant Chernykh for 250 000 roubles.
48. It should be noted that the Zakupsbyt and Ural-Sibir groups are combining for the processing of raw materials. The joint board will contain representatives of both organisations.
49. The joint co-operative societies of the north-eastern area at Perm have bought the firm Igolnoye tovarishchestvo for 300 000 roubles, cloth trade of Tikmin for 250 000 roubles, cloth trade of Izhboldin for 240 000 roubles, and the bread trade of Fayzulin for 200 000 roubles.
50. The Yenisey Co-operative Union has acquired the property of Supruy near the station Tayshet, a site at Yeniseysk for building the workshops and a soap factory in Kansk.

Mining:

51. A significant expansion in working is envisaged for the Chelyabinsk area, building a rail link Orsk–Troitsk and completing the Orsk–Orenburg line to facilitate the transport of anthracite from the area of Poltava and Bredinsk.
52. According to the newspaper *Altay*, oil has been discovered by P.I. Yegorov within the town boundaries of Biysk.
53. It is proposed to found in Siberia a section of the Russian Geological Committee; at the present moment 155 000 roubles have already been assigned to meet the estimated expenses of the Committee.

Labour questions:

54. The Commissariat for Labour and Industry in Irkutsk is proposing to attach labour sections to the district *zemstvo* authorities.
55. In Irkutsk an army order has established rules for using the labour of prisoners of war. This has been instituted because some prisoners of war let out to work have abused their freedom.

Commercial and Industrial News, No.2, 18 October 1918

Industry and Trade:

1. The Society of Leather Industry Specialists has resolved to press for the abolition of the monopoly in leather, to recognise that there is no justification for the action of the Omsk Area Committee awarding to the meat traders' union a contract for collecting meat, and to propose to the members of the Society that they should hand over the stocks they hold to authorised personnel of the District Co-operative.
2. A Society of Leather Manufacturers has been formed with the name 'Badan', whose object is to assure the supply of leather manufacturing materials to members of the Society.
3. The Barnaul Military-Industrial Committee is negotiating for the purchase of 35 000 sheepskins for sheepskin coats for the army.
4. Until special arrangements can be made it is forbidden to export *valenki* [felt boots] and winter coats from Altay Province until further notice.
5. The Ministry of Food is taking in hand the distribution of 500 wagon loads of goods which were being sent to Soviet Russia and were confiscated in Chelyabinsk. These goods are being distributed to co-operatives.
6. At the trade market in Omsk there was discussion about organising the planned purchase in the Far East of goods for the army and the public...
11. The Directorate of Migrants is proceeding to set up works for producing rosin and turpentine 30 *versts* from the town of Tara.
12. The *zemstvo* of Tomsk province has announced a prize competition for designs of pottery ware.
13. On former government land near the station of Ileysk, intensive preparations are in hand for the construction of a sugar factory.
14. Representatives of the Baltic Shipbuilding Works are discussing the construction of a large machine tool factory in Barnaul.
15. The Zakupsbyt and Ural-Sibir groups are coming together for the preparation of raw material.

Finance:

16. The Siberian, Ufa, Samara and Orenburg Credit Unions have reached an agreement to carry out all purchases on the Russian and foreign markets throughout the Siberian Credit Union.
17. The Kurgan *Zemstvo* is discussing the question of founding in Tomsk a peasant land bank.

18. In all there are up to 600 poods of gold in Siberia. During the war in the whole of Russia the gold reserves reached 2000 poods.
19. The Ministry of Finances has organised a department to restore the educational committees which used to be attached to the ministry...

Communications:

27. To struggle against mass incidents of illegal wood cutting in Tomsk province, mobile bands of armed guards are being formed.

Co-operatives:

28. Some co-operatives have turned to the credit unions with a request to help exploit the mineral wealth of Siberia, in order to prevent those riches being transferred into private hands or abroad...
32. The Altay Union of Co-operatives has started to build an electric power station at its leather factory in Barnaul.
33. Zakupsbyt is busy discussing the question of the development of the chemical industry in Siberia. The board had decided to move quickly to establish a soda water plant and a wool washery...
36. A project has been put forward to equip a Co-operative Palace in Omsk, which would house the town's co-operative societies, plus a museum, library and other services.
37. A project has been advanced to establish a pension fund for employees of the Union of Credit Unions for Siberia and the Urals...
40. In Russia there are 26 000 consumer co-operatives, with 9 million members and an annual turn-over of 5 milliard roubles.

Commercial and Industrial News, No.3, 21 October 1918

Finances:

1. The financial situation of Siberia is improving: a foreign loan of 200 million roubles has been concluded, which will be received in Russian banknotes...
4. In Siberia state regulation of the economy has been established, independent of the disruptive executive authorities...
11. Irkutsk has received from the Nadezhdinskii mine in the Lena region gold weighing 600 poods, almost 74 million roubles' worth, if each bar is valued at 32 roubles.
12. The amount of gold taken by the Bolsheviks from Blagoveshchensk to Alekseevsk is 200 poods.

Industry:

18. The leather monopoly has been replaced by state regulation of the leather industry. All aspects of leather production will come under the Ministry of Supply.
19. Zakupbyt has begun to produce various sorts of medical soap in its soap works, and is organising the purchase of other pharmaceutical items...

Production and Supply:

28. The speculators' price for kerosene has reached 9–10 roubles a pound...
32. According to rumours, Zakupsbyt has received from the Far East several wagon loads of copper goods, which are in very short supply in Siberia.
33. The Omsk War Industry Committee has taken upon itself the task of equipping all those Allied troops which have already arrived in Siberia...

Commercial and Industrial News, No.6, 28 October 1918

Industry:

12. The Siberian government has returned the Kyshtymskii district to the Urals government, in return for 4.5 million roubles grant in metals...
20. The Council of Co-operative Congresses has formed two new departments: the economic department and the law department.
22. Since the overthrow of the Bolsheviks, unemployment has gradually fallen; thus in Troitsk there are now about 170 unemployed, compared to 4000 in the Soviet period...

Commercial and Industrial News, No.8, 1 November 1918

Industry:

9. In their Zabaikal mine the Shumov Brothers extracted 33 pounds (400 grams) of gold between 6 and 25 September. For the whole Soviet period on 1 pood 10 pounds was produced.

Co-operatives:

21. The Congress of East Siberian Co-operatives in Irkutsk decided at the end of September to establish an Industrial Co-operative Union of East Siberia, which would in turn join a similar All-Siberian co-operative organisation . . .

Labour question:

25. The Omsk *Oblast* labour commissar is trying to establish arbitration courts; in this he is being supported by the Council of Trade Unions.
26. According to figure published in *Zarya*, for the first half of 1918 the unemployed population of Siberia stood at 500 000. During the same period 113 000 refugees crossed into Siberia through Chelyabinsk.

Commercial and Industrial News, No.9, 4 November 1918

Trade:

6. *Zarya*, for 6 October, carries an article critical of the policy of price limits for bread.
7. According to *Russkaya rech* the dramatically increased flow of goods on to the market has pushed up prices in Harbin, whereas in Irkutsk the price of manufactured goods, clothing, shoes and sugar has fallen markedly.

Industry:

8. The Yenisei Congress of Co-operatives has acquired a leather works, equipped with machinery and raw materials for several months' work.
9. *Siberia* reports that the Yenisei Union of Co-operatives has acquired the former Velgurskii brick works in Krasnoyarsk; the factory can produce up to two million bricks in a season.

Commercial and Industrial News, No.10, 6 November 1918

Administrative news:

1. In issue number 51 of the *Siberian Herald* there appears a decree from Administrative Council of the Provisional Government establishing state regulation in Siberia . . .

Industry:

8. According to *Russkaya Rech*, the leather industry in Novo-Nikolaevsk died during the existence of the monopoly, and most factor-

ies closed. The biggest, the 1915 Company, has only recently resumed production...

Production and Supply:

13. *Siberian News*, number 54, reports that the Ministry of Production considers the establishment of fixed or limited prices for oil products to be irrational at the present time...
16. *Siberian News*, number 54, states that the Ministry of Finance will soon buy large quantities of sugar from abroad. The Ministry of Production will compile a plan to supply the army and the civil population. The state monopoly of sugar stays in force.

Commercial and Industrial News, No.11, 8 November 1918

Finance:

7. The newspaper *Unity* has been comparing prices in Petropavlovsk for basic necessities between 1917 and 1918: wheat flour, from 7 roubles to 25 roubles per pood; rye bread, from 12 kopecks to 1 rouble 30 kopecks per pound; milk, 1 rouble 50 kopecks to 4 roubles for a quarter bucket; butter, 1 rouble to 5 roubles a pound; eggs, 40 kopecks to 3 roubles for ten; ordinary salami, 40 kopecks to 3 roubles 50 kopecks; fresh fish, 30 kopecks to 3 roubles; sugar, 35 kopecks to 8 roubles per pound; tea, 2 roubles 60 to 19 roubles per pound...

Stock exchange news:

17. The United Credit Co-operatives intend to produce in Siberia: 26 000 mowing machines with rakes; 27 000 harvesters; 5000 bailers; 8500 reapers; 7500 binders; and 240 000 poods of binder twine.
18. Irkutsk co-operatives have received 100 000 roubles through the department of the Moscow Narodnyi Bank to supply the current account of the Czechoslovak staff.
19. Professor S.N. Nikonov has put forward a plan for the establishment of an Institute of the Co-operative Economy in Vladivostok.

Commercial and Industrial News, No.12, 11 November 1918

Finance:

1. In Vladivostok a plan is being worked out by representatives of the Allied powers and financiers to establish an International Bank for Siberia...

8. According to *Siberia*, Zakupsbyt has prepared for export supplies of butter, horse hair, furs and other goods to the value of 10 million roubles. The foreign currency earned in this way will be given to the Siberian government...

DOCUMENT 1.10

Of course, the Higher Supply Council of the Allied Armies was not only concerned with the economy. Its primary concern was with mobilising an effective anti-Bolshevik army and gathering intelligence upon which that army could act.

The following telegrams, intercepts and reports give a flavour of this material, and stress the point made repeatedly by members of the Directory, after its overthrow, that there was no military reason for Kolchak's action; mobilisation and supply were going well. Note also the bleak description given of life in Soviet Russia.

RGVA, *f*. 39459, *op*. 1, *ed. khr.* 48, *ll*. 2, 5, 21, 26, 28

Higher Supply Council of the Allied Armies, 1918.

Telegrams

1. Omsk, 14 September
According to information received, mobilisation in Nizhne-Udinsk is proceeding with excellent results. The morale of those enrolled could not be better. They do their training willingly and with good heart. The population is also well disposed to the mobilisation. There is no disorder anywhere.

2. Omsk, 14 September. One of the radio-telegrams we have intercepted announces that, according to the newspaper *Kievskoe utro*, among the 121 persons to be shot by the Bolsheviks in the event of more attempts on the life of Bolshevik commissars are the names of the royal princes Dmitrii Konstantinovich, Pavel Aleksandrovich, Georgi Mikhailovich and Gavril Konstantinovich. Thereafter stand the names of well-known bankers and officers.

Temporary Deputy for the Head of the Military History Section

From intercepted radio-telegrams

Omsk 17 September

A Bolshevik radio-telegram from Tashkent announces that in Tashkent a Cheka [Extraordinary Commission for Combating Counter-revolution, Sabotage and Speculation – or secret police] has been founded with the widest powers. This will draw up a list of all the bourgeoisie, the counter-revolutionary classes of the population, persons of a Rightist Socialist tendency and all officers of the Tsarist army. Lists of the above-mentioned persons will be held by the central authorities. Commissions of this type are being established in all the administrative districts of Turkestan.

The same radio-telegram announces that a general meeting of the Communist organisation for foreign citizens in Tashkent, consisting mainly of former prisoners of war, adopted a resolution in favour of supporting, defending and strengthening Soviet power.

A radio-telegram from Moscow announces that according to Rostov newspapers there have been heated attacks in the Soviet of People's Deputies in Tiflis on the Georgian government's nationalist policies.

According to Bolshevik communiqués in the North Caucasus a ruthless contest is under way between Soviet troops and the Volunteer Army.

A State of Emergency has been declared in Tsaritsyn in connection with the Bolsheviks' mobilisation of two age groups.

Temporary Deputy for the Head of the Military History Section

Omsk, 18 September

Young soldiers' training is proceeding very successfully thanks to the enthusiasm of the men under instruction. Cases of desertion have lately almost completely ceased. The people react extremely unsympathetically to desertion. Thus, for example, in the Ishim District young men who have run away are brought to the military commander by their own parents.

Temporary Deputy for the Head of the Military History Section

From Orenburg I am transmitting the following information from a person who has just arrived from Moscow:

The position in Moscow is desperate. Not only is the city out of bread, but there is not even dried fish. There are not many of the Bolshevik army in Moscow. It would not be difficult to overthrow Soviet power, but systematic terror has robbed the Muscovites of any power to act. The Embassies of Germany, Bulgaria and Turkey have left Moscow as they consider the position unstable there. The Soviet government has barricaded itself into the Kremlin, surrounding itself with international regiments, principally Chinese. Ten thousand officers have been arrested in Moscow. From Petrograd officers are sent to Kronshtadt. The people do not know that we have taken Kazan and in general know nothing about what is happening. Bread prices in Moscow have gone up to 600–800 roubles per pood. Most Soviet troops have been moved to the Volga, mainly towards Kazan.

The newspaper *Delo naroda* states that in the Ukraine there is constant friction between the Austrian and German authorities, which sometimes goes as far as armed conflict. Thus, for example, in Odessa German and Austrian officers quarrelled in the Hotel London and the Austrians as a protest proposed a toast to France. The German officers themselves think that if we manage to hold the front for another two months Germany will be decisively defeated.

Refugees from Penza say that the people of Penza are badly informed about what is going on. The Catering College is being evacuated to Vyazma. Instead of flour they are being issued with 2 pounds of rice a head. There is exactly the same severe shortage of other foodstuffs. All powers lie in the hands of the Cheka. For any talk against the Soviets people are shot by this Commission. Grain requisitioning provokes risings everywhere and the Councils of People's Deputies are constantly having to send out punishment squads. According to Press reports which the refugees have seen there is a definite change in the feelings of the German masses: the changing situation on the Western Front where one defeat is following another is leading them to demand that Russia should make territorial and economic concessions. It is generally acknowledged by all concerned with military affairs and by middle-class and other circles of society that it is absolutely essential for peace to be preserved on Germany's Eastern Front. According to all our reports, breakdown of the country's administrative apparatus, of its military power, and social structure have gone much further than was previously supposed. Food supplies in Austria are also very difficult.

Telegram

Omsk, 4 September

According to reports from the Tyumen and Yalutorovsk Districts the number of recruits reporting to their assembly points has, as in other Districts, exceeded the estimated number by one thousand or more.

Mobilisation is proceeding smoothly. The recruits and the population at large take it very seriously, fully realising that it is essential for saving our country.

DOCUMENT 1.11

So far all the documents discussed have been from the records of the Bolsheviks' democratic opponents in the summer and autumn of 1918. As the many comments in document 1.10 show, the Bolshevik position in the summer of 1918 was precarious, and they had to resort to the most ruthless use of terror to survive.

The Bolsheviks managed to cling on to power by the skin of their teeth. Not only did the SR Party stage its uprising in Samara in June 1918, but in July 1918 the Left SR Party, up until then allies of the Bolsheviks, staged an abortive uprising in Moscow and in Simbirsk on the Volga. The second of these was the more important, for although unsuccessful it weakened the Bolshevik position on the Volga and helped Komuch's People's Army capture Kazan on 8 August 1918. The door to a rendezvous with General Poole seemed to be open.

However, Lenin, it will be recalled, had offered an economic treaty to Germany and as soon as it was clear that the bait had been taken on 10 August 1918, he was able to transfer every available loyal soldier from the demarcation line with the German occupied Ukraine to Kazan, which was successfully reconquered in early September 1918. But to forge an army to reconquer the Volga the most brutal methods had to be used. Trotsky talked openly of executing every tenth man in units which refused to fight, and there can be no doubt that the sort of terror used to keep the civilian population under control in August and September 1918, referred to in document 1.10 and glorified at the time and since as the 'Red Terror', was copied at the front.

The following directive concerning the use of torture speaks for itself. The Special Section in the army played the equivalent role of the secret police, the Cheka, in the civilian population.

RTsKhIDNI, f. 17, op. 65, ed. khr. 155, l. 16

14 August 1918

Secret

Saratov, no.60

Directive

To the Special Section of the 10th Army

Comrades, I consider it essential to direct your attention most seriously to the following.

From the time when we first set up organs for the struggle against counter-revolutionaries we have more than once observed cases of physical torture of these latter, with the objective of getting important information which we need to obtain concerning the external or internal enemy.

This sort of 'investigation' has its natural causes.

1. In this matter, as in so many others, one can see shameful traces of the old regime, which, during our captivity, subjected many of us to inhumane tortures and torments.
2. We find here that we are unconsciously copying the enemy, who has no scruples about the means he employs in fighting against us.
3. Underlying the instances to which we have referred, there may be a quite understandable sense of revenge against our enemy.

In actual fact methods of physical abuse (beatings or torture) have most commonly been observed in organisations either recently created, or alternatively already starting to fall apart. Furthermore, the higher the standard of organisation achieved in the apparatus, the more strongly do its leaders react against physical means of conducting our struggle.

There are good reasons why the Cheka instruction emphasises this matter in a separate point.

I know of one case when comrade Dzerzhinskii, going round among prisoners, saw traces of blows on the face of one man under investigation. The investigator was sent for, and although he tried to excuse himself by the strain of work and several sleepless nights, none the less he got a severe dressing down and warning from the Chairman of the All-Union Cheka.

Investigators who are weak, inexperienced, or perhaps simply ill, have recourse to methods of physical intimidation, apparently not trusting to their skill, and giving way to a simple thirst for revenge. The result is that the strongest of those under investigation suffer torture to no good purpose, and reveal nothing, while those who are innocent or weak bring false testimony against themselves and others, as often used to happen under the old autocracy.

To sum up, it is very doubtful whether anything positive results from this, while there is a very marked negative result in the political sense. Worker-Peasant Power is compromised, as is the Party which directs it.

In addition – and this is undeniably crucial for the organs of our struggle – 'physical methods' of investigation halt, and even reverse, progress towards acquiring the proper habits and skills which facilitate swift and unerring investigation.

He who relies on his fist and physical strength for conducting an investigation is inevitably in danger of forgetting his own mental capacity.

An experienced and skilful investigator will always obtain better results by his skill than any ham-fisted amateur. Indeed, the more an investigator uses physical force, the less hope he has of becoming skilled and really useful in his job.

I am telling you, comrades of the Special Section, to take to heart everything that I have demonstrated above and to apply it thoroughly and without exception.

Any personnel conducting an investigation who allow themselves to use violent methods of beating, torture or anything similar I shall hold strictly to account, and shall see to it that they are kept under guard in a hospital or prison with their name published in the press.

You must set up a body of men with the highest reputation, who strike down the secret enemy assuredly, accurately and in good time. Our apparatus must be without the slightest taint of any unscrupulous methods, but all the more terrible for the enemy.

With comradely greetings

Member of the RVS of the 10th Army, i/c Special Section

DOCUMENT 1.12

This document is of exceptional interest, since it shows clearly the instability of the Bolshevik position in October 1918. Despite their reconquest of Kazan and Samara, their hold on power was threatened from the South East by cossack forces which in October 1918 still recognised the Directory. This gives added credence to the Komuch assertion that Samara was on the point of recapture in October–November 1918 (see document 1.4), and that Kolchak's coup dislocated the front at a moment when progress was being made.

RGVA, *f.* 33987, *op.* 2, *ed. khr.* 25, *l.* 23

Cypher telegram from Voronezh, 5 October 1918

To Chairman of the All-Russian Cheka Dzerzhinskii:

I must point out the serious position on the sector of the 8th and Southern Armies. Cossacks with no large forces have seized Pavlovsk and are moving towards Liski. Our units on this front are demoralised and cannot put up any effective resistance. There is no properly defined plan of action for the military command. Most of the commanders are not up to their work. It is difficult to sort out what we owe our losses to, whether they be due to treachery, stupidity or sabotage by those in charge. Reinforcements must be sent to that sector as a matter of urgency, otherwise in the near future Voronezh will be threatened by the same fate as Kazan.

Inform comrade Trotsky and the Council of People's Commissars. Please reply urgently.

Voronezh Province Cheka

DOCUMENT 1.13

Admiral Kolchak's coup in Omsk on 18 November 1918 had radically transformed the nature of the Russian Civil War. No longer would it be a struggle between a Bolshevik dictatorship and democratic forces loyal to the Constituent Assembly, but a struggle between a Bolshevik dictatorship committed to progressive social reform and reactionary generals bent on restoring the old social order. However, the ending of the First World War had an equally dramatic impact on the course of the war.

The defeat of Germany's fellow Central Powers, Bulgaria and Turkey, meant that Allied intervention no longer needed to be focused on Archangel or Vladivostok, but could reach Russia through the Black Sea. With the end of the war the initial justification for Allied involvement in Russia – that of reopening the Eastern Front – disappeared. The British Cabinet thought long and hard about whether it was right to continue to support the Russian democrats once the First World War was over, but decided to do so on the grounds that humanity could not tolerate what had happened in the Red Terror. The decision to intervene, and to exploit the Black Sea route, was taken before Kolchak's coup; but having taken a decision in the name of democracy and humanity, the government seemed at first happy enough to allow its forces to be used by the proponents of dictatorship and reaction. These press summaries transmitted to Trotsky are again self-explanatory. The arrival of the Allies signalled a new era in the civil war, while the report from the Kuban, on whose forces the Allies would soon come to rely, clearly shows the continued popularity of the Constituent Assembly and the Directory's programme even after Kolchak's coup.

RGVA, f. 33987, op. 2, ed. khr. 25, l. 138

To the train of the Chairman of the Revolutionary Military Council of the Republic

Urgent. Secret.

[Note in margin:] To Trotsky. For information.

Summary of information from the press of the occupied provinces of Department 1 of Section 1 of the Registration Directorate of the field staff of the Revolutionary Military Council of the Republic, 26/27 November 1918 5/c.

Arrival of Allied ships:

On 23 November about 3 p.m. the English light cruiser *Liverpool*, the French cruiser *Ernest Renan* and two destroyers No.79 and 54 came into Novorossiisk. The representatives who had arrived, with the French mission Captain Ernichet, with the English mission General Blackwood, and the commanding officers of the *Liverpool*, Captain Tommy, and of the *Ernest Renan*, Captain de Maynard, declared that the Allies would furnish all possible means to restore a united Russia, while General Erdeli announced that he had brought millions of rifle cartridges and shells, besides several thousand rifles.

According to the newspaper *Yuzhnyy kray*, on 25 November under the command of the English Admiral Colson there arrived in Sevastopol the English cruiser *Canterbury*, a French destroyer, *Bisson*, and an English destroyer, *Nortess*. The paper also announces that units from New Zealand and Senegal disembarked on 23 November in Novorossiisk and that General Bodero has been appointed commander of the Allied troops in the Kuban.

The Allies have chosen Constantinople as their base. The general staff of the Allied fleet is there and the staff of the French 122nd Division, commanded by General Pocard. The forts of the Bosphorus and the Dardanelles have been occupied by French units, who have artillery at their disposal. English units have occupied the Gallipoli peninsula.

On behalf of the Crimean government the Chairman of the Council of Ministers of the Crimea has come to Sevastopol to meet the Allied squadron. Welcoming the Allies he declared that the main aims of his government are the fight against Bolshevism and the restoration of Russia.

Kuban:

The paper *Gomelskaya zhizn* of 29 November announces that the Kuban Regional Parliament has adopted a resolution which declares that the restoration of Russia may take the form of an All-Russian Federal Republic, which the Kuban Region should join as a full member. The Parliament sees the fight against Bolshevism as its first priority and for this to succeed considers it essential to form a single front under a single command. The form of government of the Russian State as it will be revived depends solely on the will of the people as expressed in the All-Russian Constituent Assembly. It is essential that the South Russian States should organise a united representation for the forthcoming peace conference, and with this in mind a South Russian Union must be created on federalist principles.

Head of the Registration Directorate, Aralov

Member of the Revolutionary Military Council of the Republic, Teodori

Head of Section 1 (signature)

2 The Don Rebellion

THE SETTING

In this second collection of documents attention is focused on the cossack rebellion in the Don region of southern Russia in the spring of 1919. This was a crucial episode in the war, since it enabled General A.I. Denikin and his White Volunteer Army to break out of the distant Kuban area to which they had been confined throughout 1918 and advance through the Don and up the Volga to Tsaritsyn; from there the great armaments work at Tula was under threat and the gates of Moscow seemed to be open. In other words, the Don cossack rebellion almost resulted in the Bolsheviks' defeat, and many lessons were learned as a consequence. These lessons were more political than military in nature and related in particular to how to adapt the iron certainties of Bolshevik dogma to the realities of winning the confidence of the rural population.

Late in November 1918 the Bolshevik Central Committee decided that henceforth the needs of the Southern Front would take precedence over all other theatres of war. This was an inevitable decision. The ending of the First World War and the consequent defeat of Turkey and Bulgaria enabled Allied intervention forces to abandon the arduous sea journeys to Archangel in the north and Vladivostok in the east and reach Russia through the Black Sea. They could thus make contact with the Volunteer Army of General A.I. Denikin, and this did much to restore the morale and fighting capacity of what had become by the autumn of 1918 little more than a demoralised rabble.

The situation on the Don had been complex in 1918. The Volunteer Army had first been formed a year earlier by General M.V. Alekseev and General L.G. Kornilov in November 1917, but this attempt to turn the Don cossack lands into a counter-revolutionary power base had ended in failure; by January 1918 the key towns of Rostov and Novocherkassk were under Bolshevik control and the Volunteer Army had retreated into the Kuban, with both generals perishing in the process. Bolshevik control of the Don region, however, did not last long. It was lost in May 1918 as a consequence of the Treaty of Brest Litovsk signed between Soviet Russia and Imperial Germany in March 1918; the Don cossack leader (*ataman*), General P.A. Krasnov, retook control of the area and established an anti-Bolshevik administration there with the agreement of the Germans. So, when the Germans evacuated the region in November 1918, Krasnov's anti-Bolshevik forces remained in control of an area which extended almost as far north as Tsaritsyn. The end of the First World War put an end to the differences between the pro-Ally Volunteer Army in the Kuban and the pro-German forces of Krasnov but, soon after their arrival, British officers insisted on putting Krasnov's forces under the overall control of General Denikin's Volunteer Army.

Thus by January 1919, under the leadership of its new commander, General Denikin, the Volunteer Army was able to transform itself from a disorderly, if pro-British, rabble into an effective fighting force; and in a series of swift and dramatic operations it succeeded in freeing from Bolshevik control the whole of the North Caucasus from the Kuban to the Caspian. In the process they had routed the whole of the Red Army's Caucasus-Caspian Army Group, defeating both the 11th and 12th Armies. The 12th Army had found itself surrounded, but the 11th Army broke up in panic. This triumph in the North Caucasus, however, was not matched by success on the Don.

The problem in the Don region was this. The British insistence that Krasnov's Don forces be subject to Denikin simply re-opened old wounds, for ever since the formation of the Volunteer Army on the Don in November 1917 the cossack rank and file had made it clear that they were more interested in defending Don autonomy and the cossack way of life than overthrowing the Bolsheviks. If the British had been able to live up to their promises of additional military support, the situation might have been different, but by the beginning of 1919 morale among Krasnov's Don cossacks was low and there was little enthusiasm for continued anti-Bolshevik operations. By January 1919 several of Krasnov's cossack units had opened talks with their Red Army opponents, and on 24 January the Red Army's 9th Army could announce that four companies of cossacks had come over to them in full strength. As the cossack army began to melt away, Krasnov resigned as *ataman* and was replaced by A.P. Bogaevskii, who had closer relations with both Denikin and the British; but a majority of cossacks ignored Bogaevskii and prepared to welcome the return of 'Soviet Power'.

The self-dispersal of the cossack army enabled the Red Army to reoccupy the Upper Don District, meeting very little resistance. But whether or not the Red Army should have advanced into the area soon became a new source of tension, this time between the the Red Army and the cossacks. Those cossacks who had opened the front to the Bolsheviks argued that they had done so on the understanding that the Don area would not be occupied by the Red Army, but left to run its own affairs; and since the cossacks who had opened the front had not been militarily defeated but had returned to their villages with their weapons, they had a point. Thus control of the Don area was as much a political as a military issue; and soon the two clashed. From a political point of view it made sense for the Bolsheviks to make concessions to the cossacks; militarily the Don region needed to be crossed to further the pursuit of Denikin. The military, logically enough, insisted that the cossack regiments be disarmed rather than simply being allowed to disperse under arms to their villages; but as these documents show this military necessity was compounded by a political line designed to alienate rather than conciliate the cossacks.

When the remnants of Krasnov's army retreated across the Donets river it numbered some 30 000 men, less than half its original strength. Most cossacks would have accepted 'Soviet Power' if it had left them alone. But within weeks Bolshevik heavy handedness had prompted a rebellion on the Don which led to the rout of the Red Army and Denikin's spectacular advance. What changed the situation was not the Allied aid arriving with Denikin, but the rebellion of the Don cossacks, provoked by Bolshevik sectarianism. The Bolsheviks abandoned all ideas of Don autonomy, incorporating the area fully into Russian territory, and on the basis of a Communist Party Orgburo decision of 24 January 1919 began a policy aimed at 'the wholesale destruction of the upper elements of cossack society': in other words, class struggle on the Don. On the basis of this order zealous Party activists began a policy which came to be known as 'decossackisation'.

The Party's decision was to be implemented by two separate organisations. After the collapse of Soviet rule on the Don under German pressure in May 1918 the Party had established a Donburo to run underground Party activity; with the re-occupation of the Don in February 1919 this took over political responsibility for the region. However, given the proximity of Denikin and the Southern Front, a rival source of political authority also existed in the region, the Political Section of the Southern Front; the two did not always agree. Although appointed directly from Moscow, the Donburo was kept away from the front, based first in Kursk, then Kozlov and finally Millerovo, and only able to operate in the rear. It could scarcely be in touch with the feelings of people in the heart of the Don territory, a situation made worse by its preference for sending to the region communists from outside the region who would not be tainted by local sympathies when it came to implementing class war policies amongst the cossacks (in practice, the indiscriminate elimination of all cossacks of military age).

Even when the rebellion began on 10 March 1919, a quick change of policy might have brought results, for the rebels declared: 'The rebellion is not against the power of the soviets and Soviet Russia but only against the Party of the Communists who have taken power into their own hands in our native land' (P. Kudinov, 'Vosstanie verkhne-dontsov v 1919g: istoricheskii ocherk', *Volnoe kazachestvo*, Prague 1931, p. 81).

These documents explore the reasons for the successful rebellion and highlight what was to be a key problem for the Bolsheviks: winning the allegiance of Russia's rural population to the urban-based nostrums of primitive Marxism. In its aftermath, the Bolsheviks began to show greater flexibility and less dogmatism in dealing with the rural population. Very tardily Lenin protested against harmful extremism in his telegram of 3 June 1919:

> In its order no.27 the Revolutionary Committee of the Don *Oblast* has abolished the [cossack] term [for a village or settlement] *stanitsa*, replacing it by the [usual Russian] designation *volost*, in accordance with which it is dividing Kotelnikov region into *volosts*.
>
> In various districts of the *oblast* the local authorities are forbidding men to wear traditional cossack trouser stripes and are abolishing the word 'cossack'.
>
> In the 9th Army horse harness and carts are being requisitioned wholesale by comrade Rogachev. In many places of the *oblast* the usual local peasant fairs are forbidden. Austrian prisoners of war are being appointed as commissars in the *stanitsas*.
>
> We must point out how essential it is to be particularly careful about interference in suchlike details of daily life, which has absolutely no effect on politics in the wider sense and at the same time greatly annoys the local population. (V.I. Lenin, *Sobranie sochinenii*, 5th edition, 1965, Vol.50, p. 387)

At approximately the same time the Politburo issued a manifesto which stated:

> The worker-peasant government ... has no intention of decossackising anyone by force, it is not against the cossack way of life, but leaves the honest working cossacks their *stanitsas* and villages, their lands, their right to wear whatever uniform they like. It preserves their crafts and trades, permits local enterprises, which may employ paid workers up to ten in number, and gives assistance to these enterprises, allowing them to trade their products at fairs, markets and shops. (I.M. Borokhova et al. (eds), *Borba za vlast sovetov na Donu 1917–1920gg, sbornik dokumentov*, Rostov on Don, 1957, document 365)

The Don Rebellion 49

But by the end of May and beginning of June 1919 the damage had been done. On 30 June 1919 Denikin captured Tsaritsyn and looked set to march on Moscow.

DOCUMENT 2.1

The first part of this document is a report to the Communist Party's Organisational Bureau drawn up by G. Ya. Sokolnikov, a long-term critic of sectarian policies, expressing criticism of the 'terrorist' tactics used towards the cossacks by the Donburo and its leader, S.I. Syrtsov. An important element in the debate is the different social conditions among cossacks in the north and south, and the possibility of the Bolsheviks finding allies among the predominantly poorer cossacks in the north; this is gone into in some detail. The other major theme of the document is the extent and arbitrariness of the terror against the cossacks, from executions down to petty harassment. As the report shows, part of the trouble was that the Bolsheviks put their rapid occupation of the Don *Oblast* down to military prowess, rather than a change in attitude among the cossacks which could rapidly disappear.

A major issue raised in the report is that of social engineering through resettlement. The idea of resettling peasants from outside the Don region on land taken from the cossacks was hardly likely to be popular, but was a constant element in Bolshevik thinking and one endorsed in a decree by Lenin of 24 May 1919.

The second half of the document is the Donburo's response to the criticism expressed in Sokolnikov's report, and its anger at the decision of the Central Committee, on hearing Sokolnikov's report, to create a Don *Oblast* Revolutionary Committee in a move directed at taking power away from the Donburo. The Donburo was unwilling to confess its errors, and quite ready to blame the Central Committee for not acting on its original proposal for administering the Don. The suggestion that the region be dismembered and the bulk attached to Tsaritsyn Province shows their scant regard for cossack feelings. Their other proposed solution was equally bureaucratic: to set up a new administrative unit in the east. Clearly, the Donburo felt its policy of dismemberment and decossackisation could still be successful if firmly implemented.

It is interesting to note that initially many Bolsheviks were prepared to take a soft line with the cossacks, before the Donburo brought them to heel. Since June 1918 it had been Bolshevik policy to rely not on village soviets in the countryside, which could all too easily fall into the hands of ideological opponents like the SRs, but 'Committees of the Poor'; thus giving a political voice only to the poor and landless, deemed the most likely to support the Bolsheviks. Thus a willingness to establish 'cossack soviets' rather than Committees of the Poor, enfranchising all cossacks, was a considerable concession and a clear departure from class-war based policies.

The delay in the receipt of telegrams and other communications was a perpetual problem in this and other theatres of war.

RTsKhIDNI, *f.* 17, *op.* 65, *ed. khr.* 34, *ll.* 85–169 [extracts] [precise date unclear, late June 1919]

To the Orgburo of the Russian Communist Party (Bolsheviks) (RKP(b)) Central Committee: a Report

Before the formation of the Don Revolutionary Committee, civilian life in those areas of the Don *Oblast* cleared of the enemy was in the hands of the Civilian Directorate of the Southern Front. This organisation was headed by Comrade Syrtsov, who was the chief of the Civilian Administration and who at the same time led the work of the Party's Donburo. Uniting in one pair of hands ideological Party work and practical work in establishing Soviet power could and has in the past had a certain use; but in other circumstances and for implementing other policies. In the given situation, this unity resulted in colossal harm for the RSFSR. Instead of controlling the work of one organisation through activity in another, instead of implementing a line drawn up from experience and healthy thought, there was united work, dominated by a single will, but a will which falsely understood the situation in which that work was being carried out and the tasks which stood before them.

Comrade Sokolnikov replied thus to the question of the causes of the uprising in the Veshenskaya region:

> The uprising in Veshenskaya region had its origins in the adoption by the military political chain of command and revolutionary committee of a policy of mass terror towards the cossacks, who had risen against Krasnov and opened the front to Soviet forces.

Comrade Sokolnikov is a member of the Revolutionary Military Council of the Southern Front, in other words someone responsible for work of a political nature and for the revolutionary committees in the region, and the actions of the army loyal to him. He cannot be suspected of partiality or bias. All the more so since the information I have been able to collect fully confirms the view of Sokolnikov. This information shows the clamouringly negligent and criminally frivolous attitude of the Party's Donburo and Civilian Administration to its duties. Instead of a serious analysis of the situation, the work of these institutions was imbued with decisions taken hurriedly and in an off-hand way.

To take just the main and basic point, the attitude towards the cossacks. According to the report of the Donburo (Comrade Syrtsov), based, apparently, on the local situation and local circumstances, the Don Committee of the Russian Communist Party worked out its line for Party activity. I will not dwell on the results of that activity, the Central Committee already knows about it, but I must say a few words about the arguments behind that policy, arguments defended by the Party's Donburo.

The Donburo based itself on two considerations: (1) the counter-revolutionary nature of the cossacks in general; and (2) the victorious advance and power of our army. The cossacks were open counter-revolutionaries who had to be destroyed and the Red Army was capable of doing this – that was the main thought of the Donburo.

The groundless accusation that the cossacks were counter-revolutionary is, of course, the product of immature reflection. Being determines consciousness, that is the truth that has always guided us. The being of the cossacks in a good half of the Don *Oblast*, all the northern and eastern regions, is far from a reality which would inevitably push them into the camp of the counter-revolution. The cossack land allotment in these regions averages 2–4 *desyatins* [1 *desyatin* = 1.09 hectares], and cossack privileges concerning trade and industry have no relevance here, for trade and industry is very poorly developed. Cossack conditions of life are no better than in the adjacent provinces of Voronezh, Tambov and Saratov. As well as this, in the Don *Oblast* there is one circumstance which is very beneficial for Soviet Russia, the fact that material benefits are very unevenly distributed between the north and the south. The land allotment in southern regions averages 20–25 *desyatins*, while in the north, as already stated, it is only 2–4. The cossack privileges of tax-free trade and the right to organise industrial or mining concerns is of great importance in the Cherkassk area and in other industrial areas, but these rights are of no use in the north. Similarly, the fishing rights are of use in the villages spread along the lower Don or on the Azov Sea but have no importance in northern areas like Medvedinkii or Khoperskii.

In a word, all the cossack properties and privileges which made the cossacks a loyal bulwark of the Russian autocracy are concentrated exclusively in the south of the *oblast* and were created more or less artificially. Southern *stanitsas*, like, for example, Novocherkasskaya, were constantly to the fore in administering the Don *Oblast* and quite consciously took an interest only in the well-being of the southern *stanitsas*, at the expense of the north. Land from the official reserve allotment was divided almost exclusively among the *stanitsas* of the south, which explains the astounding difference between allotment sizes in the north and south.

There was more than enough material to split the cossacks, to fan old antagonisms between the north and the domineering south. The Donburo and the Civilian Administration paid no attention to this and did not bother to get to know the life of the region in which they were establishing Soviet power; for this the region paid dearly, such disregard of our usual Bolshevik practice and experience.

The Donburo still considers that it was expedient to replace the power of the soviets with repression, and healthy thought and Marxist analysis with perfunctory decisions.

Comrade Syrtsov states in his report on the insurrection in the Veshenskaya region that any policy other than the quick and decisive neutralisation of the counter-revolutionaries, other than the policy of terror, would not have controlled the situation; but that terror could not be made sufficiently real 'for a number of reasons'.

Just how real the terror was can be seen from Syrtsov's report where, a few lines after the cited passage, he informs us that in the Veshenskaya region 600 people were shot. If you consider that the other revolutionary committees were not that far behind the Veshenskaya committee, and that in the building occupied by the Morozovskaya revolutionary committee 65 *mutilated* cossack bodies were found – which there had not been time to bury – then the picture of terror in the region controlled by the Donburo and the Civilian Administration is imposing enough. It should be noted that Boguslavskii, the president of the Morozovskaya revolutionary committee, who has since been shot after being sentenced by the Tribunal, was an old Party worker.

To illustrate the relationships created on the Don, I also think it necessary to inform the Central Committee that, as part of their agitational propaganda, the insurrectionary cossacks used the circular letter put out by Party organisations on the necessity of using terror with regard to the cossacks, and the telegram sent to Kolegaev, a member of the Revolutionary Military Council of the Southern Front, which mentioned destroying the cossacks without mercy. Of course, they could not have invented better agitational material.

The second basic mistake of the Donburo and the Civilian Administration was that their view of our military situation was quite inaccurate. Our victories in the Don *oblast* could be explained in the main by the dislocation of the cossacks, and changes in their mood. Instead of using this change of mood and strengthening the undoubted pro-Soviet attitude among the cossacks, the Donburo decided to rely on the bayonet and cut off the branch which supported Soviet power on the Don. These two mistakes, bordering on crimes, which we made on the Don completely shuffled the pack and complicated the situation. A lot of effort, and a lot of tact, was needed to put the situation right. Above all it is now necessary to remove from Don work all those compromised by the previous policy, the comrades of the old line. We need completely new people, with new constructive policies; only then will it be possible to hope for success.

The bases for this new constructive policy must be the following principles: the policy of repression, in regard to all cossacks, must be firmly and definitively rejected; however, that should not hinder the merciless prosecution *through the courts* of all counter-revolutionaries.

We must abandon the thought of settling in the Don *Oblast*, as soon as it has been liberated, peasants from the northern provinces. Such a resettlement would be difficult to implement, politically harmful, and, of course, would provide a permanent justification for insurrection. Resettlement, in the form in which it has been carried out so far, without any properly worked out plan or special organisation, is a crime of the highest order against those resettled, whom the cossacks simply butcher, and against the Soviet Republic, which by resettlement, among other reasons, prepared the Don insurrection.

During the first months in which Soviet power existed in the Don *Oblast* we should have limited ourselves to resettling cossacks from the northern regions to the south, to equalising cossack shares with the land allotments of peasants already living in Don villages. Resettling cossacks from one region to another is nothing new for cossacks, since such a policy was practised once before in trying to equalise allotments, until it was ended thirty years ago when the dominant southern stanitsasages decided not to give more land to the north. Allotting land to peasants already living in the Don would also be possible peacefully enough, since there was talk of this when the Tsar was on the throne and such talk did not meet with great opposition.

By resettling northerners in the south we will attract to our side both those who are resettled and the *stanitsas* from whence they are taken, since their land share will increase. This way it would be possible to create a definite cadre of 'Soviet cossacks'. However, such a task must be undertaken with great attention and care.

The striped cossack military trousers and the very words 'cossack' and 'cossack *stanitsas*' conjured up the archetypal cossack, but their life-style was ignored; it needed to be deeply analysed and agitational and propaganda material prepared which would show the dark side of cossack tradition and the bright future offered by the Soviet system. Then the cossacks would have ceased to be 'cossacks'...

[The report then moves on to how liberated regions were administered, and in particular the poor quality of personnel in Khoperskii region.]

Office workers of the old regime found themselves nice little jobs where it was especially harmful to put people with the old working traditions, like in the department of wards and guardians.

There was no proper application form, from which it would have been possible to learn of their unsuitability or black hundred views. Thus the composition of office staff served to slow down the proper speed and energy of the Soviet administration. Apart from that, there was a whole series of occasions when commissars were not called to account for stealing from villages and homesteads, getting drunk, abusing their authority, using all sorts of force against the population, seizing cattle, milk, bread, eggs and other products for their own use; they would also denounce people to the Revolutionary Tribunal if they complained. In June this bacchanalia prompted the Revolutionary Committee to issue its pronouncement 'Commissars, smarten yourselves up!'

Commissars from the Revolutionary Tribunal's investigation and searches department routinely confiscated goods quite illegally, on the basis of their own personal whims; thereafter, as notes taken at the time show, the confiscated items disappeared into thin air. Such requisitioning, and this is confirmed in written and oral testimony, was accompanied by physical force. The actions of the investigation and searches department so angered the local population that it was recognised as essential to disband the institution as quickly as possible; this was not done, however, since the insurrection took hold and the region had to be evacuated as Denikin's band advanced.

The activity of the Revolutionary Tribunal was based, despite the relevant decrees, on the mixed principle: it was a revolutionary tribunal and Cheka combined, issuing sentences behind closed doors without right of appeal or the participation of the defence. Its activity was so obviously outrageous and so divorced from the spirit of the Party and

Soviet power, that it must be seen as one of the main reasons for the insurrection in the Khoperskii region. Its activity was undoubtedly one of terror towards the peaceful population, inspired by the incorrect direcives of the Civilian Administration and blindly implemented by the Tribunal leadership, first of all its president German, and then Marchevskii, with the enthusiastic support of its members Tsislinskii and Demkin.

The point is that every day the Tribunal handled some 50 cases, showing just how carefully they must have gone into them. Death sentences were handed out in bundles, so that often those who were shot were quite innocent old men, women and children.

[Some details of these miscarriages of justice are given.]

Only towards the end, by 1 June, did the shootings cease, especially – it is my belief – after popular pressure and the growing anger of the population began to be felt and the Donburo demanded that the Revolutionary Committee change the policy of the Revolutionary Tribunal. Even the Civilian Administration felt the need to lessen the policy of terror, on the specious grounds that more peaceful times had arrived, but actually, it seems to me, because they could see the results of their actions in letting the Revolutionary Tribunal go too far. From the moment of my arrival, with the help of other communists from the centre, I undertook a determined struggle against the Donburo and the Revolutionary Committee, insistently demanding a change in the composition of the Revolutionary Tribunal and demanding that it be brought to court. This almost succeeded, but the insurrection and evacuation overtook events and the question was postponed...

Resolution on the Question of the Report of Comrade Syrtsov

The Donburo of the RKP(b), having discussed the report from Comrade Sokolnikov on the Central Committee's decision to establish a 'Don *Oblast* Revolutionary Committee', considers it necessary to inform the Central Committee of its view on the question.

The January and February advances of our forces, marking the start of the liberation of localities in the Don *oblast*, raised the question of forming a Soviet Centre to undertake Soviet construction, a centre strong enough to undertake such construction.

The absence of such a centre meant that the question of creating organs of power was being undertaken haphazardly. The political departments of divisions, specially organised commissions of such departments for peasant or town work, commissars and political workers from various units, all established local organs of government, acting as they saw fit and without any overall plan which could be dictated by a Soviet Centre. This haphazard and unsystematic work meant that in many areas elected cossack soviets were formed, as well as committees of the poor, despite the instruction of the Donburo that it was essential to create revolutionary committees based only on trustworthy elements.

The Donburo, recognising the necessity for a Soviet Centre, acted promptly and turned to the Central Committee with the suggestion that a proposal be put through All-Russian Executive Committee of the Soviets establishing a Temporary Revolutionary Committee for liberated localities in the Don *Oblast*.

The Donburo's proposal was turned down. The question was decided in the negative. It was decided, without any intermediate body, to submit all the military and civilian authorities in the area to the Revolutionary Military Council of the Southern Front, which was told on questions of Soviet construction to work in contact with the Donburo. To establish that contact, Syrtsov, a member of the Donburo, was told to go to Kozlov, to the Revolutionary Military Council of the Southern Front (telegram of Comrade Sverdlov).

With great difficulty and considerable friction the leadership implemented the establishment of regional revolutionary committees, as far as was conceivable in the specific circumstances of being in Kozlov.

At the present moment, when the sphere of our influence covers a huge territory, four-fifths of the Don *Oblast*, our organisational work requires two centres: for the north-east and the west.

The economic and social situation of the population in these two parts is very different. The north-east part has long gravitated towards Tsaritsyn, and is populated by peasants and cossacks who are much poorer than those in the south and for that reason less counter-revolutionary, closer to the situation of the peasantry.

The Donburo at one time put forward the proposal that this region should be attached to Tsaritsyn province. Such a unification would have made a good deal of political sense. The passive cossacks would, in terms of organisation, be cut off from the influence of the southern cossacks and would be transformed into simple peasants. As a percentage of the population at large they would decline from 45 to 30 per cent, and they would be linked to Tsaritsyn, a town with an appreciably sized proletariat and a Soviet apparatus of considerable size and experience.

This proposal was welcomed in principle by the Central Committee and given practical confirmation from the People's Commissar for Internal Affairs.

This project met with no objections in principal from the Revolutionary Military Council of the Southern Front and as late as March it agreed, with some reservations, to the separation of the left bank of the Don *Oblast*.

The only communication put out by the Revolutionary Military Council on the matter concerned the fear of losing influence over policy in the region. But that fear was quite unfounded if the Centre was subject to the Revolutionary Military Council and had its representatives on it.

Now, when there are 11 regional revolutionary committees and the centre running these committees is the Department of Civilian Administration based in Kozlov, the current situation has become unthinkable. The following illustration of what can happen in these circumstances is characteristic: telegrams sent from Kozlov at the end of March and early April are arriving only now in the middle of May.

Apart from political motives, the very separation of the western and eastern parts of the *oblast* make it essential that two organs be created to serve both parts. In particular, the Department of Civilian Administration concluded it was essential to have an organ for the western part (the Civilian Administration Bureau) based in Millerovo. The experiment was successful. Instead of the long and tiresome red tape of contact by courier with Kozlov, it became possible for the five revolutionary committees linked to Millerovo to decide issues quickly on the spot.

The creation now of a Don *Oblast* Revolutionary Committee (turned down once before by the Central Committee and whose very existence hinders the dismemberment of the Don *Oblast*) when:

1. in effect the eastern part is already linked to Tsaritsyn and the western part has its temporary centre in Millerovo;
2. workers and peasants have already taken on board the idea of dismembering the *oblast*;
3. there is every reason to believe that the eastern and northern cossacks have accepted the idea of abolishing 'a united Don'.

This is a big step backwards. This decision can only disorganise work on the ground. (Incidentally, it should be taken into account that organising the Revolutionary Committee and making contact with all the localities will take a considerable time. Even once it is organised, it will not be able to serve both parts of the *oblast*, and depending where it is based, will serve only one half but not both.) It will lead to confusion in the consciousness of the worker and peasant masses, who accepted the slogan of 'decossackisation'. And finally, by giving organisational expression to the line of agreement with the cossacks (Comrade Sokolnikov's point of view), it will create among the mass of cossacks (including those ready to accept the dismemberment of the *oblast*) the illusion that it will be possible to retain both 'a united Don' and the cossacks in general. To create an organ of power for the whole *oblast* at this moment – the proposal of those favouring agreement and 'not repelling the cossacks' – is to contradict the essence of the principled line adopted by the Central Committee when it confirmed the Donburo's resolution on relations with the cossacks.

That meeting of 8 April and the confirmation of its resolution on relations with the cossacks by the Central Committee obliges the Donburo to ask the Central Committee for clarification as to whether that resolution is to be implemented in full or has now been reconsidered by the Central Committee.

There is one further side to this question, which is of the essence. The circumstances surrounding the creation of a Don *Oblast* Revolutionary Committee do not of themselves make it possible to establish a proper mutual relationship between the committee and the Donburo, the sort of mutual relationship which has been established by practical work of Soviet and Party organisations throughout Russia.

For all these reasons, the Donburo considers this step a mistake for which it cannot take responsibility. It considers it essential that all its attention and all the activity of its members should be focused on strengthening organisational and political work to create a firm basis (of party organisation) for Soviet work.

DOCUMENT 2.2

The document is a detailed report written after the event by T. Khodorovskii in which he outlines the reasons for the Bolsheviks' failure. He concentrates on the weakening material strength of the army, in particular the ravages of illness, the failure to provide adequate reinforcements, and the need to transfer units to fight the insurrection. His focus is the front line on the river Donets, and it is very clear from the document that those at the front line felt that the commanders in the rear had only the haziest of notions of the real situation at the front; of the military lessons learned, the most important was that of the need to fight cavalry with cavalry. For most of the document Khodorovskii concentrates on military matters and concludes that the reason for the defeat was the Red Army's organisational failure and the organisational abilities of Denikin. When political matters are raised, it is clear this man at the front was as hardline as any theorist in the Donburo, having no time for any cossacks; more decossackisation rather than less was his solution, inflaming a class war. The distinction between the poor cossacks in the north and the rich in the south becomes a common concern in all discussions about whether some cossacks could be conciliated.

RTsKhIDNI, f. 17, op. 109, ed. khr. 44, ll. 135–42 [extracts]

Moscow, 12 August 1919

Why we were Defeated on the Southern Front

Memorandum

Copies of this have been sent to comrade Lenin, comrade Trotsky, members of the Central Committee and members of the Revolutionary Military Council Comrades Sklanskii, Gusev and Rykov.

Our successes on the southern front in January–March 1919 can be explained by the following:

1. our numerical superiority over the enemy and our technical advantage compared to theirs;
2. our ideological advantage compared to the enemy, and also the ideological cohesion and upsurge of our army, which was, in a significant degree, the result of intensive political work; and
3. demoralisation among the cossack ranks, caused, for the most part, by Krasnov's attempts to drag those cossacks attached to their villages and homesteads, into a distant march northwards, beyond the borders of the Don region.

That was how things stood in January and February. Starting in March, however, the situation began to change noticeably, in a way harmful to us. Steadily, but at a rapid tempo, numerical superiority and technical advantage began to move from us to the enemy. The dislocation among the cossacks turned to cohesion and organisation. Our ideological advantage over the enemy was preserved, but this factor could only produce a successful outcome for the campaign if combined with material strength, and this did not happen for our forces weakened daily. In these circumstances no political work could do what needed to be done to keep the necessary number of regiments supplied and up to strength.

The Dying Army

During January and February, in never-ending battles, the armies of the southern front marched up to 500 *versts*, not having at their disposal a single railway (they were all destroyed). The wounded, the ill and the exhausted left the ranks daily in large numbers. From the end of February the armies of the southern front were struck down by an epidemic of typhus, which got daily worse as we continued deep into the Don *Oblast*. In the Don *Oblast* itself typhus had already taken hold of the population, affecting work in the villages and stanitsasteads. Naturally this strengthened the grip of the epidemic on the army as well. I remind you how the Chief Health Officer of the Southern Front, Doctor Fishman, asserted more than once in his reports to the Revolutionary Military Council of the Southern Front that, although typhus could be observed in all the armies of the front, there was no epidemic; only separate cases in almost all units. He accompanied these reports with figures which purported to prove his findings.

When I arrived with the 9th Army at the start of April I was horrified at what I found – barracks, hospitals, shelters overflowing with victims of typhus. For every division of six regiments (and if the division had three brigades then there were nine regiments) there was one, or at best two doctors, and the regimental 'coolers' were being used as a medical unit. Not only were there no doctors, but no medical orderlies and no nurses. On a tour of inspection I asked about medicines, but everywhere the picture was the same; there were no medicines and any bandages had to be re-used repeatedly. This was taking place when the Chief Health Officer could report that he had ample supplies for the biggest evacuation of the ill and wounded ever undertaken; but there was no such evacuation.

[The author describes the evacuation he organised, and gives details of the difficulties involved in the journey, loading stretchers on and off boats, over pontoon bridges, etc.]

I confirm that the Health Office of the Southern Front did nothing to help the proper evacuation of the ill and wounded ... The Chief Health Officer, Doctor Fishman, claimed that there was no typhus epidemic in the army, when in fact there was the most terrible epidemic. From regiments numbering 400–500 men, 30–40 a day were succumbing.

The Don Rebellion 61

Absence of Reinforcements

But no reinforcements arrived. By the end of April and beginning of May the strength of the 9th Army was as follows:

14 division	on 30 April	5 353 bayonets	920 sabres
16 division	"	3 428	373
23 division	on 13 May	2 225	809
	total	11 006	2 602
			[*sic*: 2102]

or in all 13 608 men.

At that time, intelligence reports gave the enemy's forces deployed against the 9th Army as 10 190 bayonets and 11 720 sabres, or 21 910 men. And, in fact, if you take into account that between 30 April and 12 May many men fell out of the 14th and 16th divisions, the actual position was even less favourable to us.

Overall, the enemy had roughly double our resources on 12 May. And, in the situation on the Don front the advantage in cavalry was particularly important; the enemy had 11 720 sabres against our 2602. During the course of May the army continued to shrink, partly because of typhus, partly because of the bitter battles for control of the Don. It was quite clear to the Revolutionary Military Council of the 9th Army that with such forces the Army not only could not attack, but could not hold the left bank of the Donets, which from the middle of May was already subject to occasional cavalry raids. During April and May the Revolutionary Military Council of the 9th Army sent a series of telegrams to the appropriate authorities.

[These telegrams are reproduced, all asking for reinforcements in increasingly urgent tones.]

These telegrams had no impact until the moment when catastrophe was already upon us, even though the Revolutionary Military Council of the 9th Army had sent the Southern Front not only these worrying telegrams, but also detailed figures concerning the state of the army. I do not know who to blame, but these figures were not taken on board by the organisations to whom they were addressed and the southern front continued to believe that our early numerical superiority had been maintained, even though in the course of March up to 15 000 men had been transferred from the 8th and 9th Armies to fight the insurrection, which was bound to weaken these armies on the main front even more.

What did we do in March, April and May

During March and April no organisational work was carried out in the Staff of the Southern Front, which of itself weakened the controlling apparatus, both of all the armies and each army individually. By 10 March the 8th and 9th Armies had come to the line of the Donets, and with that our successes on the southern front came to an end. The Supreme Commander Vatsetis gave the command of the southern front the task of liquidating the enemy in the Donets Basin, and to this end the Commander of the Southern Front Gittis was ordered to move to Kupyansk to take over direct responsibility for operations to occupy the Donets Basin.

I do not want to be so brave as to criticise this plan, but must point out that the trip of Commander Gittis to Kupyansk and his absence for more than six weeks from Kozlov (the HQ of the Southern Front) meant that the work of the Southern Front practically stopped, something quite inevitable since no one can take the place of a front commander when there are crucial organisational and supply problems which can only be resolved by someone with sufficient military and business experience. I must, however, make clear that, while Gittis was in Kupyansk and later Izyuma all armies, with the exception of the 13th, were without leadership or direction from the front, and in the Front HQ itself chaos reigned, which Gittis could not immediately put right on his return. Mechanically each army was given directives, without taking into account the extent to which the army was in a state to carry out these orders. The HQ of the Southern Front was completely unaware of the real situation at the front.

The following example shows this. On 23 May the enemy crossed the front on the Donets held by the 14th and 23rd divisions. Gittis sent the following telegram to the commander of the 9th Army:

> The break in the front must be liquidated what ever happens and in the most energetic fashion. The enemy opposite the 9th Army is weak, occupying the right bank of the Donets with a weak scrappy line, broken in places and reinforced by a small, mobile group moving from place to place. It is this group that has crossed the front.

We were astounded by this telegram. The next day we informed the Front HQ that interrogations of prisoners, fugitives and captured documents made clear that opposite the 9th Army stood the Third Khoper Corps comprising five to six mounted divisions and an infantry brigade, as well as seven more mounted divisions, plus a further five to

The Don Rebellion

six divisions in the process of being moved there. Either the HQ or our Army were misinformed; whichever was the case, such a situation was unsatisfactory. Self-evidently, when the Front HQ is so out of touch, its directives become fanciful and out of touch with reality.

[The author adds as a footnote that when in July 1919 he was in Moscow, he was asked by Gusev, a member of the Revolutionary Military Council, why the 9th Army had delayed in carrying out Gittis's order: he then pointed out in person how bad it was that the commander was so poorly informed about the true state of his forces.]

The lessons of the months of fighting on the Don were poorly learnt: those working with the Don armies knew that it was impossible to fight there without cavalry, that in a war of field manoeuvres cavalry is essential, even more so in an area where there are no railways and vast roadless expanses have to be crossed. Last winter Krasnov beat us because of his mounted units, and this summer Denikin inflicted a heavy defeat by the same means. And we, the armies of the Southern Front, occupied the Don *Oblast* for three months, had at our disposal a vast quantity of suitable horses, but did not create a cavalry. Someone in the Field HQ of the Republic got the strange idea into his head to destroy the remains of our cavalry. Nevertheless, I cannot name that order from the Field HQ of the Republic in Serpukhovo by which the independent cavalry units were destroyed and the remainder brought together in divisional groups where they played a service role for the infantry. Thus we destroyed our cavalry, at a time when cavalry was deployed against us not only in divisions but in army corps, which we had to oppose with a few squadrons, a division at best.

Nothing was done to improve our strength. In no way could we come to terms with the fact that, on the Don, close at hand was the richest of unused human material. Oddly enough, there was no mobilisation in the Don *Oblast* until the very last minute (although some exceptions were made in the Millerovo and Kamenskii regions). From Morozovskaya (the HQ of the 9th Army) I repeatedly proposed to the Revolutionary Military Council of the Southern Front that we should mobilise the non-cossack peasantry in the Don *Oblast*. The majority of my telegrams were left unanswered, and Comrade Sokolnikov, a member of the Revolutionary Military Council of the Southern Front, in talks with me over the wire expressed the apprehension that mobilising the non-cossack peasantry could lead to them demonstrating against us. For me it was obvious that the Revolutionary Military Council simply would not agree to mobilisation. At the same time, work at the front among those same people convinced me that mobilising them and the workers of the Don region could pass off successfully: on 23 May I sent the following telegram to Trotsky, President of the Revolutionary Military Council:

> On several occasions I have proposed to the Revolutionary Military Council of the Southern Front that they decide as a matter of urgency the question of mobilising workers and peasants on the Don aged under 40. Until now no decision has been made. The mobilisation would certainly be a success, taking into account the embittered attitude of the peasantry to the insurgent cossacks, the opinion of all living near the front and of local leaders. If we do not introduce mobilisation immediately, then our enemy will in due course do it for us, mobilising in its turn all the able population. The Don peasantry will willingly accept mobilisation in the struggle against the counter-revolutionary cossacks and it would be a great mistake to delay further. I await your orders. Member of the Revolutionary Military Council, Khodorovskii.

At last, on 26 or 27 May, that is when the front was already broken, Commander Gittis told me over the wire that at Southern Front HQ they were working on a plan for mobilising cossacks in the northern sectors of the Don *Oblast* to be sent to the western front – there was no word of mobilising other sections of the population to fight on the Don. Only when our armies had cleared out of a good half of the Don *Oblast* did we receive orders from the Revolutionary Military Council of the Southern Front to mobilise all those under 37 in a band some 50 *versts* wide behind the front.

Of course, mobilisation carried out in these circumstances did not succeed. We took people from the fields and the work shops, gave them no uniform or boots, and put them in no cohesive military units, and threw them at the front. No useful purpose was served, and the losses were colossal. At the same time, much of the local population, as the enemy approached, simply fled, and escaped our mobilisation. In fact it is generally true that a retreating army cannot carry out a mobilisation. But this mobilisation could have been implemented calmly and in a planned fashion. Everyone working on the Don thought it was essential; the population itself, young and healthy people, could not understand why they were not mobilised, while we continued to stand there with our thin little divisions, losing the last of our strength in the daily fighting.

The Don Rebellion

For some reason it is believed our defeat on the southern front was due to some sort of dislocation in our units, and that that in turn was the result of weakening political work. I know nothing of the situation in the Ukrainian Armies, but as far as our armies are concerned, those which took the Don, the 8th, 9th and [number obliterated] we continued, right up to the last moment of our stay on the Don, to maintain the discipline, order and military preparedness of the 9th Army, and in a fighting retreat of 500 *versts* I know of no example of any part of the army not fulfilling orders. Political work in these armies was of the usual kind. We were unable to make any demands of our Red Army men; nevertheless, they carried out their orders honourably, with a clear conscience and even with selfless devotion. From this point of view the situation in the armies was quite firm, but they were weakened and emaciated to the highest degree. No political work could make good these mistakes. We were defeated as a result of the most dreadful organisational collapse, the absence of any kind of creative military thinking for the whole time we were on the Don.

What did our Enemy Do

During this time our enemy worked feverishly on organising and increasing its forces. The dislocation in its ranks and the mass surrender of cossacks ended at the moment when we left behind the middle Don, when it became quite clear to the enemy that we would not be satisfied with an amicable end to the fighting on the middle Don, but intended to clear the whole Don *Oblast*. From that moment almost the whole male cossack population rose up as we approached and left their stanitsasteads and villages for Novocherkassk and Rostov. This happened in the first and second Don regions, and the Upper Don, Salsk, and Morozov regions. According to the most conservative figures, 100 000 men left for Novocherkassk and Rostov, all of whom were enemies already armed.

For some reason many responsible workers ignore this factor, which in fact has enormous significance. The newly mobilised Don cossacks were disciplined and motivated for war, since they were going into a campaign to take back their own villages and homesteads. Of even greater significance was the appearance against us on the Don of Denikin, who not long before had liquidated our Caucasian Front and freed his hands for action on the Don. By then Denikin's army had ceased to be a volunteer officers' army but one based on the mobilisation of the male population of the areas he passed through. By this means Denikin had mobilised by March-April considerable numbers of

Kuban cossacks, Chechens, Ingush, Kalmyks and others. It was indeed the Kuban cossacks and Kalmyks who dealt the worst blows to us in our final retreat.

According to our information, by the last ten days of May Denikin had on the Southern Front from 120 000 to 150 000 men in formations which were well commanded and supplied, but also capable of agile manoeuvres. Denikin's good supplies were based on his control of the rich Kuban. Supplies in terms of arms, ammunition and technical support were also good. Denikin's army, when compared to the Red Army, was co-ordinated and organised, and based on an HQ which comprised well-known specialists (Dragomirov, Lukomskii, Romanovskii, Plyushchevskii). Denikin's Army was composed primarily of cavalry. Every day this army expanded; newly formed regiments, divisions and corps appeared transforming the old units – in a word, organisational work never stopped for a second, which was not the case with us. Acting with an army of this type, organised on these lines, Denikin took the initiative from us and picked away at our weak spots, always having, as he did, sufficient mounted superiority to beat us. His victory over us was a victory of organisation of disorder, initiative and creative military thought over a vacuum.

Our Attitude to the Cossacks

There is no doubt that the insurrection which began in March greatly complicated our military and political situation on the Don. But it would be a mistake to think that this insurrection was caused only by our political activity on the Don. I have had the chance for several months to reconsider the situation, and am firmly convinced that there were no groups among the cossacks with whom we could have come to an agreement. Among the Don cossacks, those in the north just as in the south, there simply do not exist the people described in our papers as 'working-class cossacks'. All cossacks on the Don are well off. From this point of view we can promise him nothing by way of attraction: cossacks have never had it so good. Political slogans are for them a distraction. On the Don we can only rely on the non-cossack peasantry, something correctly stated in the Central Committee's first directive on our Don policy. The mistake was not this directive, but that we tried to implement it with insufficient force. Once and for all it must be understood that we are engaged in a struggle not for the cossacks but **with the cossacks**; our task is the **total subjugation and pacification of the Don**. That is only possible with adequate military resources.

It is wrong to engage in a light campaign; what is needed is to leave stationed in all large villages and homesteads a garrison which will keep order for a long time to come. We did not do this and that allowed the cossacks to stage an insurrection. That insurrection would have occurred whether or not we had carried out a policy of terror in the Don, for to deny our essence and not to carry out our economic programme, even in the most reduced and limited way, was impossible – and it was that which was the basic cause of the insurrection. Of course, it was also caused by the fact that the organs of Soviet power on the Don, the revolutionary committees, were not really in place and were ill-prepared for the responsible tasks placed on them; but this played a secondary role. Our policy on the Don should have been based on our military strength and a relationship with the non-cossack peasantry. The attempt to win over the northern cossacks (Khoperskii and Ust Medveditskii regions) against the southern cossacks must be recognised as an utter failure. The northern cossacks are rich enough, and we will not win them over with economic slogans. Basing ourselves on them, in the light of past experience, is hopeless. The northern cossacks only surrendered to Mironov because they no longer wanted to fight. When we tried to mobilise them, they took to the forests, and during our retreat the much praised northern cossacks rose up, intercepted our convoys, shot our people and forced us to fight to occupy every village and homestead.

At the time of the March insurrection we had no clear understanding of its real scale. Very soon it became clear that before us were not isolated groups of rebels but a mass counter-revolutionary movement in which the whole population of dozens and dozens of villages and homesteads was taking part. The population was armed and well organised into squads, regiments and divisions. Some of our units sent to put down the rebellion were weak, not united in an overall command, and as a result their activities were random. Only at the end of March, when the uprising had taken hold of a large area, did the commander of the Southern Front take charge of the forces confronting the rebels, in Army Command 9. This order was a fateful mistake and this is why: at the moment it was issued almost the whole of the Army HQ, and equally all the army apparatus, was based in Mikhailovka, but the Army Commander with several executive officers was in Morosovskaya. To command an expeditionary force, not yet formed into any final units, in the absence of the Army HQ and executive command, presented huge difficulties.

A whole month passed and only at the end of April was the order of the Southern Front complied with to establish and supply a counter-insurgency force of two divisions, the expeditionary division of the 8th Army and the expeditionary division of the 9th Army. This order would have been good if it had not been six weeks too late, but, irrespective of this, it was impossible to lay on Army Command 9 the additional command of the expeditionary force. This meant splitting the attention of the army command in two, when it already had enough to do on the front on the Donets. In effect Army Command 9 was given the command of two different armies, which, with a weak and scattered HQ, turned out to be almost impossible. A separate, special command should have been created for the expeditionary force. This the Southern Front did only in the middle of May, in other words almost two months after the outbreak of the rebellion. It was already too late. It proved impossible in just a few days to liquidate a rebellion which had taken hold in a large area. Ten days later our defeats on the main front began.

T. Khodorovskii

DOCUMENT 2.3

This is a pessimistic report concerning vanishing forces written by A.L. Kolegaev, a member of the Revolutionary Military Council, to Lenin on 21 May 1919. The Revolutionary Military Council had been created to oversee the Bolsheviks' war effort in September 1918, as the Red Army retook Kazan from the People's Army of the Directory (see Chapter 1); Kolegaev was unique among its members in being a former member of the Left SR Party.

Kolegaev is defensive – 'We were not to blame that at the beginning of the rebellion we were unable to pull out good forces to suppress it' – and clearly believed he was following a coherent strategy of gathering reliable forces before making a decisive counter-attack; the problem was that he never obtained sufficient reliable resources to make such an attack. The document clearly shows the lack of reliable troops, particularly when it came to fighting the cossack rebellion rather than Denikin's army; that troops from the defeated 11th Army (see above) were being used to confront the cossacks simply highlights the point. It is also clear that Kolegaev was aware of the collapse in the rear brought about by the work of the Donburo and wanted to have a figure of Sokolnikov's standing, and moderation, to try to improve the situation. However, there is no hint of his allegiance to the Left SR Party making him any more conciliatory to the cossacks. The document also shows clearly how stretched the upper echelons of the Southern Front command were when faced with both the Don rebellion and the war against Denikin, and how aware the Front HQ was of the communication problems referred to in document 2.2.

RTsKhIDNI, f. 17, op. 109, ed. khr. 44, l. 23
Telegram to Lenin, Moscow, Chairman of Sovnarkom (copy)
21.5.19
(indecipherable code number)
Your No.204/S.

First of all Comrade Beloborodov must take every possible step on the spot to establish communication with our units, so that orders reach them more speedily. For its part the Front had released some telephone equipment, depriving Front HQ both from the political and technical point of view. This has been done to help the HQ of the Counter-insurgency Expeditionary Force (sent there are: Comrades Plyat, Sokolnikov and Nerelson; also sent there are Beloborodov and Potamoshev, with Paremykov and Khovansko as political workers and three young men recently arrived from General Staff as technical workers). Front HQ has parted with Comrade Khvesin, former Commander of the 8th Army, Comrade Khigur, Divisional Commander, former Brigade Commander Alekseev, and a former lieutenant colonel. This goes to show that the Front is taking steps to ensure the smooth functioning of communication with the units: we are giving away staff to our own loss. Those working on the spot must get the necessary technical personnel.

In the second place the fuel which has been sent for the armoured cars cannot be effective, since the rains of the last few days are going to prevent them operating for a couple of days yet.

In the third place, Khvesin, Head of the Counter-insurgency Expeditionary Force, informs us that the thousand cadet commanders who have arrived along with the other reinforcements, barely cover our losses from sickness or desertion.

The 33rd Division has just arrived. I think it would be completely wrong to throw the whole or part of this division against the insurgents, since we do not yet know its true worth: we must first establish how far it is battle-worthy, whether it is politically reliable and how far it is technically prepared, since normally from the 11th Army, whence it has been transferred, units arrive in a demoralised state, and we shall not allow ourselves to send reinforcements to the enemy rather than to our own units.

We have sent people to carry out an inspection of the political mood, the disposition of forces and the state of the stores. They will give us their findings in a couple of days, and then if everything passes muster we shall move the better parts of the troops. By that time we shall also have arriving the armoured cars which Trotsky assigned to us. We have had plenty of trouble with the Kronshtadt Regiment (1500 infantry, which is a large force for us) and the Serdobsk Regiment. The former was transferred to us from Orienbaum and when launched immediately into action the men fled. The other regiment, which had also come from the rear, surrendered.

You may reproach us for being too slow, but we cannot now risk committing these men against the insurgents. Even though we may have to hear your reproaches, we must prepare a final blow and wipe the enemy out at one go. If operations fail for political reasons, we shall have to pay very dearly in political terms. We were not to blame that at the beginning of the rebellion we were unable to pull out good forces to suppress it: our front is constantly in a difficult position and it is only now that reinforcements are beginning to reach us.

At the time of my arrival in the last days of April you yourself thought that Lugansk could not fall. I must take this opportunity to say that I consider it a serious mistake to keep Comrade Beloborodov with the counter-insurgency forces in Boguchar, when he has been appointed Chairman of the Don Revolutionary Committee. There is someone with sufficient authority, namely Sokolnikov, while the need to organise our rule on the Don and the work of the Revolutionary Committee is tremendously important, in the sense that we need to establish a realistic and permanent set-up for putting our policies into practice.

This work is at present not being done and we are exposing our rear areas. What had been achieved is now falling apart, with four out of five members of the Revolutionary Committee absent, and particularly Comrade Beloborodov. I would even state the problem thus: if you need to have your own responsible representative with the counter-insurgency forces, then delegate this duty to someone, but do not keep Comrade Beloborodov there. I physically am not able to see to the Civilian Administration (Revolutionary Committee), since I am taken up with looking after the delivery of supplies through the Food Supply Administration, and now I am the only member of the Front Revolutionary Military Council (RVS).

I am bringing to your attention and for your approval what has been said at the beginning of this telegram about the note which we received on inspecting one of the regiments (divisions) who have arrived from the Ukrainian front:

> Discipline has been completely lost. More than 30 per cent of the Red Army men have run off. Practically the whole command staff are not fit to hold their posts from the regimental commander down. The commission concludes that the regiment cannot exist with such a command staff.

If the regiments of the 33rd Division turn out like that, then we cannot send them against the rebellion, but will need to work them over.

Signed, Member of the RVS A. Kolegaev, No.5465

DOCUMENT 2.4

This document comprises extracts from a letter to the Central Committee from an Army Commissar, N. Suglitskii. Much of it is routine, if surprising, giving the importance the Bolsheviks attached to political work. He highlights the difficulty in organising political work among the soldiers on the Southern Front: not only were there shortages of the most basic supplies – such as newspapers and textbooks – but the stretched political workers had their time cut out working in the villages, rather than among their proper constituency. Despite such problems he is up-beat about morale and prospects.

Yet when he moves on to discuss the military situation, he has a depressing tale to tell of typhus, losses in battle, the failure to cross the Donets, and the superiority of the enemy's forces. The tale is so depressing that this section of his report soon starts to contradict the picture of political reliability he had begun by painting; lack of basic clothing had prompted a mutiny and an outbreak of thieving from the local population which had had negative political consequences.

Despite painting such a negative picture, Suglitskii, no doubt like other political commissars, tried to see the wider picture; the poor supplies to the Southern Front were no doubt the result of the need to fight Admiral Kolchak in the East; but the feeling that he and his comrades have been forgotten is hard to disguise. His conclusion that Denikin's men were butchers who could still be easily defeated reflects a naive and ironic optimism based largely on wishful thinking, for a Bolshevik rout was only moments away.

On the crucial question of the political attitude to be taken towards the cossacks, Suglitskii is clearly out of sympathy with the Donburo. He clearly believed there was a future in winning over the 'working class cossacks', and his brief reference to the cossacks' 'sympathy for the idea of a commune' reflects clearly the view that, if treated sympathetically, the cossack tradition of radical self-administration dating back to the Pugachev revolt against Empress Catherine II could be allied to the cause of Bolshevism. It is interesting to note, in the context of the struggle for hearts and minds, the role played by aeroplanes in propaganda leaflet drops.

RTsKhIDNI, *f. 17, op. 65, ed. khr. 157, ll. 61–6* [extracts]

Written in pencil. Signed on l.66: 'N. Suglitskii, Head of Political Section of 23rd Rifle Division of 9th Army, Southern Front.'

19 May 1919: To the Central Committee

I am taking advantage of comrade Nagar's going on sick leave to Moscow to write at least a short account of how our work is going, and generally to report on the 23rd Rifle Division of the 9th Army on the Southern Front.

By writing direct to you I am breaking the proper chain of command, since I ought to report to the Army's Political Department, but I do make detailed daily reports to them on the state of each unit. From force of habit I still want to write to the Central Committee about the general situation in the Division and an overall picture of the front as a whole.

The Division was formed by bringing together [Red Army commander] Comrade [F.K.] Mironov's Division with the Brigade of Comrade Sievers and the Ural Division. After I had typhus during our spring offensive I was entrusted with the task of organising the 23rd Division's Political Section. Up to then there had been no Party work carried out in the Division. Although work should have been carried on mainly in our units, all the political workers were dispersed round the villages, and there simply was no Political Section...

Now the Division has no units without at least a small communist cell and a group of sympathisers... Shows are put on... There is a desire to create schools for literacy, but we have had to postpone that, because we have no alphabet books or writing materials. There is only one such school – in a cossack section, formed from cossack prisoners who have volunteered. Comrades Courts are being formed to sort out minor cases. To deal with crime a Divisional Section of the Army Tribunal has been organised, which we draw on for administrative purposes, using the personnel as advocates for the prosecution or defence. I am arranging a 50 per cent contribution to the Central Committee, which I am sending you through the post...

I may say that as far as politics go the mood of the Red Army men is generally very good... all grounds for misunderstanding are being cleared away. In general there is a good standard in the Division's political attitude; there are no politically unreliable units in the Division. The Red Army men show a tremendous interest in newspapers, but unfortunately papers reach us only very irregularly, and with two weeks' delay – that is, when things are at their best – a month ago the Red Army men got no papers for a whole month or more. This was explained by the fact that the cossacks had blown up almost all the bridges and the railways were completely cut off. Supplies came through tremendously in arrears, since they had to be carried over 3–400 *versts*.

I shall now proceed to deal with the Division's fighting capacity. Comrade Mironov's division, and in general the united group under Mironov's command, have distinguished themselves. In a brief space of time we swept victoriously from Borisoglebsk to Kamenskaya. We have been held up at the Donets, at first because of the ice melting and ice floes coming down, and now with the scanty forces that we have we cannot push across the river. I must tell you that our strength has now come down to 80–100 infantry per regiment, instead of the former strength of 2000 as they were in the winter. Spanish influenza and typhus have accounted for many of the losses and we have suffered many casualties in battles. When we tried to force the Donets – because there was no reserve and only our division got across on it own – we lost up to 2000 men – prisoners, drowned and killed. The men who were exhausted, without any support from nearby units, had to retreat willy-nilly under pressure from the enemy, who were six times stronger. He threw 4 divisions against us, and two very strong detachments of Kalmyks and men from the Kuban'. Our Red Army men withstood quite extraordinary pressure from the enemy, beating off up to five attacks. Men were dying who had had no sleep and nothing to eat. Some regiments had not slept for four days and would go to sleep as soon as they halted. In the end one regiment faltered and made us retreat with loss across the Donets, leaving many of our comrades drowned...

We are looking forward to receiving reinforcements, and can see that it will be a long time before that moment comes, since all our forces are directed against Kolchak. The men are without footwear or clothing, since it is impossible to offer them any articles of uniform. Because of that they have refused to advance, making their demands as follows: 'first of all put some clothes on me, and after that if I refuse, you can insist and shoot me if you wish'. In the 203rd Regiment alone there are no less than 600 men who are barefoot, men that we had no right to send into the front line in rain and cold, making them lie in their trenches night and day without any relief – and they expected to get kitted out with some uniform while they were in the rear.

The Southern Front greatly encouraged the High Command by its success, whereas no one pays any attention to it now, but you ought to see what the soldiers look like. They are simply in rags – there is no other word to describe them. Faced with the lack of uniform they requisition things from the local people, sometimes by robbing them, and that poisons people's minds against us. I have shouted and made a great fuss to get someone to attend to this, for there is neither tobacco, nor sugar, nor fat bacon, to say nothing of uniform or forage for the horses. Now they have taken heed and they are making promises. We'll wait and see.

The state of morale in the enemy army is highly favourable for us. They are held together only by the Kalmyks, the officers and some of the men from the Kuban'. Men are refusing to be conscripted, particularly the Ukrainians in the Taganrog District. General Shkuro's punishment squads have come along to compel them to go. They are real butchers: under the name of 'wolf squadrons' they came into the villages, putting up gallows and carrying out the following trick: they'd lay hold of a man who refused to go, put a noose round his neck, hang him for a few seconds, let him down, and, jeering at him, would ask – was it a good idea to go? And which would be better – to go or to be hanged? They would continue this practice until the man died. I am reporting this from what eyewitnesses have said.

In the Taganrog District 17 areas in all have refused to go, and have been forcibly mobilised; now they are coming over to us, whole units at a time. The unwilling conscripts free our prisoners and help them to escape. The officers, in spite of being under orders not to shoot prisoners, nevertheless do kill our men, particularly any cossacks who fall into their hands. There is strong feeling against those in command. An underground organisation existed in Rostov and Novocherkassk, and it is interesting that most of them were students or from the minor intelligentsia. Some of them were doctors, who exempted some men that appeared before the medical board. [The cossack *ataman*] Bogayevskii and Denikin have a very limited number of troops. He operates in the main by concentrating his forces in one place, inflicting defeats in the local area, but not undertaking any strategic offensives. One may see these as the last convulsions of Denikin's forces, with their morale being destroyed. If we could just add a little to our strength we could break them in the near future. We shall not be able to drive them back if we attack at 80 points.

The cossacks are dropping appeals from aeroplanes; I am sending two of them to you. I have never seen our aeroplanes flying at all. That is greatly to be regretted, for, although our soldiers laugh and do not pay any heed to cossack appeals, on the other hand our appeals have a good effect on the enemy. You must send as many as possible here, especially the newspaper the *Working Class Cossacks*. In the forward areas there is a most active campaign of agitation work. Meetings are enthusiastically supported...

The cossacks are a bitterly deceived mass of people, who are even fully in sympathy with the idea of a commune, for that was the way they lived. But, due to a tremendous persecution and actions by the communist authorities which sometimes were quite wrong, this mass is becoming corrupted and have turned to be our enemies. We need experienced Party workers here, not the sort who come to make propaganda and say such awful things that I throw them out neck and crop from here... Do not leave my voice unheard, like 'the voice of one crying in the wilderness'.

N. Suglitskii

DOCUMENT 2.5

This telegram is simply a footnote to document 2.4. The shortage of decent political commissars in the 9th Army had been noted as early as February 1919.

RTsKhIDNI, *f.* 17, *op.* 65, *ed. khr.* 157, *ll.* 182–4

1 February 1919, 9th Army

Concerning artillery units of 9th Army

Army's complete lack of commissars. Political Section of Southern Front has none. We must have eighteen battalion commissars, not essential to have artillery specialists. Position serious. Urgent measures essential.

DOCUMENT 2.6

Like document 2.4, this is a report from a political commissar to the Central Committee drawing attention to the forthcoming disaster on the Don. It concentrates on the shortage of food for the soldiers and forage for the horses, but again notes that even at its most successful, the army was too weak to consolidate its positions on the far side of the Donets – a military situation which made it all the more important that there should not be a rebellion in the rear.

RTsKhIDNI, *f.* 17, *op.* 109, *ed. khr.* 44, *l.* 16

From the Political Commissar of the 2nd Artillery Division of 1st Brigade of the Inza Division of the 8th Army

To the Moscow Central Committee of the Party of Communists

7 May 1919

I wish to draw to your attention that the situation on our front will be disastrous if exceptionally energetic measures are not taken to improve supplies, both of food and of forage for our horses. I personally quite realise my shortcomings in both these respects, but nevertheless would suggest that you must find more adequate solutions to our difficulties. The reality is that there is absolutely no proper forage, which is a sorry state of affairs. It is not always possible to use pasture, and horses are too weak to stand, which severely weakens the army's fighting capacity. The men have nothing to eat for two days at a time and it demands superhuman skill to keep up their morale.

Let me quote you an example: battery no.5 in the course of six days received one day's forage; but it has not remained in one place, going rather from place to place, as tactical demands necessitated. When we crossed the Donets the artillery could not move 10 *versts* in 24 hours. The other batteries are in the same state. To sum up: I am using the word 'disastrous' without any exaggeration, absolutely using the full meaning of the word. The men are so worn out with cold and hunger that we really may expect dire consequences if no one is able to supply the men and their horses. There is a great lack of horses.

Divisional Political Commissar (signature illegible)

RKP(b) Central Committee Secretariat, 26.5.19

Information input 5433

DOCUMENT 2.7

The following two extracts from reports by the Red Army Supreme Commander in Chief, I.I. Vatsetis, remind us that the Don disaster was just part of a much broader picture. The first self-justifying report to Lenin gives an idea of the state of the High Command as the Don Rebellion developed in April 1919. It clearly shows the devastating impact on the High Command of the defeat of the 11th Army in the North Caucasus in January 1919: the use of the remnants of the 11th Army in the fighting on the Don has already been mentioned in document 2.3 where it was criticised by Kolegaev; here Vatsetis first points out that he had sent these units for political retraining before returning to the front, and then gives a long defence of his own association with these men since the autumn of 1918 when he became Supreme Commander. He, like Kolegaev in document 2.3, seems to be saying 'it is not my fault'; perhaps he was already aware of political moves against him, for he was dismissed on 3 July 1919 after Denikin had captured Tsaritsyn on 30 June 1919, a direct consequence of the disaster on the Don. Vatsetis's concern for the past rather than a willingness to confront the current danger reads rather strangely. In the final extract Vatsetis insists almost petulantly that he has moved to the Southern Front all the troops that could be spared.

In the second part of his report, he again bemoans the many problems he faced in ensuring that all parts of the Red Army were properly supplied, in particular how this resulted in clashes with L.B. Krasin, appointed by Lenin to head the Extraordinary Commission for the Supply of the Red Army. Clearly Vatsetis felt his authority was being undermined at this level as well.

RTsKhIDNI, f. 17, op. 109, ed. khr. 4l, ll. 1–5 [extracts]

Report by Vatsetis to Lenin; copy to Chairman Defence Council

April 1919

Almost the entire 11th Division surrendered at that time, about 10 000 men with 35 guns... The Revolutionary Military Council (RVS) of the Southern Front stated that the 11th Division was completely unfit to send into action...

In what circumstances was this division formed? This case will be brought before the RVS of the Republic at its coming session... If the commander of 9th Army knew that this division was unfit for action, then he had no good reason to push it into a battle. He should have left that division in reserve in Balashov, where I had directed it for more political work to be carried out...

We must not on any account accuse the Nizhnii Novgorod Provincial Commissariat of sending a division to the front which was unfit for active service, because that division started to be put together in August [1918]... I came twice to Nizhnii Novgorod. The Nizhnii Novgorod Military Commissariat in a comparatively short space of time managed to mobilise six regiments, get some artillery together, including heavy artillery, and to procure horses. At the same time they were going on with their political work, which made it possible for them to instil politically conscious discipline and get the mass of soldiers to obey them...

Besides all that, this division at its full strength found time to go through training for active service. The Nizhnii Novgorod Military Commissariat, comrades Kraevskii, Kogan and member of the General Staff Lyubushkin, were working literally to exhaustion – we all remember only too well the month of August. They had to form the division, to prepare the defence of Nizhnii Novgorod, and at the same time to wrestle with the Food Supply Commission, which was not providing proper food for the men and was starving the unit's horses. I carried out an inspection of that division in Nizhnii Novgorod – on 15 October [1918] if I am not mistaken – and the results of that inspection are contained in my Order of the Day... At the inspection I congratulated the men on their readiness to proceed to the front, which remarks they greeted with great enthusiasm. So I had the impression that this division was a tightly knit large military unit, such as were rare in Russia at that time, with the exception of the Latvian Rifle Division, which had been created by me...

After the inspection the Provincial Military Commissariat reported to me – and to Kobozev, a member of RVS of the Republic, who was with me at that time – that many soldiers of the 11th Division, as they set out for the front, were leaving their families in very difficult circumsances. That division was made up almost entirely of workers. Very many of them are leaving their families without the means of subsistence, food at that time in Nizhnii Novgorod being in extremely short supply. As for the People's Commissariat of Social Services, no such body existed in Nizhnii Novgorod... For the soldiers to go on active service, without making any provision to help them as a matter of urgency, means to leave their families at the risk of starving to death...

Comrade Kobozev and I decided to give one million roubles to the Provincial Military Commissariat to distribute to the families of the Red

Army men departing for the war... There were no reserves at all on the Southern Front at that time and the cossacks were threatening to cut our lines of communication with Saratov...

[Vatsetis concludes this section of his report by noting that, despite these preparations, the 11th Division came to grief because of the enemy's superiority in numbers.]

At this point I must comment that the situation for realising our strategic objectives at the fronts and the lack of central stores (either of arms or food) sometimes necessitates my personal intervention to avoid bureaucratic delays. Such was the case with sending arms to sections of the front where unexpected disaster blew up, as equally happens with supplying provisions for military units which are urgently transferred from one front to another...

There was one such case, just limited to quartermaster's stores, when I gave the order to despatch five wagon loads of flour and five wagons of forage to follow the Latvian regiments which had been moved across from the Eastern to the Western Front. And at that time comrade [L.B.] Krasin [who had since 2 November 1918 been head of the Extraordinary Commission for the Supply of the Red Army] found it possible to countermand this order of mine. The flour was unloaded in Moscow and used for a completely different purpose. The Latvian regiments set off for Pskov without taking any supplies with them. To avoid a disaster we had to take urgent measures to bake bread in Moscow and send it to Pskov to distribute to the regiments – and you can just imagine the state of this bread when it was delivered to the front line in frosty winter weather after lying for several days in goods wagons. In that case too I did not receive from comrade Krasin any notification that he was changing my order. All I got was a copy of his telegram to the Central Supply Administration, to the effect that some persons, including the Commander-in-Chief, were acting out of order by issuing instructions for food and forage, and at the end of the telegram there was even a threat to complain to Sovnarkom...

Those of my subordinates who get instructions from me in such cases are duty bound to report about this only to the central supply bodies, and it is impermissible that these latter could change my orders without even letting me know anything about it...

The whole attention of the Eastern Front is focused on Perm. At the present juncture I do not have at my disposal any strategic reserves, who are ready to go into action. Besides which all forces that are in any way disposable have at the present moment been drawn off for the Southern Front.

True signature C-in-C Vatsetis

DOCUMENT 2.8

This further report from Vatsetis to Lenin makes clear that by the beginning of May 1919 the Commander in Chief had grasped the seriousness of the situation on the Don. But it is equally clear that his eyes were still as much on Kolchak and the Eastern Front; all available reserves had been concentrated there, for Kolchak had begun his offensive against Ufa in March 1919 and on 28 April the Red Army staged what was at first a successful counter-attack. Had there not been a rebellion by the Don cossacks, Vatsetis's concentration on the Eastern Front would have been perfectly sensible; for it was the Don rebellion behind the Donets front line which enabled Denikin to advance so dramatically, and that rebellion was the result of a political rather than a military failure.

That Vatsetis was becoming aware of this is clear from his comments on the situation in the Ukraine. Although the Bolsheviks had been able to make dramatic advances into the Ukraine as the German occupying forces left at the end of 1918, their hold on the area was precarious. Not only did they have to contend with nationalist forces under S.V. Petlyura, but the same sort of 'class war' policies which had so alienated the cossacks were also being deployed against the Ukrainian peasantry, with the Bolsheviks using the decisions of Committees of the Poor to justify the requisitioning of grain. This policy back-fired against the Bolsheviks in May 1919. Antonov-Ovseenko had conducted much of his campaign in the Ukraine with the support of guerrilla commanders who had begun their careers harrying the German occupying forces. In the spring of 1919, during the campaign to oust the French intervention force, these commanders had retained a large degree of autonomy, so that in May 1919 it was not difficult for the most active of them, Major Grigoriev, to organise a rebellion and establish a 'soviet' but non-Bolshevik Ukraine.

The Don Rebellion 81

RTsKhIDNI *f.* 17, *op.* 109, *ed.* khr. 41, *ll.* 12–14 [extracts]

To: Chairman of Defence Council, Comrade Lenin

Copy to comrade Trotsky

7 May 1919, Serpukhov. *Urgent. Secret.*

In the last few days war in the south of the RSFSR has taken a turn for the worse. In the eastern parts of the south, i.e., in the Don *Oblast*, we cannot strike a decisive blow, in spite of sending down there the last forces we have at our disposal at this time. On the Southern Front the enemy already has a numerical superiority over us. The military units which we are sending to the Southern Front are not in sufficient numbers to make up for our losses in killed, wounded and illness in the 8th, 9th and 13th Armies, whose ranks have been greatly thinned in ceaseless bitter battles . . .

The armies of the Southern Front are getting no more than 40 per cent of the necessary replacements . . . In the area of the Donets Basin our units have been forced back step by step . . . To the west of the Manych the 10th Army have come up against an enemy superior in numbers. The successes achieved by our 10th Army have evidently reached their maximum, due to their superior spirit, and from now on they will have to go over to the defensive . . .

The threat of Kolchak on the Volga has required all our reserves to be transferred there, thanks to which we have managed to check the further advance of his armies . . .

The Ukraine, advancing along the path of independence, appears weaker than had seemed at first glance . . . My precepts about the need to form a strategic reserve met with statements from [V.A.] Antonov[-Ovseenko], Commander of the Ukrainian Front, that to create this he would have to clear out the whole Ukraine . . . Petlyura is threatening Kiev from the north west . . . The uprising to the north-east of Kiev is evidently growing . . . We have had to send the 3rd Division which was stationed in Chernigov Province . . . According to Antonov's reports the rebels have 8 guns . . . This rebellion in the rear of the Ukrainian Front now makes for the same unfavourable circumstances as were created in the rear of the Southern Front in the Don *Oblast* . . .

3 The Kaleidoscope of War

This chapter seeks to give a kaleidoscopic picture of the many and varied aspects of life at the height of the Civil War during the summer and autumn of 1919, as the Bolsheviks gradually moved from the defensive to the offensive and ultimate victory. It is sub-divided into five parts, dealing with different aspects of the fighting.

THE GREENS

The first issue to be addressed in this chapter takes up the question of how the Red Army should cope with rebellions behind the White lines, the issue raised in document 2.8. Ultimately the Bolshevik victory had a lot to do with their ability to form alliances with 'Green' groups operating in the rear; but establishing these alliances was fraught with difficulty, for more often than not it meant coming to some sort of deal with representatives of peasant socialist or peasant anarchist groups, whom the Bolsheviks had been fighting in the first stage of the civil war in 1918. The Bolsheviks' experience on the Don showed how difficult party cadres found it to relate to the aspirations of peasant farmers. Thus these alliances were always unstable marriages of convenience, which in the last resort broke down.

Document 3.1

This document is a report on the Bolsheviks' relations with *ataman* Grigoriev early in May 1919. Nikifor Grigoriev, a flamboyant former Tsarist officer, had formed his own partisan unit which; at the start of 1919; co-operated with the Ukrainian Red Army Commander Antonov-Ovseenko in re-establishing Soviet power in the Ukraine as the German and Austrian forces left once the First World War was finally over. During March 1919 he was responsible for driving French and Greek intervention forces out of the Ukraine. However, he rebelled against Antonov-Ovseenko on 7 May 1919, declaring his intention of forming a 'Soviet Ukraine without commissars'. This revolutionary, almost anarchist, slogan was accompanied by a populist denunciation of the Bolshevik commissars as Jews, and Grigoriev unleashed a wave of pogroms against 'Jew-Communists' in the provinces of Kiev, Kherson and Poltava. Outraged by this pogromist element to Grigoriev's rebellion, the anarchist leader in the Ukraine, Nestor

Makhno (see document 3.2), invited Grigoriev to a public meeting in the village of Sentova in July 1919; after what Makhno's supporters described as a 'reactionary' speech, a fight broke out and Grigoriev was killed. Grigoriev's forces were then invited to join those of Makhno.

What is interesting about this document, written by the Army Commander on the Southern Front, Antonov-Ovseenko, is that it is dated before Grigoriev's rebellion began, at a time when it was clearly felt that a deal could be done with him. The author, unlike every other commentator, notes Grigoriev's humble origins, rather than his spell as an officer in the Tsarist Army, and accepts that his ideas and those of his followers are at one, a local man true to the aspirations of the middle peasants; and there is no mention of anti-semitism, other than to say he tried to avoid it. (The pogroms Grigoriev unleashed occurred in June.) However, as with all commentators, Grigoriev's 'headstrong' character is noted.

Equally important is the reference to the Left SRs. The left wing of the SR Party had always been strong in the Ukraine, and from March 1918 onward the Party had been committed to organising a peasant insurrection in the Ukraine aimed at driving out the German and Austrian forces and re-establishing Soviet power; however, by Soviet power the Left SRs meant re-establishing the authority of the village soviets and not the 'Committees of Poor Peasants' through which the Bolsheviks had been seeking to unleash 'class war in the countryside' since May 1918. Food requisitioning, always justified on the grounds that the 'poor of the village' were sending grain to 'their allies the proletariat of the cities', was clearly enabling the Left SRs in this part of the Ukraine to continue to operate as a viable force, even though their party had been banned in Russia proper. That Grigoriev's forces were so well supplied is perhaps also worthy of note.

The conclusion – that Grigoriev should be worked with – was overtaken by events, but it is noteworthy that at least some Bolsheviks had recognised that using force against the peasantry would not work; and that someone of Antonov's stature had reached this conclusion was especially significant.

RGVA, f. 33987, op. 2, ed. khr. 72, l. 33

Secretariat of the Chairman of the Revolutionary Military Council.

Commander of Armies Copy of the Ukrainian Front. *Secret.*

2 May 1919, No.823

To the Chairman of the Council of People's Commissars, Comrade Rakovskii

To the People's Commissar for Military Affairs, Comrade Podvoiskii

Note on Grigoriev

From direct experience I have ascertained and confirm that:

1. At the present moment Grigoriev has no hostile intentions towards the Soviet regime; he has the same kind of character as the middling peasantry of the Aleksandria District from which he and his troops originate.
2. The Left SRs are carrying out intensive anti-Soviet agitation throughout the whole Aleksandria District. Their work is not contested as it should be because our political work is weak and in places Soviet power is not properly established. Their propaganda feeds on the discontent provoked by the tactless behaviour of some agents of the Cheka or the Food Requisitioning Organisation and by the Soviet authorities' lack of contact with the local population (thus, for example, the leaders of the District Executive Committee are from Moscow).
3. Grigoriev has a tremendous influence in this district as a local man who has always stood up against the oppressors of the peasantry here. He has strengthened his influence by surrounding himself with the most influential people from the various districts.
4. The main body of Grigoriev's troops are 'middling peasants', as are the vast majority of the peasants in this region.
5. Grigoriev's headstrong character has not yet been brought under control as it should be by the Political Commissars – Comrade Ratin is well-intentioned but weak.
6. An inspection of the stores in Grigoriev's workshops revealed that they are turning out daily up to 600 pairs of trousers made from tent canvas, while the armoury repairs up to 40 rifles and 3 machine guns a day. There is nothing surplus in the stores: they have absolutely no footwear but they have enough leather for 2000 pairs of boots and (coarse) cloth for 15 000 sets of underclothes. They are very short of cartridges and there are no rifles in store. They have up to 10 000 shells for three-inch and other guns. The supply administration is a model of organisation: it is obvious that the quartermaster aims at perfect accountability.
7. Grigoriev keeps his subordinates in fear of him; he can lay about him physically and is quick to mete out summary punishment.
8. He has averted pogroms in Nikolaev and Odessa, as also similar attempts in Aleksandria.
9. He himself lives like a townsman of modest means, not with any great

extravagance, and he has acquired nothing for himself. He has given cloth out to the widows of Red Army men, to the soldiers themselves, to schools and the poor.
10. Political commissars are allowed in, and work without hindrance.
11. There are few excesses, no more than in any of the regiments from central Russia. They are caused by the provocative behaviour of the Left Socialist Revolutionaries and partly by that of the local authorities.
12. Grigoriev is vain, has considerable military ability, and has undertaken not to set up his own rule. It should be quite possible to keep him under control.

Conclusion:

1. We need to put in the most intensive political and organisational work in the Aleksandria District in order to eliminate the middling peasants' distrust of us.
2. Forcible measures will not achieve our objective and are bound to fail.
3. Grigoriev should be used as a military force (he is now proceeding under orders to Bessarabia). We must send him reliable commissars and political workers.

Commander of the Units of the Ukrainian Front, Antonov

For the Secretary, Molokhovskii

True copy, Departmental Secretary of People's Commissar for Military Affairs (signature)

7 May 1919

Document 3.2

The anarchist partisan force commanded by Nestor Ivanovich Makhno, the Revolutionary Partisan Army, had been fighting the Austrian forces which occupied the Ukraine under the Brest-Litovsk Treaty since the early summer of 1918. The Bolsheviks had first made contact with Makhno in March 1919 when the Bolshevik commander P.I. Dybenko sent representatives to seek a possible agreement; Dybenko had long favoured the encouragement of partisan as well as regular army units. However, reaching an understanding with Makhno proved difficult because the Bolsheviks insisted on describing Makhno's movement as *kulak* (rich peasant) dominated, since it refused to recognise the authority of Lenin's Committees of the Poor; the Bolsheviks became particularly worried in June 1919 when

Makhno, ignoring the Committees of the Poor, attempted to organise a Ukraine-wide congress of peasant soviets. The Bolsheviks' commitment to class war in the villages meant their relations with Makhno were already strained as Denikin began his dramatic advance from the Don.

The Bolsheviks hoped to use Makhno to cover the western side of Denikin's advance, but in late May 1919 Denikin's cavalry cut through Makhno's troops, who fled in disorder. Moscow declared Makhno a traitor who had opened the front to Denikin; while Makhno accused the Bolsheviks of having done the same. However, in the first days of October 1919, Makhno suddenly raced back across the river Dnieper to his home base at Gulyai-Pole, from where he could raid Ekaterinoslav Province. He even briefly captured the provincial capital where he put his anarchist theory into practice. Although Denikin was able to drive Makhno off, it was only at the cost of committing his reserves and stripping units from his front line. Thus, when in October 1919 Makhno and the Bolsheviks really were operating in tandem, they were able to make rapid progress; Makhno successfully destroyed Denikin's rear and helped the Red Army force Denikin to retreat beyond the Don.

However, relations between the Bolsheviks and Makhno remained strained. After Denikin's defeat, the Bolshevik authorities in the Ukraine denounced him as an outlaw in mid-January 1920, and although they welcomed his forces in the joint struggle against General Wrangel later that year, they again denounced him when Wrangel had been defeated; by the end of 1920 Makhno's forces had been annihilated by the Bolsheviks.

What is interesting about this document is first and foremost the recognition of Makhno's revolutionary credentials, followed by the series of signals that a deal with him might be possible. It was clearly a positive sign that there was tension between the anarchists and the Bolsheviks' main ideological opponents, the Left SRs; it was also encouraging that Makhno upheld the anarchist principles of freedom of information to the extent that he allowed communist literature to circulate freely (the Bolsheviks had long since stopped allowing anarchist literature to circulate) and that the anarchist principle of electing officers was dying out in practice. The Bolsheviks were clearly also encouraged by Makhno's absence from the Third Congress of Peasants, Workers and Partisans; it had been the resolutions passed at this congress which had led to the breakdown in relations with Dybenko and the start of the allegation that Makhno headed a *kulak* organisation. As points 18 and 19 make clear, relations between Dybenko and Makhno seemed fine in May when action against Denikin began.

Antonov's clear conclusion that it would be possible to work with

Makhno if the campaign against him were dropped did not materialise in the early summer; for it was only after Denikin's initial victory that Makhno and the Red Army began to collaborate in the autumn. It is also of interest how well equipped and organised Makhno's forces were, and the recognition that anti-semitism was not in evidence.

RGVA, f. 33987, op. 2, ed. khr. 72, l. 34

Commander of Armies of the Ukrainian Front

Copy. *Secret.*

May 1919, No.822

Active service army

To the Chairman of the Council of People's Commissars, Comrade Rakovskii

To the People's Commissar for Military Affairs, Comrade Podvoiskii

Note on Makhno

From direct experience I have ascertained and confirm that:

1. Makhno himself, his main military aides and his regiments are imbued with the desire to smash the counter-revolutionary cossacks and officers.
2. Makhno and Marusya Nikiforova [his common law wife] are carrying on a campaign to create 'a united revolutionary front against counter-revolution'.
3. They do not care for the Left SRs.
4. Makhno admits our party literature and has accepted political commissars.
5. The principle of electing leaders is gradually dying out in the units. Order No.12 reduces the regimental committees to the functions of supply acting as quartermasters.
6. Makhno has played no part in anti-Soviet agitation; he was not at the Third Congress in Gulyai Pole and did not sign the resolutions of the Congress.
7. He protests in the press against agitation for pogroms.
8. He does not let Marusya Nikiforova into military affairs, and maintains that her role should be confined to care and nursing.
9. Makhno and his staff live at an extremely modest level; there is no sign of banditry.
10. One can see some organisational work in the district: they are

setting up children's collectives and schools. Gulyai Pole is one of the strongest cultural centres in New Russia, containing 3 institutions of secondary education and so on. Thanks to Makhno up to 10 military hospitals have been opened for the wounded. They have got a workshop going which repairs pieces of ordnance and makes locks for them.

11. The wounded are bright faced and eager to get back into the fray. The poor fighting efficiency of certain units can be attributed to weakness in their commanders.

12. Makhno's forces consist of 4 regiments with up to 6000 infantry, up to 20 machine guns, 5 three-inch guns, 2 40-inch guns [sic] and 2 4.5-inch guns, one armoured train, very few cartridges. Half the rifles are Italian; the position with uniform is very difficult; half the men are barefoot. The 8th Regiment is quite badly disciplined.

13. The units are all ex-soldiers, of outstanding quality (men who returned to Gulyai Pole from the war always came back at least as NCOs). They are excellent material but need further indoctrination.

14. To make up losses in Makhno's units (apart from anything else there are up to 1000 wounded in hospital) one regiment stationed three *versts* from Kuteinikov summoned a congress of 72 districts to declare 'voluntary mobilisation', or more precisely voluntary recruitment.

15. Attached to Makhno, rather in his rear, there are some rogues who from time to time behave disgracefully. Because discipline is being strengthened in Makhno's units bandit elements are deserting from them and fouling the rear areas. There is one famous man, a cripple with no legs, who organises fighting units; he is no bandit.

16. Our political workers in Makhno's units are weak and cowardly, unable to stand up to the harmful elements.

17. Attacks on Makhno infuriate the local population and his men.

18. According to Dybenko and Makhno the story of the attack on Aleksandrovsk is curious nonsense: no one was attacking – a battalion was going to rest; the idea of an attack was just made up by some locals, prone to panic.

19. The retreat from Mariupol' was due to the 9th Division running away. Makhno's brigade was 27 *versts* from Taganrog and three from Kuteynikov.

Conclusion:

1. Makhno will not move against us.
2. We need to do our political work throughout the area and that is quite possible. Any campaign against Makhno ought to be stopped.

3. The area can give us enormous forces against the cossacks, but only if we get it under control.
4. We must send in the best possible workers for military organisational work in this district.

Commander of Armies of the Ukrainian Front, Antonov (signature)

Document 3.3

How difficult the Bolsheviks found it to distinguish between 'good' and 'bad' Green forces is made clear from this newspaper account. There were, of course, essentially bandit groups of men living rough in the hills and forests; but the word *kulak* was often used to describe any peasant opponent of Bolshevism who refused to accept the authority of Lenin's Committees of the Poor. The slogan, 'Long live the soviets but down with the communists', was common amongst anarchists and Left SRs.

RTsKhIDNI, *f. 17, op. 65, ed. khr. 157, l. 17* [extract]

Issue of the single sheet newspaper, Red Soldier, *organ of Political Section of 33rd Infantry Rifle Division. No clear date.*

The Green Army

Red Army comrades of No.2 Brigade are greatly interested in the Green Army, which has often been the subject of absurd rumours. There is a Green Army in the Kuban'. It is fighting for Soviet power against Denikin, and according to the latest reports has succeeded in taking Tuapse and Maykop. These are our friends. But we also find another sort of 'Green Army men', that are in the rear areas behind our front: small bands of deserters, people saving their own skins, and *kulaks*, operating under the leadership of counter-revolutionaries, who have run away from their units or are dodging the call-up. They commit burglaries and brutal robberies, and are traitors to Soviet power, although they sometimes try to hide under the slogan 'Long live the soviets, but down with communists'. We all know extremely well that the Cadets of the Upper Don and other districts are also allegedly in favour of soviet power, and yet none of us has the slightest doubt that these failed adherents of worker-peasant power are indistinguishable from the most hardened *kulaks* on the Don. The same applies to the Green Army deserters. We have to fight against them ruthlessly, and exterminate them as bandits, traitors and defenders of the old gang of landowners and bourgeois. Our struggle against them is going well. In the very near future our rear areas will be cleansed from every foul trace of Whites and Greens...

Document 3.4

This report clearly shows how by September 1919 the possible advantage of Makhno-style activity behind Denikin's lines was dawning on Bolsheviks in authority. The author is clearly impressed by the effectiveness of partisan activity, and determined to bring it under closer Red Army co-ordination; it is interesting that, apart from the obvious difficulties of getting money assigned to such a project, he recognises the necessity of establishing effective political work among such groups.

RTsKhIDNI, *f. 17, op. 109, ed. khr.* 44

To the Deputy Chairman of the RVS of the Republic

From member of the RVS of the 14th Army, S.M. Natsarenus

13 September 1919

Following on the departure of our troops from the south, partisan detachments of every kind started to operate in the enemy's rear in almost all parts of the Ekaterinoslav, Poltava and Kharkov provinces.

Besides the usual robberies and illegal activities, some of the detachments have carried on serious hostilities against the forces of Denikin and Petlyura, mainly by destroying their communications and supply trains.

The strength of the detachments sometimes amounts to an impressive total of 1000 men under arms, along with their own transport.

Thus in the Dikanskii woods there is up to a battalion of infantry, more than a battalion of cavalry with guns and machine guns. In the districts of Motols, Radyach and Zinkovsk, similarly in the woods, a force equal to the Dikanskii one, but with better supplies and arms.

These forces are active, mobile and difficult to catch, so that they may inflict quite significant damage on the enemy.

The military situation requires that the best possible use be made of these bands, and that they should be brought under a united command, and among the bands themselves there can be observed a significant tendency to centralisation, to accept military and political leadership.

Subordination to such a command will only be possible if the bands are given help by the RVS of the Republic, but that will involve expenditure, which the RVS is not in a position to meet because of the absence of the relevant credits.

Because of the necessity of taking control of these bands, I am requesting that two million [roubles] be put at my disposal for this purpose.

Only two million is being requested because, as they have done until now, the bands will supply themselves from the local population; the main expenses will consist of maintaining contact with them and sending large numbers of communists to join them, empowered to purge the band command structures of bandits and robbers. At the same time they will be instructed to carry out oral and written propaganda work.

Getting control of these bands, bringing their operations into the proper channels, getting their activities organised to support the front, this all demands action from within, getting our comrades into positions of influence and control.

But to attempt it means having sufficient material support to finance sending comrades on such a mission.

The credit I ask for is urgent and should be budgeted for without too many formalities.

S. Natsarenus

Document 3.5

This document simply reminds us of the political consequences of the Bolsheviks' failure to address the Green issue effectively. Deprived of proper cossack representation as late as November 1919, exiled groups of cossacks were the only ones able to attend the 7th All-Russian Congress of Soviets.

RTsKhIDNI, f. 17, op. 65, ed. khr. 35, l. 168

Cossack Section, 24 November 1919

To the Presidium of the All-Russian Central Executive Committee of the Soviets

Whereas the cossack lands are occupied by gangs of White Guards, which makes it impossible for cossack representatives to attend the 7th All-Russian Congress of Soviets, the Cossack Section of the All-Russian Central Executive Committee therefore requests the Presidium of the All-Russian Central Executive Committee of the Soviets to allocate seven places with full voting rights to members of the Cossack

Section at the forthcoming All-Russian Congress of Soviets, in order to give expression to the voice of working-class revolutionary cossacks of all *oblasts* and *voiskos* [districts], as was the case at the preceding six congresses.

Deputy Head of Cossack Section of All-Russian Central Executive Committee (signature)

Secretary (signature)

MORALE AND SUPPLY

The majority of these documents give a snapshot picture of the state of the Red Army in the summer of 1919, when the military situation looked at its worst for the Bolsheviks. Morale was low and so was the level of supplies. However, for comparison, the final document relates to November 1919 when the Bolsheviks were on the verge of victory, but problems clearly still remained. They serve to counter-act the propaganda vision of the Red Army propagated by the Bolsheviks after their victory.

Document 3.6

This document is a long extract from a report from the Astrakhan region to the Central Committee in Moscow. The generally low level of morale is clear and need not be elaborated on; but of particular interest are the references to political work among the non-Russian population. The report from Krasnyi Yar gives an insight into the work of propagandists among the Muslim population, while the report from Urda says a great deal about prejudice and inter-ethnic tension in the region; it was only with the greatest difficulty that the Bolsheviks could provide political education officers who lived up to their internationalist creed.

RTsKhIDNI, *f.* 17, *op.* 65, *ed. khr.* 157, *ll.* 80–6 [extract]

Secret

To Central Committee RKP(b) Information Section

Report on Political Situation for 18 July 1919, 34th Division

Base Food Shop: Mood of office workers satisfactory. Grumbling noted among labourers because they do not get Red Army ration on a par with all the office staff.

Source: Report of Political Commissar of Base Food Shop, Comrade Zakhalyavko of 17 July. Information input No.3082

Politburo of Military Sector of Railway

Akhtuva Station: The mood of the working staff of the Baskunchavskii Railway is unreliable, in view of which propaganda work has been stepped up, as has the supply of literature, and the local railwaymen's Communist Party organisation has been given appropriate instructions. The peasant population is in a counter-revolutionary mood. There have been occasions on which the *kulaks*, mistaking our flotilla for one of Denikin's, have supplied the ships with provisions. Part of the gang which has been distilling illegal spirits and cutting telegraph wires has been caught and sent to the Special Section in Astrakhan.

Source: Report of 12 July from Head of Politburo of Railway Military Education Comrade Zemskii. Information input No.3079

Politburo of Left Military Sector

Krasnyi Yar: Morale of soldiers of 1st Battalion of 199th Regiment is satisfactory. Under enemy pressure our units have retreated to fresh positions. At first the retreat was disorderly, but after a certain time proceeded in an organised way. The fighting spirit of the soldiers was affected by the retreat and measures were taken to restore their morale. The Red Army men are hostile to their command staff, in particular to the Commander Poleshko, who according to them had served in the staff of the traitor Sorokin. Poleshko has been arrested and is being sent under escort to Astrakhan. After Poleshko's arrest the Red Army men have been encouraged and spirits have risen. Propaganda and educational work is under way. The population gladly come to the concerts and meetings which have been arranged for them. Propagandists who have come from the Muslims in Astrakhan have organised a Muslim communist cell in Krasnyi Yar and are arranging meetings and lectures in the Muslim language. The Muslim agitators are also carrying on propaganda work among the Muslim population of the district.

Source: Telegram of 17 July from Head of Politburo of Left Military Sector. Information input No.3101

Politburo of Western Military Sector

Yadyki: The conference of cells of Western Military Sector has been successful. Delegates are setting off to the conference in Astrakhan.

Source: Report of 12 July from Head of Politburo of Western Military Education. Information input No.3085

Politburo of Eastern Military Sector

Urda: Military Commissariat. The Commissariat makes no effort to cooperate with the Politburo and the Political Commissar of the military sector. **It looks like a fortress which it is difficult to get into.** Its personnel do not come to work on time and do not put enough energy into their work.

The 1st Kirghiz Model Cavalry Regiment, which began to be formed back in February, at the moment presents a sorry picture of demoralisation. When it formed the regiment the military commissariat probably did not take into account that it would pass out of its direct control. When the regiment was due to be transferred to the 34th Division this could not be achieved quickly. The commissariat did not want to put it into effect, and besides that the regiment was not a fighting unit, but was more like an apparatus for maintaining that unit. Just one part of the regiment has been detailed off for the defence of the *oblast*. The remainder (who are still training) service the commissariat and the town of Urda. They carry out guard duties, guard the quarters of the military commissar, are on duty with the reserve camel train, and so on.

The Politburo, which has no specialised military knowledge, requests competent orders from the Kirghiz RVS about what is the most appropriate form of organisation. **More than 508 men from the regiment are on sick leave.** The squadron which had been sent to the military sector **is directed by a notorious bandit, appointed by the Commissariat after some of the command staff had deserted to join the Whites.** The squadron is becoming demoralised, but it is difficult to replace him, since there are no men able to carry out garrison and guard duties in the town. A meeting of the command staff of the regiment was called in order to clarify the reasons for the deterioration in discipline, and find ways to improve it. It was demonstrated that discipline suffered particularly seriously after the White officers deserted from Urda. The officers who stayed with the regiment had their weapons taken away from them. The *dzhigits* [mounted tribesmen] do not obey those who had fallen under suspicion and no help is given by measures to tighten discipline. The *dzhigits* go off to their houses, carrying their mattresses with them. They do not turn up for work, they drive their horses senselessly and so on. It is said that after the officers had deserted they were about to kill off all the Russians, announcing that the commanders' day was done, etc.

It became obvious that it was best to return their arms to the command staff, give them back their rights and restore faith in them. It was proposed that educative work should be increased, strengthening the regiment with Kirghiz who could read and write, since the better educated Kirghiz had been taken into the office by the commissariat, while the regiment was left without even any interpreters who could give good translations for their military training. The Chief Instructor maintains (and his opinion is shared by all the command staff) that **the Kirghiz people are not military stuff, that they are lazy and physically ill-adapted to military training**, etc. This reasoning of the Chief Instructor throws cold water on the command staff, gives them **grounds for justifying their lack of success and makes them approach their work with the prejudice that nothing can be achieved.**

With the help of its agitators the Politburo is setting up Comrades' Courts and Education Commissions, organising meetings and discussions. It intends to give instructions to the regimental commander about putting unit instruction on a sound basis. It would be desirable to have a corresponding order from the top, showing the fatal effect of the Chief Instructor's way of looking at things, as he has promoted it among the command staff.

We are suffering from a serious shortage of political workers, who would work on behalf of the Bureau and make reports to it. In this context it would seem desirable to make use of the colleagues who came with Comrade Umerov. Comrade Narimanov gave a letter on this subject to Comrade Umerov, but did not set out clearly what had to be done. It was on account of this that Comrade Umerov, not paying attention to the said letter, detailed four comrades for face to face work in the Regiment, but they **do not report to the Politburo**, since they consider themselves as working for the Education Section of the **Commissariat**. Without the knowledge of the **Bureau** one of them has been **sent on business to Saratov**. Now we shall have to insist that comrade **Umerov lets us have party workers to be placed under the direct control of the Politburo** for service with the front line units of the Kirghiz Regiment. In the Politburo's opinion it is impossible to avoid extra efforts to convince them, and undesirable friction. This would not be so if the Political Section of the Astrakhan Region would send us without intermediaries the most essential workers, who are extremely necessary for the forthcoming work on improving the political education of the *dzhigits*, for tightening up discipline, trying to stop desertions, enforcing conscription, and so on.

The Politburo requests the Political Section to send five or six Muslims to work with the staff of the Politburo. The appropriate measures have been taken by the Political Section. The Political Education Department of the Commissariat could be switched to work among the local population, the supply organs, and in units which have been reconstituted. The comrades who are now on courses organised by the Section could also be employed in this way. The Politburo begs you to take the **measures to carry out our request as contained in our telegram of 5 July, No.32 to the Provincial, Committee Against Desertion.**

Source: Report of Comrade Zemskii of 8 July. Information input No.3001

Document 3.7

This report on the state of the armies on the Southern Front in early August 1919 needs no elaboration. Supplies are short and morale is low.

RTsKhIDNI, *f.* 17, *op.* 65, *ed. khr.* 157, *l.* 1

Secret

Political Section of RVS Southern Front, Department of Information and Communications

Reports on state of armies on Southern Front from 1 to 8 August 1919

29th Rifle Regiment:

All companies have Comrades' Courts. The Red Army men have well-developed political consciousness and their behaviour is exemplary. Intensive political work is carried out in the regiment. In virtually all companies or small detachments there are communist cells and Political Education Commissions. There are commissions in charge of stores; supplies are poor.

5 August

103 Rifle Regiment:

The command staff are poorly directed. Discipline is weak. The majority of the command staff are relatives or come from the same area as the Red Army men, so that orders are carried out on a family basis. Low level of political consciousness. Most of the political commissars are poorly prepared. Lack of political workers. Cells organised in machine gun squad and in 2nd battalion. Political education has been organised.

[no date]

9th Army: 14th Rifle Division, 118 Rifle Regiment:

Relations between command staff and Soviet authorities are not quite as one might wish. There is a cell of 14 communists. Party work is very bad.

25 July

119 Rifle Regiment:

Military spirit satisfactory. Red Army men politically educated, apart from those who have recently arrived. A commission has been appointed to take charge of stores, but it functions badly. The regiment is poorly off for uniform; some of the men go barefoot.

[no date]

2nd Brigade:

The brigade commander, Zinoviev, a former colonel, is a weak person to be in charge of the brigade. He has no authority among the higher ranks of the command staff. He has almost no opinions of his own for the working out of operational plans. His work is characterised by inertia and a slack attitude to his duties. The Brigade Chief of Staff, Zaslavskii, is an outstanding officer, who served in General Headquarters. He has a strong influence on the unit commanders. It is really he who commands the brigade. One can very often observe him making various tactless remarks against the RVS and political commissars. The brigade is now being re-formed with men conscripted from Saratov Province. The conscripts are extremely unreliable and their morale is bad. There are deserters. There are not enough command staff in the brigade. It is essential that a large number of political workers shall be sent, to be appointed as political commissars to carry out Party work.

4 August

[Number indecipherable] brigade:

The brigade is very poorly supplied. Often there is a shortage of ammunition. Many Red Army men are barefoot and only half clothed. The brigade receives practically nothing from the Supply Department and has to make do with its own resources.

30 July

Document 3.8

Whether this letter to the editor from a certain Vasiliy Churakov was ever published is unclear, but it was certainly forwarded to the Bolshevik Party Central Committee for information. Morale in this particular unit must have been very low indeed.

RTsKhIDNI, *f.* 17, *op.* 65, *ed. khr.* 157, *l.* 182

Received by Central Committee, 12 June 1919

There are even people like this (Letter to the Editor)

It may be an unconscious, more likely a deliberate misunderstanding by some comrades of the present situation, but I do not know how to describe what I have seen in our company on the 29th of this month [presumably June]. In No.1 Company of the Voronezh Regiment a communist cell was recently organised. It was joined by several of the more politically committed comrades in our company. Working with other men from those sympathetic to communism, one of the most politically educated comrades, P. Boyko, arranged meetings in the company, and summoned to the defence of the proletarian revolution both the oppressed workers, and peasants throughout the world, to fight against the power of capital.

A few days ago we had to go as reinforcements to replace comrades who had been killed. Some of the communist comrades and also some of the 'sympathisers', members of our cell, should have gone with us. When it was suggested to them that they should go as volunteers along with their comrades, not one among them agreed to go. It was proposed to draw lots, but comrade P. Boyko even refused selection by lot, declaring firmly:

'I will not go, and to hell with the commune and all its works.'

One must ask why, when there was no demand for them to go to the front, they were so strongly in favour of the commune and Soviet power, and yet when they were proposed and had to go, they then refuse and do not accept anything. Who can we believe in and who are we to listen to, if the words of our leaders are contradicted by their actions?

Red Army Man of No.1 Company of the 30th Voronezh Defence Regiment of the Railway of the Southern Front Vasilii Churakov

Document 3.9

This short extract of a report to the Central Committee simply underlines the fact that the poor supply situation did not only effect the Southern Front.

RTsKhIDNI, f. 17, op. 65, ed. khr. 155, l. 2a

Received 26 June 1919

RVS Eastern Front, RVS 5th Army

Fifty per cent of the Red Army men have no footwear, greatcoats or underclothes. As the cold nights set in, illnesses caused by the cold are increasing every day...

Document 3.10

The final document in this part relates to the end of 1919, when Bolshevik victory seemed certain, rather than the summer of 1919 when the Bolsheviks seemed on the verge of defeat. It shows very clearly indeed that many of the problems of supply and morale continued long after that disastrous summer. If uniforms existed, they were not being distributed, and the men, and in particular the cavalry horses, still went hungry; similarly, political work hardly existed. What had changed by the end of the year was, partly, the end of the typhus outbreak, but mostly the adoption of a less sectarian policy towards the rural population; after the lesson of the Don rebellion, the Bolsheviks understood the crucial importance of not alienating the cossack majority.

The document also shows that Denikin's cavalry remained a force to be reckoned with, even though the majority of infantrymen captured were men in their early fifties. The reference to aeroplanes is also interesting.

In July 1918 Beloborodov was the man responsible for organising the execution of the Tsar and his family in Ekaterinburg.

RTsKhIDNI, *f.* 17, *op.* 65, *ed. khr.* 155, *l.* 48

Balashov [a town on the Southern Front]: Report to Central Committee

3 November 1919, signed at end 'Beloborodov'

Dear Comrades

Evidently we should conclude that the enemy has finished his operation against our army. Over the last two days our divisions have begun to push forward without encountering any resistance. Our men have occupied the stations Samodurovok and Povorino almost without a fight. As far as we can judge by the information at our disposal, the enemy is regrouping his forces in order to make a new thrust on the right flank of the 9th Army and the left flank of the 8th Army (in the area of the stations Koleno and Borisoglebsk). It is quite obvious that Denikin has exhausted his reserves of men for service. While I have been with the 23rd Division half of the prisoners who have come into our hands are old men from 49 to 55 years. The prisoners are not in any official uniform; they are going into action wearing the clothes in which they left home. If our soldiers are badly off for uniform, that is absolutely not because things are lacking, but arises from the scandalous, exasperating disorganisation of our supply system.

There is as yet no perceptible inflow of active, efficient workers into this branch of our organisation (I am taking the 9th Army as an example). For this same reason our soldiers go hungry, since in areas where military operations are actually taking place one will never see a single food supply commission charged with buying food. Cavalry units especially suffer from this, being frequently moved about: the supply commissions are completely unable to attend to their needs. Our cavalry have a miserable time through the fault of another body, the so-called 'purchasing commission'. They, too, stay far back in the rear and work slowly, at a snail's pace. The cavalry units get no remounts and the men (horsemen with no horses) are left hanging around in the baggage trains.

The army's sanitary and medical services are still in a disgusting state. The typhus epidemic has stopped and cases of typhus are now quite rare, but, on the other hand, care for our wounded is terribly badly organised, particularly any form of first aid to be given during a battle. I spent two days near our advanced positions; men who came out of the line had to drag themselves along for several *versts* before they could get a first dressing for their wounds. This was happening during very fierce fighting in the 23rd Division's sector (in the area of the station Budarino).

There is no reading matter in the front lines. I had to cover about 200 *versts* in the course of a week, and I did not see a single newspaper, even in the rear areas. Neither the Red Army men, nor the command staff, nor the commissars have any idea at all of what is going on in the world. Even the RVS has been without a newspaper for more than a week. It naturally is impossible to carry out any political work in such conditions. The radio station is taken up with operational work and thus the whole army finds itself cut off from the world outside. We are setting to work all that collection of people who are hanging about in the rear with nothing to do. If we can get some intake of Party workers from the centre it will allow us to brush up our complement of commissars, who are mainly an exceedingly uninspiring and inactive bunch.

A certain lull at the front will now give us the chance to get some reinforcements into the divisions. In the 9th Army there are really only two divisions left, the 22nd and 23rd. In the 14th Division and in each of the brigades of Divisions 36 and 21 there are only a handful of men.

The 56th Division (formerly 4th Ukrainian Division) has been completely disbanded, in view of its absolute collapse under the enemy's blows, and thereafter. The final break-up of the Division was brought about by the commanders, who were thoroughly rotten, and by its useless political workers. To crown it all, the remnants of the Division arranged a meeting yesterday, and discussed the order to advance. They sent a delegation to the RVS. The delegation has been placed under arrest and will be shot; the Red Army men are being disarmed today and every tenth one will be shot. The Division was made up of Ukrainian peasants.

Our chief affliction, as before, remains the enemy's cavalry. Our infantry have never ceased to fear it, in spite of the greater fire power on our side.

Besides their special cavalry strike units, on the flank of each infantry regiment the enemy places a squadron of cavalry (100–200 strong), and by passing round our flanks these force our infantry to fall back. Our own special commissions to deal with cavalry will not be much use, because they are too small in number. The specialists who are meant to give training to the infantry are a completely incompetent lot, less experienced than our average front line troops, and have much to learn themselves before they start teaching others. The only thing the commissions can do is to concentrate the active service commanders' attention on working out methods to combat cavalry. They will do a certain amount of good in this way.

At the present moment Army HQ is moving to Serdobsk. Here in Balashov there remain only the RVS and the Army Commander with his operations section. If the enemy relaxes his pressure the other parts of headquarters will be brought back to Balashov.

With comradely greetings

A. Beloborodov

P.S. The Army has absolutely no paper. If there was paper it would be possible to work up a strong leaflet campaign among the enemy's units. Our air force is working splendidly. I cannot praise the pilots' conduct too highly. The aircraft sometimes get up to 20 holes when they are carrying out reconnaissance and literature drops. Pressure must be brought to bear on the Head of Paper Supply to stop printing all unnecessary material, concentrating only on what is essential for our defence.

True signature B.

TERROR

From the very moment the Bolsheviks seized power in October 1917 they used the arbitrary exercise of power against their opponents. Such a policy reached its zenith in August and September 1918 when, with the Bolsheviks' grip on power at its most tenuous, Lenin endorsed the policy of Red Terror. In a bloodbath lasting about a month at least 10 000 alleged enemies of Bolshevism were executed. Although the terror reduced in intensity once the First World War was over, it remained a constant feature of Bolshevik life. Arbitrary arrest could affect any real or supposed enemy of Soviet power.

Document 3.11

This document is an abridged letter from the Red Army's Supreme Commander in Chief, I.I. Vatsetis, to Lenin concerning, primarily, the arbitrary arrest of leading Red Army generals in April 1919; it constitutes an emotional denunciation of what was already becoming an arbitrary regime. The Red Army had always been dependent on the officer corps of the old Imperial Army, and so the question of political reliability was always there; but in this letter Vatsetis makes it perfectly clear he thinks this issue is being deliberately abused and that political commissars revel in being able to catch generals out. The arrest of Teodori seems particularly inappropriate, as Vatsetis suggests, since he was loyal in the autumn of 1918, the most difficult period for the Soviet regime.

M.S. Kedrov joined the Cheka in December 1918 and in January 1919 became the Head of its Special Department.

RTsKhIDNI, f. 17, op. 109, ed. khr. 41 [extracts]

To: Chairman of Defence Council, Lenin

From: C-in-C of all armed forces of the Republic, 18 April 1919

No.17, Town of Serpukhov

Report

There are not enough command staff for the active service units. Although the courses which are run in the Republic do provide a considerable number for adding to the command staff, nevertheless in continuous ceaseless battles at the front we are losing command staff in large numbers. The percentage of casualties among the commanders is enormous, almost twice as high as among other ranks ... We have departed from the rule of trying to conserve command staff ... Everywhere and on every occasion they are in the front rank of the combatants – often out in front – and they are the first to get killed. This has a particularly bad effect on the outcome of a battle, since units are deprived of their commanders right at the beginning of the fighting, so that they are left without leaders at its end, and consequently lose much of their effectiveness in action.

In the various headquarters there are not enough people to work who have proper military training. In the General Staff we are more than 70 per cent short of the required establishment, and at the front the shortage of trained specialists may reach as high as 82 per cent. It means that in the headquarters the whole burden of work requiring military training and specialised knowledge falls on the 15 to 35 per cent who are in post. As a result of this we get a great overload of duties for those working in the General Staff, particularly when they are serving at the front, and this means they become completely exhausted, with considerable percentage of illness among these first class personnel...

People in headquarters, directing operations, are putting much more energy into carrying out their duties than was required in practice under conditions of service as they were in the old Imperial Army... One can observe that the commissars who are attached to them are often behaving tactlessly towards members of staff at headquarters. These commissars have not always been selected for this duty with sufficient care. Among the commissars, unfortunately, there are few with sufficient education to understand the feelings and the milieu over which they have to exercise control – and the process of control often turns into relentlessly following every movement of the officer they are attached to. People like this do great harm in practical and specialised work, but unfortunately there are all too many commissars of this type...

Both in print, and in the speeches of demagogues speaking to a huge concourse of people, phrases still appear persistently which are insulting for those working on the General Staff. From all sides accusations pour out that they have their price, that they are counter-revolutionaries or saboteurs. Former officers who are serving on our General Staff do not deserve this unjust attitude... Generally it was considered that the Russian General Staff was extremely liberal, always coming half-way to meet any progressive movement or swing to the left, and even under the old regime the General Staff was strongly suspected of revolutionary tendencies... Those who were monarchists have long since lined up with our enemies... Every commissar has his secret desire to catch our staff officers out in some counter-revolutionary attitude or treachery... This seems a very strange way to behave, since that sort of behaviour was a typical feature of the gendarmes of the old regime...

Recently everyone has been especially upset by the sudden arrest of Teodori of GHQ [see Document 1.13], whom all knew to be a faithful and conscientious person, working for Soviet power in a highly responsible position. Under Comrade Kedrov's instructions, in spite of the fact that all the charges against him have been proved null and void, Teodori still remains under arrest. That can only be attributed to Comrade Kedrov's arbitrary misuse of his powers... Indisputably Teodori has been tremendously helpful to us, especially in the summer of 1918 [see Chapter 1]. At that time rebellions were rife in our country, and had to be put down by the Operations Section, of which Teodori was the Military Director. Similarly, when we had to fight against the Czechoslovak

Corps... Teodori gave invaluable service as Military Director of the Operations Section, which was headed by Comrade Aralov. The Supreme Military Council, which at that time stood at the head of the military apparatus, turned out to be quite incapable of dealing with the press of practical work, and all the duties belonging to that Council were carried out by the Operations Section, with Teodori on its staff. I can bear witness to Teodori's immense contribution to our success on the Volga at that time. It was only thanks to his thrusting energy and his devotion to our cause that we managed to get our country to provide sufficient reserves... and to preserve military discipline in the staff who were forming units locally and despatching them to the Eastern Front. His services at that time should not be forgotten... Persistent rumours are circulating that Comrade Kedrov's assistant Eynduk declared there to be no charges against Teodori, and that charges would have to be made up.

In the last few days Comrade Selivachev has also been arrested, whom it was intended to appoint to command the Eastern Front. Selivachev I knew even before the war, and he was never a monarchist; quite the opposite – under the monarchy he was one of those who was persecuted. Taken together both these arrests make it look as though hostages are being taken in advance...

I request that an enquiry should be set up into Comrade Kedrov's activity, and that he should be brought to book if he is the only guilty party. Comrade Kedrov I know from his highly unsuccessful command of the 6th Army, during which time, quite illegally, without any right to do so, he ordered the arrest of the Commander of the 2nd Army, Comrade Blokhin, and the whole staff of the 2nd Army – adding in his telegram that if need be they should be shot. The 2nd Army was not under Comrade Kedrov's command, and for this act he was dismissed from command of the 6th Army... Kedrov destroyed the command of the 2nd Army, as a result of which it disintegrated...

In the headquarters of the Eastern Front they recently arrested Khrulev, who was a member of the General Staff. The Revolutionary Tribunal condemned him to five years in prison, though at the same time the man really guilty of the crime got off with just a reprimand.

In the headquarters of the Ural District the entire HQ staff were arrested without any due cause whatsoever.

On 1 April in the headquarters of the 1st Army, by the individual decision of Comrade Kal, member of RVS of 1st Army, the assistant head of the radio-telegraph [section], Vendebaum, was shot without trial or investigation.

All this emphasises what an arbitrary regime is still practised by political workers on a personal basis, both towards individuals in the headquarters, and in their treatment of specialists in general . . . Nothing but harm arises from such conditions of service, that afford no security against unfounded arrest, and this at a time when work demands such stressful concentration . . .

As a result of our temporary setbacks on the Eastern Front many people are overcome by a state of alarm . . . One can observe this among the commissars and the feeling is undoubtedly transmitted to those working on the Staff . . . We shall have to draw some sort of line beyond which it will be forbidden to show suspicion or to mock members of the headquarters staff. In the name of our final victory over our many enemies, we must guarantee complete immunity and freedom to all members of the General Staff now serving in the Red Army, allowing them to be arrested only when definite evidence is produced, and only when their immediate superiors are kept informed.

Besides this I consider it essential to review the case of Khrulev of the General Staff, who was unjustly accused, and to bring to book comrade Kalinin, who shot Vendebaum without any trial or investigation, since this kind of arbitrary behaviour damages the reputation of Soviet power.

C-in-C of all armed forces of the Republic GHQ, Vatsetis

18 April 1919, Serpukhov

Document 3.12

The exercise of arbitrary power was not only a feature of the apex of power: the security services operated at every level, either in the form of the Cheka or in the Special Sections of the Red Army. This report on the work of one such Special Section throws up much of interest: thus although much of the section's work involved standard counter-intelligence activities such as interviewing prisoners of war, as early as the summer of 1919 the Bolsheviks were recruiting networks of informants and had established norms according to which such people should operate.

RTsKhIDNI, *f.* 17, *op.* 65, *ed. khr.* 155, *ll.* 80–1

To the administration of the Special Section of the All-Union Cheka

Copies to the Special Section of the Southern Front, to Comrade Minin, member of RVS of 10th Army

5 September 1919

Report and Statement

On 3 July this year, acting on the order of RVS of 10th Army, No.326, Comrade Genkin is appointed as the new Chairman to replace Comrade Novitskii as Chairman of Special Section.

I. *State of the Special Section on 4 July this year*

Even a cursory glance reveals the state of Special Section of 10th Army to be chaotic. We do take into account that 4 July was the moment of the evacuation from Tsaritsyn, which fell to the enemy. Comrade Novitskii is handing over to his successor only a certain part of the secret papers and documents. Why does he not hand over the Special Section as a whole?

The papers which Comrade Genkin has received are no longer secret from him. They have come in as multiple copies, there are no top copies.

Information. Have measures often been taken to organise a network of informants? There are none of them in one unit. The establishment is for one or two persons.

II. *Work on organising the Special Section of 10th Army*

The Army is retreating, and together with it must retreat the steamer in which the Special Section is quartered. Taking advantage of that time an assessment of Party workers was carried out. As a result we are left with a small number of workers, but those who remain are reliable.

Work of the Information Unit

Two objectives:

1. Infiltration, i.e., through its informants, through reports, extracts from political communiqués and such like – it should gather materials which pick out criminal personnel in various institutions, units and Army staffs.
2. By drawing up reports, summaries of operations, etc., it should keep the centre and the RVS informed about the work of the Special Section.

In the active part of the section there are in all about 35 agents, of whom only 6–7 are capable of undertaking serious counter-intelligence work in depth.

The Head of Staff for All-Russia has assigned to us the responsibility of examining prisoners of war and people who have come across to us.

Managerial Unit

Department No.4 has been moved into the occupied town of Kamyshin for work in the town and on the Army's left flank.

Department No.2 is placed on the left bank of the Volga (at present in the Nikolayevsk Workers' Settlement).

Three points of the Special Section have been organised on the River Volga. They are responsible for observing all passing steamers and for military intelligence work.

III. *Coded report on the work of the Special Section of 10th Army, from 4 July to 1 September this year*

Total number of cases processed by Special Section 10th Army, 326.

Out of which cases completed:

> charged with spying 6
> charged with counter-revolutionary activities 3
> charged with dereliction of duty 69
> charged with belonging to a White Guard organisation 3.

DESERTION

Given some of the features of the war explored above – the Bolsheviks' negative attitude to the majority of the rural population, the low level of propaganda work and the poor level of supplies – it is hardly surprising that large numbers of those recruited to the Red Army simply deserted. The next four documents in this part of Chapter 3 relate to desertion, considering some individual cases and more general issues.

Document 3.13

This document illustrates how, for Party members accused of desertion, the first body to deal with them would be the Party organisation. However, once deprived of Party membership, they were handed over to the Special Section of the Army (see document 3.12).

RTsKhIDNI, *f.* 17, *op.* 65, *ed. khr.* 157, *l.* 181

Received by Central Committee, 14 May 1919

Minutes of general meeting of members of the communist cell of the Special Section of 9th Army 23 April this year; 46 members attended.

Comrade Epshtein was elected Chairman, Comrade Fokin Secretary.

Agenda

1. Deviation of fellow communists from Party discipline.
2. Current business.

The meeting heard a Report on the first agenda item from Comrade Kaftanikov, who indicated in his report the sad fact that certain communists, at the most critical moment when the White Guard pack were advancing towards Ust-Medveditskaya, abandoned their posts and fled under various pretexts to the *stanitsa* Archadinskaya. After the report, a number of speakers on the same subject pointed out this incident of cowardice, and how several of our fellow communists had attempted to run away. After long arguments and opinions exchanged from every side, the proposal was adopted to hand over to a Party court the comrades who had left Ust-Medveditskaya.

Resolved:

To deprive of Party membership, and hand over to the court of the Special Section of the 9th Army the following comrades: Kozlovskii, Panfilov, Frolov and Romanov.

Heard Comrade Manegenov's statement concerning the stealing of some objects and various pieces of property during the evacuation of Ust-Medveditskaya.

Resolved:

To pass the matter over to the Special Section of the 9th Army for detailed clarification and to bring those guilty to trial.

Heard Comrade Suslov's application to be admitted to the category of 'sympathisers', attached to the cell of the Special Section of 9th Army.

Chairman (signature)
Secretary (signature)

Document 3.14

This document relates to July 1919 when the Bolsheviks were at their lowest ebb, and gives some idea of the numbers deserting and the methods used to combat desertion. It also shows how reports from deserters could have useful intelligence value, and that desertion itself was sometimes hard to define. Were the four deserters from Tushilovka really deserters, or just fishermen caught up in a war?

RTsKhIDNI, *f.* 17, *op.* 65, *ed. khr.* 157, *ll.* 87–8 [extract]

To Central Committee Information Section

>Report on Political Situation for 18 July 1919

[extract]

Provincial Anti-desertion Commission

From 3 to 18 July 64 men have deserted from their units. We have brought in 30 men by cordoning off areas and searching them, and 44 men have given themselves up voluntarily. Ten of those arrested are really inveterate deserters: **150 deserters are ready to be sent on**.

Source: Report of 17 July, Information input [number unclear]

Deserters Return

The brothers A. and I. Romanov, coming from Biryuzak, have stated: on 17 June we went to our cousin [name unclear]. Ten days after we arrived with him cossacks came in and wanted to conscript us. That same night we took some flour and made off for Astrakhan.

In the Biryuzak area the main figure is Sklyanin, a former officer and merchant in Astrakhan. His force amounts to about 1980 men, including many from Astrakhan. **They gather information by means of scouts, whom they send into the black market**. They bring vodka from there and get the cossacks drunk on it. In most cases the population do not like the cossacks for their drunkenness and the way they misbehave. People hated the Chechens who were here before the cossacks because they took their cattle. Since some parts of the population still support the cossacks there are often misunderstandings between villages on that score. For maintaining contact between Old and New Biryuzak **there are two enemy aeroplanes**.

Four deserters (Mayzurov, Suslikov, Ratashchinskii and Korotenkov) who have come from Tushilovka station (near Bryansk) have stated:

>At the end of May we set off down there also **to get flour**. The cossacks kept us there, taking the sails off our boat and not allowing us to go to it. There are very few cossacks there, only scouts. Besides us there were detained about 500 people from Astrakhan,

mainly fishermen, all of them having fled from Astrakhan. The cossacks conscripted about 300 of them, aged 20–24. Some of them went quite willingly. We have heard that there is a detachment of Sklyanin's but we do not know how strong it is or what it consists of. The cossack units in Tushilovka have no uniform or footwear (they are given clothing by their own forces). We managed to escape, profiting by the lack of an escort when they were sending us to Lagan.

The deserters assure us that they went off **not knowing that men of their age groups had been called up**. They have come back to Astrakhan to defend Soviet power. They all come from **Area 10 of the Combined Fishermen's Union** (Novo-Aleksandrovskii village).

Source: interrogation of deserters 17 July. Information input [No.]

Document 3.15

This document shows how by the end of 1919 the Bolsheviks were determined to take a very hard line indeed against anybody deserting or harbouring deserters.

RGVA, *f.* 33987, *op.* 2, *ed. khr.* 32, *l.* 48

Instructions to District Anti-desertion Commissions on measures to deal with those who harbour deserters

Secret.

Ratified at the session of Central Anti-desertion Commission, 18 December 1919.

1. The following are to be considered deserters: all those who without authorisation absent themselves from military units, factories, institutions and enterprises, when the staff of same have been declared as mobilised by decrees of the Defence Council, those who overstay any sort of leave, and those who do not report when mobilised.
2. Those who aid deserters must be considered those who give shelter to a deserter, all those who know the whereabouts of the said deserter and do not take any steps to deliver him over to the proper authorities.
3. From those mentioned in category 2 the highest degree of guilt is borne by the owners of houses, the chairmen of house committees,

among whom the deserter is living, their nearest neighbours and the chairmen of local councils.

Document 3.16

This final document on desertion links forward to Chapter 4. Ironically, despite the measures referred to in document 3.15, once the civil war was clearly over and Denikin and Kolchak defeated, there was a mass wave of desertions. What was the point of remaining in the Red Army? Bolshevik ideologues might dream of world revolution, but the spring sowing had far greater attractions to the majority of Red Army men.

RGVA, f. 33987, op. 2, ed. khr. 32, l. 4

Telegram No.109

To Comrade Danilov, Central Anti-desertion Commission

At our meeting yesterday one of the comrades stated that desertions amounted to 75 per cent from troops going to the front. Please inform me what is the average percentage of desertions and how is the exceptionally high percentage of deserters arrived at in some exceptional cases.

Chairman of the Revolutionary Military Council, Trotsky 13 January 1920

[Pencilled note at foot of telegram: 'Early reply expected'.]

EVERYDAY LIFE

Inevitably documents relating to every day life are chosen more or less at random. However the documents in this section give some idea of the frustrations of life on both sides of the lines. For reasons of consistency they again refer to the Southern Front.

Document 3.17

The Civil War did not put an end to the age-old practice of trading in illegally distilled alcohol. However, this document also reminds us that the Cheka was not only responsible for counter-revolutionary activity, but also serious crime.

RTsKhIDNI, f. 17, op. 5, ed. khr. 10, l. 125 [extracts]

19 December 1919

I am sending this to the All-Russian Cheka. I cannot refrain from drawing attention to this completely wrong way of working. I have written letters like this several times, but just torn them up, because if the people I am writing about get to know, they may kill me [and] may find me by my handwriting, and so I just won't sign it...
In the area of Yangildskii sub-district in every small or large village they are making illegal spirit and trading in it. In all the villages there are people who have run away and deserters. Village soviets know quite precisely where the deserters are. The village soviets have only had three months' experience of normal administration, and therefore they are all hiding deserters. The policemen know who is trading in illegal spirits. In the large village of Ishaki the following people are trading liquor: Nikolai Trofimov, Nikolai Osmanov, Avdotya Mironova, Mikhail Chusmaroev, citizen Chibachevoi. Irina Osipovna answers for all those who trade in or make illegal spirits. Acting on their own authority the police arrest Irina Osipovna, she gives them money, they release her, she feeds them with meat. You just go and ask Irina Osipovna, she will tell you how many times the police have caught her with spirits.

Document 3.18

That supplies were a problem on the White side of the lines as well as on the Red side is clear from this document. It is more or less self-explanatory; clearly the capitalists on the White side did not always find it easy to agree among themselves when it came to competing for lucrative Army contracts, and there is more than a hint at underhand activity in this complaint.

GARO, f. 865, op. 1, ed. khr. 235, ll. 1–23 [extracts]

To His Excellency *Ataman* of the Almighty *Voisko* of the Don The Office, 31 July 1919

From the undersigned members of the group of footwear manufacturers of Rostov on Don.

RE: Contract to supply the army with 40 000 pairs of soldiers' boots and the actions of the District Quartermaster of Rostov District, Colonel Sotsevich.

Request

Resulting from the Army's pressing need for footwear the *Ataman*'s Order of 11 February 1919, No.299 declared the mobilisation for defence of all footwear workshops and leather factories.

The Order gave notice of three months' incarceration for any owners of footwear workshops who evaded this mobilisation.

Such was the *Ataman*'s order. The Quartermaster's Department showed a different attitude to the Army's need for footwear...

When the footwear manufacturers approached the District Quartermaster of Rostov District, Colonel Sotsevich, he, Colonel Sotsevich, either failed outright to receive them or absolutely refused to see them ... The reason for this became clear when the undersigned manufacturers, having formed themselves into the group Armyboot, went to Novocherkassk to the Principal Head of Military Supplies, General Kirianov, with their proposal to supply 100 000 pairs of boots to the Army within half a year at 205 roubles per pair...

It appeared that Colonel Sotsevich had concluded an agreement with a group of leather manufacturers to supply the Army with boots at 235 roubles per pair, i.e., millions of roubles dearer... The group of leather manufacturers who took on this contract had never produced any footwear, had no workshops for making boots, and so of course was completely incapable of carrying out the contract it had entered into. In this affair the group of leather manufacturers could only act as an intermediary and, not having its own workshops, had to entrust the actual carrying out of the contract to other persons...

What is even more strange about this transfer of the contract to an intermediary (with a loss to the Treasury of millions of roubles) is that the footwear manufacturers on more than one occasion made direct proposals to Colonel Sotsevich to conclude a contract with him and Colonel Sotsevich knew full well that the leather manufacturers would not be able to carry out the obligations that they had taken on themselves.

Colonel Sotsevich, as a result of the agreement that he had signed, had on 7 March to call a meeting of the owners of footwear workshops, but not with the purpose of asking them to conclude a contract with the Treasury... but in order to persuade the footwear workshops to take on responsibility for fulfilling the Treasury contract on terms proposed by the leather manufacturers.

The Quartermaster's persuasion was backed by an unambiguous threat:

General mobilisation will be carried out in the near future. Woe to those shoemakers who are not agreeable to the terms laid down by the leather manufacturers. They shall all be sent to the Front. At the moment we are proposing that you should agree voluntarily to our terms, but we can also use force to compel you to work for the Army – everything for the Army.

Our group refused... Having studied the state of the leather market, our group came to the conclusion that there was a sufficient quantity of firm leather on the market, and we made a proposal to the Management of the Quartermaster's Department of the *Voisko* to contract for making 40 000 soldiers' boots within three months...

From then on our case was held up at every step in the Quartermaster's Department of the *Voisko*. The Quartermaster's second in command, Colonel Lesnikov, did not receive us; negotiations about the terms of the contract were carried on through one of the officials. When the terms were finally worked out and our group asked for the contract to be forwarded as soon as possible to the auditor, it turned out that there was only one typist working and there was no one to transcribe the contract. When we ourselves had transcribed it, we were informed on the following day that the contract had nevertheless not been sent to the auditor, since the Quartermaster's Department had had second thoughts and found it necessary to cross out a number of the conditions...

We had to raise a complaint with the Principal Head of Military Supplies. General Kirianov was most attentive to the proposal we made. He gave instructions that the contract should be sent to the auditor and despatched an urgent telegram to Rostov to exempt the craftsmen in our factories from call-up. Only on 26 March did an answer come by telephone from the Quartermaster's Department that the contract had been returned from the auditor. But when we went on the morning of 27 March to acquaint ourselves with the auditor's remarks we were informed by Colonel Lesnikov: 'In view of representations made by Colonel Sotsevich the Principal Head of Supplies has refused your contract.'

Since the Principal Head of Supplies was now a new appointment it was easy for him to be misled by Colonel Sotsevich's explanations which had no basis in reality.

In view of what we have demonstrated we have the honour respectfully to request Your Excellency:

1. To entrust to us the fulfilment of the contract for 40 000 pairs of soldiers' boots and this should be done as rapidly as possible since summer is almost upon us. Thanks to the quite unfitting attitude of the Quartermaster's Department to our proposal the Army has already been deprived of several thousand pairs of soldiers' boots in the course of last month.

2. To set up an enquiry into Colonel Sotsevich's behaviour on account of his markedly partial preference for the group of leather manufacturers to the detriment of the Treasury and the Army.

We entrust the transmission of this request to the Deputy [word indecipherable] Serovda Grigor'evich Chalkhutyan.

[4 signatures]

Document 3.19

It was common practice when the Whites took control of an area to invite local capitalists to pay a voluntary levy to the Army, in recognition of the fact that the Bolsheviks had been driven out of the district; the Bolsheviks were after all committed to nationalisation of the economy. Private businesses usually paid up, since they welcomed the free trade regime and recognised that the White administration needed a quick influx of cash before any more stable system of taxation could be introduced. This document relates to implementing such a levy in Rostov on Don. While voluntary, firms were expected to pay.

GARO, f. 865, op. 1, ed. khr. 225, l. 7 [extracts]

The Special Commission of the Society of Factory Owners of Rostov and Nakhichevan for Collection of the Self-imposed Tax

30 April 1919

Pursuant to the decree of the Commission which has been established . . . we inform you that for the above mentioned tax your overall assets have been determined at 2 500 000 roubles. Wherefore, not later than five days after receiving this notice, you must deposit 25 000 roubles, as 1 per cent of the sum assessed by the Commission, in the 'Special account for collection of the self-imposed tax', at one of the local banks [two banks named]. . . .

You must inform the Commission at the address Bolshaya sadovaya 35, premises of the Society of Factory Owners, that the money has been deposited.

Document 3.20

The co-operative movement in Russia was not confined to Siberia (see Chapter 1), but operated throughout the country. The co-operatives were not run by private capital, nor were they particularly fond of the White regime, since most were sympathetic towards the abandoned Directory and Constituent Assembly; avoiding politics, they busied themselves with public works. Not surprisingly, then, they were unwilling to pay a voluntary levy which celebrated private industry's support for Denikin.

GARO, f. 865, op. 1, ed. khr. 225, ll. 10–11 [extracts]

The Council of Co-operative Congresses of the South-East Region

To His Excellency, Governor-General of the towns of Rostov and Nakhichevan

At the suggestion of Your Excellency industrial and commercial circles of Rostov and Nakhichevan on Don have acknowledged the necessity of collecting by their efforts 25 000 000 roubles to be placed at the government's disposal to meet the expenses of the war, by means of a once-for-all tax on large properties. The commissions formed to effectuate this self-imposed tax, the Society of Merchants and suchlike committees, the Societies of Factory Owners and others, headed by a Supreme Commission . . . have decided to also include local co-operative organisations among those liable to pay the tax . . . Several of the latter have received invitations to pay within a five-day time limit advance sums amounting to 1 per cent of the assessed value of their capital. Furthermore these demands in most cases emanate from two Commissions, each of which makes an independent assessment of the assets . . .

The Council of Co-operative Congresses of the South-East Region considers it its duty to bring to Your Excellency's attention that not the entire population of Rostov and Nakhichevan is liable for tax, but only the commercial and industrial classes, as being those very people who hold large amounts of private capital, the value of which has been enormously increased under the abnormal conditions of economic life of the last four years, and this is particularly noticeable when contrasted with the general impoverishment of other classes of the population.

It is an undoubted and well recognised fact that co-operative enterprises . . . exist as common social organisations for mutual assistance, not seeking any accretion of capital. In their aims they are the complete opposite of private enterprises. The co-operative movement serves three-quarters of the whole population, and mainly its poorest and middle classes. The property and capital of the co-operatives belong to the people, just like the property of state, municipal and community enterprises, and, as is well known, they are treated, in view of this, quite differently from private capital. One must also allow for the fact that the capital of co-operative enterprises, consisting of very small individual shares, is extremely limited, so that co-operative organisations have to operate largely on borrowed funds.

From this point of principle the efforts of the Rostov and Nakhichevan industrial and commercial circles to transfer part of the self-imposed tax on to the shoulders of the co-operative movement cannot be deemed correct.

The co-operative movement . . . has always willingly contributed from its resources quite large sums for separate items of culture and education, and general communal needs. Thus, for example, Rostov and Nakhichevan Co-operatives have of late organised and maintained at their expense a feeding point in Rostov station for people suffering from typhus.

The Council of Co-operative Congresses of the South-East Region wishes to present to Your Excellency their request that you should make it clear to the Commissions for Collection of the Self-imposed Tax that local co-operative enterprises should not be subjected to contributions to the Self-imposed Tax, or at least be exempt until this question is resolved in the Don's Government and Legislative Bodies.

Chairman of the Council (signed) Nikitin
Aide to the Chairman (signed) Zdanovich
For the Secretary (signed) Shishenko

Document 3.21

As we saw during the campaign on the Volga and Siberia in 1918, accommodation was a constant problem as armies moved to and fro. Rather like the story of the British Consul in Chapter 1, Lidiya Tkhorzhevskaya eventually got what she wanted, but only after an enormous struggle.

GARO, f. 865, op. 1, ed. khr. 225, l. 27

To Chairman of Council of Executive Heads of the Almighty *Voisko* of the Don

Request from Lidiya Ivanovna Tkhorzhevskaya, wife of Lieutenant of the Pavlovsk Guards Regiment to free her apartment from requisition orders.

In 1918, using every last penny from my parents and husband and borrowing some more, I acquired a little house at 10a Konsistorskaya Street, consisting in all of two apartments. I had in mind to provide somewhere to live for myself, my parents and my wounded husband, and that, by letting one of the apartments, I could cover my expenditure on the house, besides having some resources to back up the insufficient salary which my husband receives as a volunteer. Although I have had higher education I myself cannot work on account of my illness, namely a weak heart.

Lieutenant-Colonel V.A. Dmitriev, working in Army Supplies, installed himself without any agreement in the lower apartment of the said house — which has running water, a bathroom, electric light and other amenities. Not willing either to quit the apartment, nor to pay for it, Dmitriev without my knowledge wangled through the Apartments Requisitioning Commission the right to have assigned to him the whole apartment that he had occupied, consisting of 5 rooms, instead of the 3 rooms for which he has authorisation. He ceased paying me anything for the apartment, but at the same time he kept permanent tenants there, paying full board.

In reply to my complaint that Dmitriev was occupying the whole apartment instead of 3 rooms the Apartments Requisitioning Commission decreed to requisition a room in my apartment, and then, after Dmitriev's former tenants moved out, installed there, by their allocation order of 22 February 1919, the family of 7 persons of Lieutenant-Colonel Popov, who is employed in the Office of the District *Ataman* of the Donets District, although Mr Popov himself was living in Sulin.* In reply to the order made by the C-in-C, General Denisov, that the money for the apartment should be paid over directly to him, Dmitriev yesterday, 30 January, paid into the Town Office 250 roubles for two months, but at the same time he presented the Office with a demand to pay him 639 roubles for those same two months, as though he were owed for coal and electricity. (I append a copy of Dmitriev's application to the Office.) One may easily realise that after an application like this the Office paid me nothing. From then on neither Dmitriev nor Popov have paid in any money whatsoever.

[* Popov's family have complete board with Dmitriev, including laundry.]

As a result I have been placed in an impossible situation: as the owner of the house, and the wife of an officer twice wounded (at Torgovaia and Armavir), and now serving at the front, I find myself compelled, not having received a single kopeck from October 1918, to keep in my house two families of officials serving in the rear, and to pay bills for water and electricity, meeting quite disproportionate expenses incurred by the tenants (no less than 12 persons in all).

At the same time the families of Dmitriev and Popov dominate the house and, feeling themselves in some measure protected, they permit themselves in their dealings with both me and my parents to use expressions, threats and actions which should not be permitted among people living together in any well ordered house. Furthermore, Dmitriev himself (by now a full Colonel) stirs up petty complaints with the police, and has recourse to the Citizens' Conciliation Commission, turning up in person at the hearings, and so on.

The aforementioned actions of Mr Dmitriev are completely destroying my interests and can hardly be regarded as normal, to say nothing of the moral side of all this. Mr Dmitriev, who has a permanent place of residence in Novocherkassk and his own house (at 67 Kolodeznaya Street), can hardly be included in the category of 'temporary resident' in the town, and therefore has scarcely got the right to requisition an apartment that he had been occupying for rent, even if it was without any proper conditions. Then, having got an order on the premises without my knowledge, or even informing me or the Town Office, Dmitriev should not have the use of 5 rooms instead of the 3 he had been allocated, and into the bargain kept tenants in them, using water, cleaning services, etc., for which I was paying. In any case Dmitriev cannot escape paying me for the apartment over the period from October 1918 to the present day, i.e., for 9 months he has deprived me of the means of existence. In the same way the family of Mr Popov, as someone who lives and works in Sulin, has not really the right to requisition premises in Novocherkassk.

In consideration of the above I earnestly beg Your Excellency, as the highest upholder of the laws which apply equally to all inhabitants of the Don, to understand my position and to make the following disposition:

1. to exempt from requisition my house at 10a Konsistorskaya Street,
2. in the shortest possible time to free the living space in this house, at present occupied by Messrs Dmitriev, Popov and their families, and
3. to compel Mr Dmitriev finally to pay me the money owing to me from

15 October 1918, at least to hand over the rent allowance money he has received from the Treasury (as a supplement to his pay), and to make good, without the necessity for a separate account, the expenses for heating and lighting, not having recourse to the Citizens' Conciliation Commission or the Arbitrators, since in both of these bodies I am of course powerless against Mr Dmitriev and his machinations.

(signed) wife of Guards lieutenant L. Tkhorzhevskaya 1 June 1919

[handwritten postscript] In view of this I beg earnestly to exempt the said apartment from requisition.

Lidiya Tkhorzhevskaya, 1 August 1919

[appended response]

To Administration of Council of Executive Heads of the Almighty *Voisko* of the Don

Returning the correspondence herewith, I wish to inform you that Colonel Dmitriev in compliance with the Order of the Director of Military and Naval Sections has from 21 August vacated the apartment of Mrs Tkhorzhevskaya which he had occupied.

24 August 1919

Head of Administration of the Principal Head of Military Supplies Major-General

Document 3.22

The abuse of drugs is something referred to by participants on both sides in the civil war. Here a young member of the Cheka becomes corrupted by the easy money to be made when arbitrary power has replaced the rule of law; the mother's plea that her son is simply a teenage rebel in need of help and re-education engages our sympathy.

RTsKhIDNI, *f.* 17, *op.* 5, *ed. khr.* 5, *ll.* 91–3 [extracts]

Moscow, 21 September 1919

Dear Paulina Markovna [presumably a Cheka or Party official]

Although I have not yet met you personally, my faith in you seems to justify my appealing to you with this letter.

A terrible thing has happened to my only son, Vsevolod, who has just passed his seventeenth birthday on 8 August this year... Vsevolod has flung himself into practical work with great enthusiasm – he played a most active part in various committees and organisations of his schoolmates in the High School... When Kolchak advanced he decided to go to the front...

About the end of July or beginning of August we learnt from a document which Vsevolod happened to leave on the table that he had been appointed commissar with the Secret Operations Section of the Moscow Cheka... At the end of August he would be away from home for three or four days at a time, and then completely disappeared for a week.

At our wits' end to guess what had happened to him, we find out by chance that our son has been arrested, and is being held by the Moscow Board of Criminal Investigation for conducting a search without proper authorisation. By further enquiries we managed to find out that he was with three or four young men (all immature youths aged from 16 to 20). They wanted to carry out a search in some sort of opium smoking den, evidently thinking they could get money thereby, by letting the criminals off a summons. They were arrested on the spot, and brought to the Commissariat, where they confessed everything, and also that this was not the first occasion... Under the martial law of our revolutionary time there may be a threat of capital punishment, execution by firing squad.

And all this has happened in the brief space of three or four months. Still just a child, he writes his mother a letter from prison, in which he asks her: 'Mum, when you bring me a pudding, write how many days it is for, otherwise I eat it all in one day.' It's all just an unceasing terrible nightmare.

Paulina Markovna, for your tender mother's heart I don't need to write any more. Our poor boy has been tormented these three or four months by his thoughts, and even more so by the part he has played, quite beyond his years, and consequently beyond his understanding. Even mature, comparatively stable men may have their heads turned, while he is only just seventeen – after all, he has only just come off the food ration for children. Let him be punished – that can only lead to his being reformed. He himself feels repentant, and says that he cannot remember how he spent the last two weeks when he was still at liberty, and that only now has he come to his senses – and he asks to be sent to the front to fight for the Reds, so that he can redeem his fault, but let the sentence be a just one.

Vsevolod cannot be held fully responsible, if we take his youth into consideration and his unstable psychology. Do whatever you think possible to save him. I truly believe that you will be saving not only my son but also someone who will be a useful person devoted to the good of society.

Yours sincerely

signature

4 The Labour Armies of the Soviet Republic

The Russian Civil War was to all intents and purposes over by the end of 1919. On the Eastern Front Kolchak's capital, Omsk, was taken by the Bolsheviks on 14 November 1919; as his forces retreated eastward the SRs and Mensheviks seized power in Irkutsk on 4 January 1920, and with the help of remnants of the Czechoslovak Legion arrested Kolchak as he tried to pass through the city. By the end of January the local Bolsheviks had persuaded the SRs and Mensheviks to co-operate with them and put Kolchak on trial, but on 6 February he was summarily executed to prevent him being rescued in what seemed, momentarily, to be a White counter-attack. The Red Army finally secured Irkutsk on 6 March 1920. On the Southern Front the Red Army had at last discovered cavalry (see Chapter 2), and the Red Cavalry, created over the summer and autumn of 1919, drove Denikin back to the Don and beyond, with Rostov being recovered in January 1920. Although Denikin was able to make a final stand on the Kuban river in March 1920, it was only a temporary reprieve; by April 1920 he and his forces had been evacuated to the Crimea.

In the spring of 1920 the Bolsheviks did not know that on 25 April 1920 the Poles would attack them and that this would enable the remnants of Denikin's army, led by General P.N. Wrangel, to break out of the Crimea and restart the Civil War. They were unaware that this final round of fighting would so exhaust the country that by the time peace had been restored the country would be faced by rebellions of workers, sailors and peasants in the spring of 1921, and that the certainties of communism would be surrendered to the pragmatism of Lenin's NEP. So, before the fighting resumed, the Bolsheviks could plan the reconstruction of the country according to their own communist agenda. The first months of 1920, therefore, are a fascinating period in the history of Soviet Russia when the Civil War seemed to be over, and the construction of socialism could begin.

During the war the economic life of the country had been organised according to the premises of what was known as 'war communism'. This involved the banning of private industry and trade, the requisitioning of grain and the partial elimination of money through rationing; dressed up with a lot of talk about the abolition of money, war communism was an *ad hoc* response to the vicissitudes of war; in the words of Alec Nove (*An Economic History of the USSR*, Allen Lane, 1969, p. 74), 'a siege economy

The Labour Armies of the Soviet Republic 125

with a communist ideology'. But peace meant the experiences of war communism could be rationalised and put on a firmer footing. That was the importance of the experiment with Labour Armies to which these documents relate. The idea of the Labour Army was the Bolshevik leadership's response to the question of how to make war communism a permanent feature of Soviet Russia's peaceful economic development. Many issues raised at this time, before the NEP was adopted, were issues which would resurface in Russian history when Stalin ended the NEP.

The Labour Army experiment began when the 3rd Army of the Eastern Front asked to be renamed the 1st Revolutionary Army of Labour. As these documents show, the proposal came from the Revolutionary Military Council of the 3rd Army itself, but fitted in with discussions already under way in Moscow. The initiative was supported by Lenin and Trotsky, and on 17–18 January 1920 the Politburo decided to prepare such armies for the Kuban and the Ukraine, and the towns of Kazan and Petrograd. The Labour Army would be formed by merging active service units with reserve forces. As the process got under way the 8th Army became the Caucasus Labour Army, the 7th Army the Petrograd Labour Army, and the 4th Turkestan Army the 2nd Revolutionary Labour Army and so on, with other Labour Armies or units being formed for the railways, the Donbas; in all, nine labour armies were formed between 1920 and 1922, as well as other labour units at various levels.

As the documents show, their organisation was complex. Each one was headed by a Revolutionary Council (*sovtrudarm*) which comprised representatives of the Defence Council, the All-Russian Council of National Economy, the Commissariats of Production, Land, Communications, Labour, Internal Affairs, the Supreme Council for Army Supply and the High Command. These *sovtrudarms* were responsible to the Revolutionary Military Council of the Republic, and for operational purposes the Council for Labour and Defence. Although *sovtrudarms* were nominally responsible to local economic organisations, in practice their activities were highly centralised. Eventually, particularly in those areas situated a long way from Moscow, like the Caucasus and the Ukraine, they had virtually dictatorial powers over the economy.

Although the documents reproduced here relate only to the period of peace – January, February and March 1920 – the Labour Armies continued to operate throughout the period of the Polish War and Wrangel's break-out from the Crimea, and once peace was restored the Bolshevik leadership found itself split between those, like Trotsky, who wanted to continue with the mobilisation and conscription of labour, and his opponents who did not. Thus began the trade union controversy in the Bolshevik

Party which so dominated the autumn of 1920 and dogged preparations for the 10th Party Congress; it was only resolved by the political crisis of March 1921 which forced the Bolshevik Government to adopt the NEP. On 30 March 1921 the Labour Armies were brought under the control of the Commissariat of Labour and, although they continued to exist until January 1922, it was clear that by this decision they had lost their former significance.

There are four themes to these documents. The first is the organisational confusion caused by trying to get military organisations to liaise with existing economic organisations, while retaining any meaningful role as military reserves. The second is the determination to portray what was taking place as a *socialist* experiment; there is an undeniable element of utopianism in the assertion (document 4.10) that this is 'the first step to a socialist economic organism', and many of the documents' authors were sure that revolutionary enthusiasm could compensate for poor organisation. The third theme, the obverse of the second, is the clear sub-text that much of the reality of the work of any Labour Army would be in requisitioning grain from the peasants.

The final theme is not so much a theme, since it only really emerges in one document, and then as an unspoken assumption. In document 4.20 Zinoviev links the question of Labour Armies to the need for continued preparedness for war and the imperative of world revolution. World revolution was at the very top of the Bolsheviks' agenda in the summer of 1920 when the war against Poland swung in their favour and the gates of Warsaw seemed to be open. But in the spring of 1920 the formation of Labour Armies meant that there was a ready Red Army reserve to be called on when world revolution demanded. Four months after Zinoviev's confident prediction that the revolution was about to cross the Caucasus and embrace the peoples of the East, the independent Soviet Republic of Gilan was established in northern Persia.

DOCUMENT 4.1

This document makes clear that, while the Third Army did indeed take its own initiative in establishing the First Labour Army, the Bolshevik Government was already thinking along these lines, with Trotsky being the most overtly enthusiastic. However, there was equally clearly a great deal of confusion at this meeting as to what precisely was being proposed: was the army to be put to large-scale unskilled work and, if so, to what work precisely, or was the key task to try to mobilise the skilled workers who had left the cities during the civil war and were now living in the countryside; if the latter were in deed the case, it was important to identify which skilled workers were already in the army. The most radical proposal was put forward by Sereda, who suggested that the army should be used to take over large empty tracts of land in Siberia and become actively involved in farming. The common context for all involved in the discussion was the alarming supply situation and the need to put those receiving the relatively generous Red Army ration to good purpose.

RGAE, f. 3429, op. 1, ed. khr. 1527, ll. 1–8

From the minutes of the meeting of the Commission on the Introduction of Labour Conscription and the Mobilisation of the Work Force

No.1, Moscow, 30 December 1919

Present: Comrades Trotsky, Krasin, Sereda, Tomsky, Shmidt O. Yu., Shmidt, Vladimirskii, Lomov, Milyutin, Popov.

Trotsky: Let me declare the session open. The chief question which our commission has to face is to work out a plan for introducing conscription of labour embodied in the swiftest possible measures for mobilising the work force, making use of the military chain of command and military units which are being released from active service.

Tomsky: Our first task must be to establish how many workers we have and then to organise the unskilled workers... We are short of qualified workers everywhere. So we must both train some workers and also take them out of the army.

Milyutin: Counting the work force is not the most essential thing. We have to think in the first place about food, about how to assure food supplies for 3 million workers... We must apply labour discipline and the military units which are being released to the most urgent work. It seems to me there are four types of work to be undertaken in the first instance: (1) stockpiling fuel, (2) loading and unloading, (3) cartage, (4) agricultural work. It is essential to make use of those who are receiving an army ration. We shall not have enough to provide rations for other groups called back into the work force.

Shmidt: The problem outlined by Milyutin is real, but he has forgotten the basic question – the revival of industry. To achieve this we need to count and assign to tasks the available qualified personnel and to mobilise unqualified labour in the country, the army and the towns. We must mobilise them for work in the four categories which comrade Milyutin has mentioned. And in this matter it is the military department which bears the main responsibility for bringing specialists out of the army and counting them.

Krasin: Apart from those works which comrade Milyutin has mentioned, building work is extremely important and also a number of other works: breaking stones, burning lime, construction and repair of communications. No particular qualifications are required for this kind of work. For bringing the mass of workers under labour discipline we shall have to take two elements from the military sphere: first their methods and tempo of work, and second their cadre of workers. At the same time we must remember... that what works in the military sphere will not always work in industry.

Trotsky:... To assign the work force we must first know its precise numbers. Pulling qualified workers out of the army as has been the practice hitherto is the crudest form of improvised calculation... Besides those tasks which Milyutin has named we must add some others as, for example, clearance of snowdrifts. Getting people for that work has really so far been done without any calculation or plan...

Sereda: We have two tasks before us: to apply labour discipline as a system for getting production back on its feet, and using labour discipline for specific urgent needs. This latter must have a definite place in agriculture. For agriculture we could set the task of using large army units on areas of land which have no small proprietors and follow a technique of transferring these units from one area to another. We could thus achieve the result of building up a reserve of grain which would make it possible for us to maintain a permanent work force. We must give the work force equipment which we can obtain from the army. The organisation of repair shops has already given good results. Our agriculture should be based on mobilisation of the work force...

Lomov: I think that in the present circumstances we can draw a fair number of workers from the country, but I would like to point out that it is not possible to get carried away with the idea of mobilising a large work force, since a work force demands a definite quantity of food, which is in short supply. We may thus be faced with the dilemma: should we not supply food to those parts of industry which are already working and demobilise the mass of soldiers in the army?

Shmidt: A purely military framework should remain for the organisation of our Food Army. For that purpose we need to have perhaps 100 000 men. As far as food goes we'll manage to procure it for the army. It is obvious that we'll manage the food problem if the army is occupied elsewhere...

Popov:... It is absolutely essential that we make a count of the work force and we must also interest ourselves in calculating the number of workers. Before the war there were 6 million workers; at the end of 1918 there were $2^1/_2$ million inside our republic; and now there are about $1^1/_2$ million. Many workers are living in the country and thus are doing work which has nothing to do with their specialisation. We need to make a precise count and work out how many specialists there are in the army. We could make such a count quickly through the organs of the military command. Then we need to carry out a count of the whole population, using special commissions, following which we can assign special ration cards for each person who has a specialisation. That will come up to about 5 million cards. We could carry out a census like that in about $2^1/_2$ months...

Milyutin: I have already indicated that I am prepared to see certain defined categories of workers withdrawn from the army... It all depends on the food supply. If we could feed an army ration to a million workers at this present moment that would be an excellent way to solve the problem; but without this supply of food these questions cannot be solved. But I should like to leave all that aside; as things are now it is impossible. For that reason I am devoting special attention to those areas where we can increase productivity, without supplying an army ration and where we can instil a new sense of life. These are definite tasks which we should concentrate on...

As for the references to taking two or three hundred workers out of the army, that is a comparatively minor factor, which is not significant on a state-wide scale and which has only a limited local significance. Therefore, if we can dispose of hundreds of thousands of men, it seems to me essential to put our first effort into those areas where we can increase productivity without supplying food.

Tomsky:... To try to ensure the food supply military food detachments have been created, which prey upon agriculture. Who do these food detachments consist of? They are made up of skilled workers... Apart from the food detachments, skilled workers are going into all sorts of work as commissars, into agricultural communes, working co-operatives, to craft industries, particularly after the decrees on craft industries which led to a massive flood of workers into home-based industry...

Trotsky: My thinking is along these lines: in the military sphere we are working on preparation for demobilisation. That is a complicated business. Demobilisation may come a year from now or two months from now. We are faced with the question: what are we going to do with the demobilised men? Are we just going to let them go wherever they fancy or are we going to apply them to other tasks facing the country? My theses are drawn up with this in mind. They will be abstractions if demobilisation comes about after two years and they will be timely if it comes in two months' time. Some of my theses will still be effective no matter when demobilisation comes, and I reserve the right to bring forward in general discussions those proposals which may have actual significance at the time.

I would like to draw your attention to the service record book for Red Army men, several million copies of which are being issued. We resolved to introduce it by the first of January; perhaps it may extend over into February. There is a heading in it about what trade the man had before entering the army and this should be significant.

Sereda: I want to say that I consider the most important main task to which we must direct our system of mobilisation and organisation in the army is the realm of agriculture. I am not talking only about state farms. I think that the area of land which cannot be sown because there is not sufficient labour amounts to no less than 3 million desyatins (3 million × 1.09 hectares). That land could feed 10 million people, i.e., the whole urban proletariat could be well fed with this resource. Now we are informed that in the Uralsk *Oblast* the land is not being worked by anyone. The state ought to take this land into its charge and work it by applying forced labour, which should be based on military units. Unless we do this our other tasks cannot be satisfactorily resolved. The other tasks, those of industry, are on a longer time scale.

We have to decide the food question this year, come what may. The other tasks take second place and we shall deal with them when we have resolved the question of agriculture. In military units we can find not only our work force, but also livestock and the means to make agricultural equipment. The People's Commissariat of Economic Affairs must help in this by supplying metal, coal and other essentials. The experience of last year has shown that the areas brought into cultivation can be extended. Thus in Tver Province the area under crops increased up to 4000 *desyatins*. Therefore I propose that we speedily organise military units as agricultural teams to be transferred into areas where they are needed to organise agricultural labour.

[The general discussion was closed and the members proceeded to practical proposals.]

DOCUMENT 4.2

The resolution adopted at the end of this session shows that very little of the confusion referred to above had been resolved, but the key decision was to involve the Army High Command overtly in economic affairs, a decision signalled by inviting General M.D. Bonch Bruevich to join the commission; Bonch Bruevich was the Bolsheviks' first Army Chief of Staff, who in the first half of 1918 headed the Supreme Military Council until replaced by I.I. Vatsetis when the Revolutionary Military Council of the Republic was created in August 1918.

RGVA, f. 3429, op. 1, ed. khr. 1527, ll. 14–15

Resolution of the meeting on the Introduction of General Labour Conscription and the Mobilisation of the Work Force

Moscow, 30 December 1919

Present: Comrades Trotsky, Milyutin, Krasin, Sereda, Vladimirskii, Tomskii, Shmidt O. Yu., Shmidt, Lomov, Popov.

1. The Commission proposes to the All-Russian Council of National Economy that it present, even in the roughest outline, a general plan for meeting the most urgent and essential economic demands of the country in the industrial sphere, defining needs for labour in the basic categories.
2. The Commission resolves to give this task also to the People's Commissariat of Transport Communications.
3. The People's Commissariat of Agriculture shall present a plan for the exploitation of areas of land which are empty, unsown and unexploited; shall state the work force necessary to carry this out; and present a plan of general measures for the improvement of agriculture, along with the corresponding demands to be made on the work force.
4. A general calculation should be made of the work force needed in all basic categories of labour, to work out ways and means for its rational exploitation, and where the labour should be recruited (from the army, the country, from Soviet institutions, etc.). An evaluation should also be made of ways of re-establishing a work force (professional

schools, training, etc.), with responsibility for this going to a commission drawn from the People's Commissariat of Labour, the Central Council of Trade Unions, and the Central Statistical Office. This commission should invite to its first sitting a representative of the All-Russian General Staff, as also a representative of the field staff with the purpose of introducing not more than one or two additional questions into the Red Army man's service record book, so that when an agreement is reached these extra questions may be immediately transmitted by telegraph to all the appropriate military commands [the administrative census directorates].

5. The People's Commissariat of Internal Affairs is to clarify whether the basic positions arrived at by our first commission have been accepted, in which it had worked out instructions for stockpiling fuel and clearing snow from rail and road. It should also present to the next session of the Commission on the Introduction of Labour Conscription the basic positions worked out by the first commission. If the All-Russian Chief of Staff has not participated in this commission its instructions should be sent to him for consideration.

[point 6 omitted]

7. The military department is to clarify:

(a) How many qualified workers could the army release now who would be capable of acting as the organiser of an enterprise.

(b) What military units could be released immediately for productive work of one sort or another; where can they be found; how long can they be released for.

(c) What additional means of transport and other resources can be spared by the military department for work in agriculture and elsewhere.

8. The commission resolves to co-opt Mikhail Dmitrievich Bonch-Bruevich as a permanent member...

Chairman of the Commission, L. Trotsky

DOCUMENT 4.3

This document simply records the initial proposal of the Third Army Command.

RGVA, f. 164, op. 1, ed. khr. 4, l. 7

From the minutes of sessions of the Revolutionary Military Council of the Third Army of the Eastern Front concerning the proposal by Comrade Gaevskii, as a member of the Revolutionary Military Council for the formation of a Labour Army

No.649, January 1920

Present: Army Commander Matiyasevich and members Gaevskii and Lokatskov.

Discussed:

3. Comrade Gaevskii's proposal for re-organising the Third Red Army as the First Revolutionary Labour Army of the Russian Soviet Federal Socialist Republic.

Resolved:

3. The Revolutionary Military Council agreed in principle with Comrade Gaevskii's proposal.

Commander of Third Army Comrade Matiyasevich

Members of Third Army Revolutionary Military Council Gaevskii and Lokatskov

DOCUMENT 4.4

This document shows that when the Third Army's proposal was first communicated to Trotsky there was no suggestion that the idea should become a model for the whole country, only that in the Urals there was a well established, but wrecked, industrial base and sufficient supplies of food to maintain the army while it set to work; it was 'a happy chance'. Just as for the Directory in 1918 (Chapter 1) there was a strong temptation to believe that if only the economic resources of Siberia could be harnessed, all other problems could be rapidly resolved.

It is also important to note the clear implication in the points made, particularly in points 4 and after, that the army would in practice be controlling all aspects of economic and social life; even though in point 9 this is expressly denied.

The suggestion that the Labour Army would call up and train workers not already in the Red Army shows that the originators of the Labour Army idea shared some of the confused ambitions of the Moscow politicians referred to in document 4.1.

RGVA, f. 7164, op. 1, ed. khr. 7

Telegram from the Revolutionary Military Council of the Third Army of Eastern Front to Chairmen of Council of Defence and Revolutionary Military Council of the Republic

No.02539, January 1920

The military successes of the last few days and the ever greater economic ruin confront Soviet power with two tasks: to finish off counter-revolution in our country, providing a strong Red Army screen on our Western frontier and protecting us from the puny jackals of Allied imperialism, and to use the armies then released to organise production, to restore transport and to introduce general conscription of labour.

The armies who are released with this objective in view should be directed especially into those industrial areas where they can easily be assured of food. For reasons which you know our Army is the first to be released from the hard task of war. It includes tens of thousands of completely healthy men, thousands of specialists, hundreds and thousands of communists and responsible political workers, firmly united by their life in action and skilled at directing the masses.

By a happy chance the Army is situated in the very sort of area from where alone it is possible to start to get the economy back on its feet. Chelyabinsk, Tobolsk and Ekaterinburg Provinces have huge food surpluses and have fuel; Siberia is close at hand with an abundance of food which there is no way of moving out at present. The Urals have metal and ore; there are inexhaustible possibilities in that area for developing industry. If we get firmly established here it is from this area alone that we can get our economy out of the dead end where it is at present.

In spite of the marvellous conditions here things have not been looking good up to now: the railways are barely working at all and the factories are dragging out a miserable existence, completely lacking fuel, food, specialists and workers.

Bearing all this in mind, and with the harsh facts before us, we must on no account leave a whole army inactive or fritter it away piecemeal.

With the object of speedily restoring and organising the economy over the whole of the Urals, in Chelyabinsk, Tobolsk and Ekaterinburg Provinces the Revolutionary Military Council of Third Army proposes:

1. To direct the Third Red Army's forces and all means at its disposal to getting transport working again and organising the economy in the said area.
2. To rename the Third Red Army of the Eastern Front as the First Revolutionary Labour Army of the Russian Soviet Federal Socialist Republic.
3. Those in charge of the First Labour Army to appoint a Revolutionary Labour Council, numbering three people headed by a Chairman, all three appointed and governed directly by the Defence Council.
4. The Revolutionary Labour Army is the highest body for overseeing and organising the military and economic organisations of Uralsk *Oblast* and is the body which is responsible for the administrative and political control of the area.
5. The main task of the First Revolutionary Labour Army is to restore the national economy in the shortest possible time by the widespread use of mass action and by introducing complete conscription of labour.
6. The military specialists of the Third Army are added to the strength of the Urals Regional Military Commissariat, which becomes the military labour body of the Third Army in charge of mobilisation and at the same time carries out the tasks of the All-Russian Chief of Staff.
7. All representatives and plenipotentiaries of Central institutions, sent to the Urals theatre of operations to bring into order some branch of the economy, come under the orders of the Revolutionary Labour Army and are taken on to its strength without the right to alter independently the tasks which Central Government has entrusted to them.
8. All technical and specialised commissions and representative groups sent by the central government to restore some branch of the economy will work in conjunction with the Revolutionary Labour Army.
9. All local district, province and other bodies remain as before. There is no change in relationships either among them or between them and central government.
10. The First Revolutionary Labour Army has a temporary status.
11. The Third Army releases immediately such military specialists as are required by the Fifth Army, still on active service.

The First Revolutionary Labour Army sets itself the following first tasks:

(a) To apply all the forces at our disposal and all the resources of our Army to stockpiling fuel and restoring the rail links Omsk–Ekaterinburg and Chelyabinsk–Omsk, to achieve which all technical manpower will be devoted to the railway; and we shall introduce partial labour mobilisation for stockpiling firewood and intensifying work in the coal mines.

(b) To build up a reserve Labour Army by a general call-up of one or two years of young men, who under the guidance of existing Party members and specialists will go to form stalwart communist labour cadres, able to work with enthusiasm and attract others to work. They should undergo military training, work under labour discipline and study.

(c) To proceed with the training of a more powerful political section for establishing the province's economy on a communist basis, to apply labour mobilisation on a wider scale, and to raise the general cultural level in the province. (We know by our experience with the army that this is easiest to achieve by mass action.)

(d) To put the railways under martial law like the army. For provisions to bring in the army supply system and norms for rations (come what may, we shall not be able to export all the grain from Siberia to central Russia).

We have the manpower, food products in plenty, a great amount of raw material and fuel. The whole region is well populated, so we are not short of human resources. We await your decision and instructions.

Commander of the Army Matiyasevich

Member of the Third Revolutionary Labour Army Gaevskii

DOCUMENT 4.5

Trotsky's response to the Third Army initiative, althouh supportive, was immediately to focus on the enormous powers that the Labour Army was to assume over local life.

RGVA, *f.* 164, *op.* 1, *ed. khr.* 7, *l.* 3

Telegram from Trotsky to RVS of Third Army of Eastern Front

No.162/a, 11 January 1920

In principle I consider your plan completely correct, capable of producing tremendous results, especially in transitional, recently conquered areas like the Urals and Siberia. It is essential:

1. to establish completely correct relations with the corresponding central economic (production) bodies concerned with the national economy at the centre;
2. to facilitate in every possible way the establishment of the right eco-

nomic bodies in the area of your activity, and as they are set up to harmonise all your work with theirs;

3. you must work out a plan for a production company, and when you have this confirmed tell the army about it, involve the local population, and set to work.

That is my view on this question. I shall consistently defend this view with the Government and I hope that you will have ample opportunities to bring benefit to the Soviet Republic in the purely economic sphere.

Trotsky

DOCUMENT 4.6

This extract from a session of the Council of People's Commissars shows that Lenin and Trotsky jointly sponsored the idea of supporting the Third Army's initiative, and both became involved in its rapid implementation.

GARF, f. R-130, op. 4, ed. khr. 1, l. 11

From minutes of meeting of the Council of People's Commissars concerning the formation of the First Revolutionary Labour Army

No.340, 13 January 1920

In the Chair: Lenin

Present: Lenin, Krasin, Avanesov, Dzerzhinsky, Ganetskii, Chutskaeev, Markov, Milyutin, Dimantshteyn, Vinokurov, Lomonosov, Vladimirskii, Bakinskii, Podbelskii, Sviderskii, Sheyman, Yakovlev, Yurev, Pokrovskii, Semashko, Kashchenko, Nogin, Sereda, Krestinskii, Chermomkevich, Anikst, Lomov, Nikolayev, Potyayev, Shmidt (People's Commissariat of Supply), Shmidt (People's Commissariat of Labour), Krasikov, Galkin, Syromolotov, Savrasov, Rykov, Sklyanskii, Rozengold, Trotsky, Kozlovskii, Karakhan, Lezhava, Voykov, Sheverdin.

Received:

8. Proposal of RVS of Third Army to convert the Red Army of the Eastern Front into the First Revolutionary Labour Army (Lenin, Trotsky).

Resolved:

To welcome the proposal of the RVS of the Third Army; to use its strength for economic tasks; to elect a commission for evolving proposals about the means and methods for usefully and properly exploiting the resources of the Third Army. Membership of the commission: Comrades Lenin, Rykov, Krasin, Trotsky, Tsyurupa and Tomskii. The commission should complete its work by Friday 16 January.

DOCUMENT 4.7

The document shows that in trying to meet Trotsky's request and clarify the relationship between local government, central government and the Labour Army, the initiators came up with an ever more complex system of interlocking responsibilities, which still gave ultimate responsibility to the military. This is reinforced by the decision to declare the whole population mobilised, and by the decision to address the question of the spring sowing. The Labour Army was seeking more and more power, and in this context it is particularly important to note the conviction of the initiators of the Labour Army that they saw themselves creating 'a socialist economic organism'.

RGVA, *f.* 164, *op.* 1, *ed. khr.* 7, *ll.* 4–5

Telegram from members of RVS of Third Army to Chairman RVS of the Republic Trotsky concerning addenda to their Regulations on the Labour Army

No.56/svs, Talitskoye, 13 January 1920

In reply to your telegram 162/a, on the first point we propose to add to the ten paragraphs of our proposition:

11. All-Russian Council of the National Economy, People's Commissariats of Supply, Labour and Agriculture each to appoint immediately at the disposal of the Revolutionary Labour Army one plenipotentiary representative for the province empowered to report directly to the Revolutionary Labour Army.

Note: All persons or special commissions sent to the province by the central organisations must place themselves at the disposal of the corresponding representatives for their department in the province.

12. All orders of central departments and people's commissars are transmitted to departments and commissariats through their representatives in the *oblast*.

13. Orders of a technical character are transmitted by the *oblast* representatives directly to local staff. Questions of an organisational character, and administrative measures or those with a wider scope must be submitted to examination by the Revolutionary Labour Army to be harmonised with the overall situation. Central government bodies may deal directly with the Revolutionary Labour Army and may directly assign it tasks.

14. The Revolutionary Labour Army retains the right to reject representatives proposed for the *oblast* and to make its own independent appointments, for the later approval of the corresponding central body.

15. For the time being there is no change in the arrangements for financing bodies in the province and no change for them in their way of presenting financial statements, estimates and proposals, but they are obliged at the same time to submit copies of same to the *oblast* representatives.

16. All orders and resolutions of the Revolutionary Labour Army which are not in contradiction with the basic laws of the Soviet Republic are effective both for local organisations in the *oblast* and also for *oblast* representatives.

17. The Revolutionary Labour Army is under the direct control of the Defence Council of the Republic. Any important measures involving basic principles are enacted by the Revolutionary Labour Army with the prior approval of the Defence Council and will have first been agreed with the appropriate commissariat.

To the four points of immediate tasks which were laid down at the end of our first telegram we consider it necessary to add:

5. We must proceed immediately to work out a plan for the speedy restoration of the whole economy of the *oblast* stage by stage, making use of the labour of broad sections of the local population and the reserve Labour Army. As the process becomes clearer, to take definite preparatory steps to prepare the mass of the population and to give effect to the measures adopted.

6. In the first place, to raise the problem of working out a plan of state help at the level of the *oblast* for the peasants in the coming spring and summer campaign, helping them with working the land, sowing, getting in the harvest, making rational use of all free lands and intensifying agricultural work.

7. To declare to the whole population of the *oblast* that they must consider themselves called up under general labour mobilisation, and, as real needs dictate, to introduce labour mobilisation by assigning labour

tasks to the people on the spot and by recruiting them into the Labour Army for transfer to other localities. To conduct a rigorous campaign to explain the measures envisaged to the population, in order to ensure the implementation of the system.

8. Drawing on our present strength of communists and sympathisers to set up immediately a series of specialist schools for teaching production tasks.

In drawing up the additional points here set out we have been guided by the following considerations:

1. The main task of the system we have expounded is to engage the whole population of the *oblast* in restoring the economy as quickly as possible.

2. In order to make rational use of the entire population we have to be aware of the whole economic system of the *oblast*, and accordingly we need to create in the *oblast* some kind of 'battery' for the economy, which must embrace all sides of the economy and bring together in itself the whole activity of all the institutions in the province.

3. It is clear that many central institutions sense intuitively the economic unity of the Uralsk *oblast* and it is for this reason that we encounter in the Urals a whole range of *oblast* plenipotentiary representatives and commissions. Their activity very often achieves remarkably little, as it is unco-ordinated and not united by any single authoritative will extending over the *oblast*. We must bring their activity together, which can be assured by the system of the Revolutionary Labour Army.

4. It has been established by military science and by the experience of many years of military practice that a commander who wishes to contribute maximum benefit to the main cause cannot exercise direct control over more than five military formations (and in general not more than ten units directly subordinated to him) [this passage in brackets crossed out in the original text]. In all countries the army has hitherto shown itself to be the most centralised and most technically perfect apparatus of the state. If we have reached this conclusion both scientifically and in practice in this domain of the state, this principle is fully applicable in every other branch of the state, and also to the complete state structure from top to bottom. It is impossible to manage dozens of provinces from one centre. The Revolutionary Labour Army is making a start to move along that path.

5. Our basic task is to convert the state into a single economic organism. The centre has already embarked on combining several of the people's commissariats. We are taking a further step forward by our system

of uniting all the commissariats and departments at the level of the *oblast* and putting them to serve the process of production.

Thus the Revolutionary Labour Army is a first step towards creating a socialist economic organism for the *oblast*. If further clarification is necessary, please have us called to the telegraph office.

Commander of Third Army Matiyasevich
Member of RVS of the Army Gaevskii

DOCUMENT 4.8

In this telegram from Trotsky to the Third Army leaders it is clear that the question of the relationship between the Labour Army and the local authorities is causing trouble in Moscow. Note also, however, Trotsky's interest in extending the experiment to other parts of the country.

RGVA, f. 164, op. 1, ed. khr. 7, l. 7

Telegram from Trotsky to RVS of Third Army of Eastern Front

No.220/13/1p, [13 January] 1920

First. Inform us: Have you discussed the plan to create the Revolutionary Labour Army in the Political Section, at meetings of responsible communists, in Party cells, or is your plan drawn up only by the RVS?

Second. Approximately how many skilled workers have you got in your Army?

Third. How many communists are there in your Army?

I think it necessary to warn you that a number of comrades have objections to the scope of your plan. Therefore the more down to earth, the more modest in form is your first *démarche*, the more advantageous in every respect. The first real practical success will give grounds for extending the experiment. And on the other hand the first serious conflict with authoritative local institutions will make it exceptionally difficult for the experiment. Do everything you can to catch the interest and draw to your side the most responsible *oblast* and local activists and local institutions.

Chairman RVS Trotsky

DOCUMENT 4.9

Once again, although this response to Trotsky's concerns is supposed to place a limit on the pretensions of the Labour Army, wide powers are retained. Note also the lack of information about specialists, and the small number of Party activists compared to the size of the army.

RGVA, f. 164, op. 1, ed. khr. 7, l. 16

Message from member of RVS of Third Army Gaevskii to Chairman of RVS of Republic

No.220/13/1P, Talitsa, 13 January 1920

On your first point: the plan has been discussed only in RVS of Third Army. Political Section of Third Army is in Ekaterinburg, which restricts close contact with responsible activists. In general I did not intend to give wide publicity to the plan until I had your approval in principle.

On the second point: we are still engaged in counting the number of specialists in accordance with the instruction of the Revolutionary Council, and still have not got results in, so I cannot give you exact figures. There are 170 000 men on the strength of the Army today. If we bear in mind that for the last half year the Army has recruited only in the Urals, there should be a very high proportion of specialists.

On the third point: because of units leaving every day I find it difficult to give you an exact number of communists. Up to 1 November, before we had the Week of the Party, the Army contained 7666 Communists and 8868 sympathisers. A few days ago the Political Section presented me with a list of responsible Party activists and commissars just in the command echelons of the Army, and there are 300 of them.

I agree with your warnings and therefore for the first stage we can limit the tasks of the Revolutionary Labour Army and set it the following aims: first, to restore rail traffic in the *oblast*; second, to stockpile firewood; third, the right to introduce general labour mobilisation; fourth, to place the Urals Regional Committee under its control; fifth, to give every possible assistance to the whole economy of the Uralsk *Oblast*; and sixth, to appoint to the Revolutionary Labour Army plenipotentiaries from the All-Russian Council of the National Economy, and the People's Commissariats of Labour and Transport Communications.

It is essential to place a strong and authoritative Party comrade at the head of the Revolutionary Labour Army. Today I am summoning Comrade Andronikov to the telegraph office in Ekaterinburg, one of the soundest officials in the Urals. I shall put the whole picture before him and try to secure his agreement. I shall ask him to bring the matter up in the People's Commissariat of the Province to obtain support for the project. I have just asked to get in telegraphic communication with the head of the Political Section of the Third Army and will try the same with him. If there is still time I may go to Ekaterinburg myself. I await your further instructions.

Member of RVS of Third Army Gaevskii

DOCUMENT 4.10

This document updates some of the figures in document 4.9, and shows how the initiators of the Labour Army plan were keen to support Trotsky in any debate about the future of the experiment, unaware of Lenin's support for the idea.

RGVA, f. 164, op. 1, ed. khr. 7, l. 8

Message from member of RVS of Third Army Gaevskii to Chairman of Revolutionary Military Council of Republic Trotsky

No.64/sve, 14 January 1920

Yesterday I spoke with Andronikov over the direct telegraph line. He said: 'In general and taken as a whole the project is quite realistic. At present the main trouble is the difficulty of delivering fuel to the factories. This in turn can be explained by the lack of fodder, mainly oats, and by traffic difficulties on the railway. If we can get your plan operating now we can avoid the factories coming to a stop in the summer. Otherwise we are going to have a whole series of factories rising against us, including some of the big ones.'

Today he will call together the responsible Party workers of the Urals for an exhaustive discussion and will let me have the results in the evening. He personally is all for the plan.

I got fresh information today: the Army as a whole has now up to 7000 communists, up to 2000 sympathisers, and up to 400 responsible Party workers.

Let me know whether the question has been discussed by the government and what are the results. If it has not been discussed then when will it be? So that we in the Urals can give you support at the right time.

Member of RVS of Third Army, Gaevskii

DOCUMENT 4.11

The government's formal decision to support the idea of the Labour Army is accompanied by the hope that its organisation should not be too cumbersome, a pious hope given the complexities of all the proposals stemming from the Third Army. (See documents 4.4 and 4.7.)

RGVA, *f.* 164, *op.* 1, *ed. khr.* 7, *l.* 9

Telegram from Trotsky to RVS of Third Army

No.264, 15 January 1920

The statute on the First Revolutionary Labour Army has been confirmed today. You will receive it in a few hours. Plenipotentiary representatives of the economic departments are brought in as members of the RVS of the Labour Army. That will give a Board of 8 members, i.e., 8 added to existing RVS, but as most of the members will be going out into the various localities to supervise the works on the spot, it must be hoped that the council will not be too cumbersome. It is essential at all costs to overcome departmental rivalries or lack of mutual trust. You must smooth out any difference of views by reaching an agreement between you, doing everything you can to avoid complaints to the centre. It is essential to give your work the character of a contribution to the cause of communism rather than just carrying out some routine burden of service. That is the only way success will be assured.

To achieve this you will have to bring in all the local communist manpower and inspire people to join the cause on the broadest possible front. You must do away with the anonymity of military units, and, quite to the contrary, in daily reports on your work each unit must be named and its merits or lapses noted. I recommend that attached to the Labour Councils of the Army you should create Technical Councils for the detailed working out of a specific plan of work. It will be fatal for your idea if military units or peasants you have enrolled are moved about in masses without any sensible aim and do not find the quarters, food or equipment they need. You must foresee all their needs and work out everything in advance.

I must repeat once more: your experiment has tremendous significance. If it were to come to grief because of some squabble or short-sightedness it would be a very severe blow for the Soviet Republic.

Chairman of RVS Trotsky

DOCUMENT 4.12

Not only did the creation of the Labour Army cause problems with local administrative authorities but, as this telegram shows, it also had an impact on relations with other army units, in this case the Fifth Army.

RGVA, f. 164, op. 1, ed. khr. 7, l. 11

Telegram from Trotsky to Field Staff of RVS of the Republic, Chief of All-Russian General Staff and RVS of Third Army

No.311, 15 January 1920

Having regard to Resolution of Defence Council about converting Third Army into Revolutionary Labour Army, all former orders and demarcations under which separate Army institutions were transmitted to various institutions in the field and at the front are suspended. Henceforth officials and separate institutions may be transferred from Third Army to Fifth only in so far as such transfer does not destroy the structure of the Third Army. Any disagreement that may occur on this question to be referred to RVS of Republic for consideration.

Chairman of RVS Trotsky

DOCUMENT 4.13

This document reminds us that, whatever the grand notions about 'building a socialist economic organism', one of the basic tasks of the Labour Army was to requisition.

RGVA, f. 164, op. 1, ed. khr. 4, l. 20

From record of session of RVS of Third Army concerning conversion of Third Army into Labour Army

No.69, 15 January 1920

Present: Army Commander Matiyasevich, Members of Third Army RVS Lokatskov and Gaevskii.

Discussed:

5. Telegram from Chairman of RVS of Republic Trotsky concerning confirmation of project of Labour Army

Resolved:

5. To await the arrival of the project itself from the centre.

Business of Secretariat of RVS

Discussed:

7. Telegram of Chief of Staff of 13 January No.8–18/211 to put at disposal of Ekaterinburg Province Food Supply Committee 2 squadrons of Tenth Cavalry Division and 100 men from Reserve Regiment of Army for collecting surplus produce from the population.

Resolved:

7. Not to send squadron of Tenth Cavalry Division but to send instead a squadron from the Inspectorate of the Anti-profiteer Detachments. Commander of Reserve Regiment to send 100 men. To indicate to Province Food Supply Committee that internal security troops can successfully be employed for the purpose they have indicated. Army Chief of Staff to carry out this order.

Commander of Army Matiyasevich
Members of RVS Lokatskov, Gaevskii

DOCUMENT 4.14

This official communication announcing the creation of the Labour Army is noteworthy on a number of counts. First, it stresses that the army 'remains under arms', ready to resume fighting should that be necessary. Second, it makes clear that the various Soviet economic institutions were there simply to provide guidance to the army, not direct its work. Third, the 'main task' of the army was to 'collect systematically all surpluses', in other words to requisition; this would almost certainly vitiate the hope that the army would establish 'harmonious relationships of comradeship and co-operation with all the toiling classes'. Fourth, the repetition of calls for strict accounting and listing of material, when combined with the appeals to end the day singing socialist hymns, gives some idea of how war communism was supposed to work as an economic system.

RGVA, f. 164, op. 1, ed. khr. 7, ll. 17–19

Order-memorandum to Third Army concerning First Revolutionary Labour Army

No.313, 15 January 1920

1. The Third Army has fulfilled its military task, but the enemy is not yet cleared from all fronts. The rapacious imperialists are threatening Siberia from the Far East; the hirelings of the Entente threaten Soviet Russia from the west; there are still White Guard gangs in Archangel; the Caucasus is still to be freed. Therefore the Third Revolutionary Army remains under arms, keeping its fighting spirit and its internal cohesion as an organisation, in case the Socialist Fatherland summons it to new military tasks.

2. But with its sense of duty and high level of social consciousness the Revolutionary Army does not want to let the time slip idly by during the weeks and months of breathing space which it has been granted. It will adapt its strength and the means at its disposal to help the economic recovery of the country, while remaining a military force to be feared by the enemies of the working class. Without losing its fighting capacity it is being converted into a **Revolutionary Labour Army**.

3. The Revolutionary Military Council of the Third Army becomes part of the Council of the **Labour Army**. Alongside the members of the RVS this will contain representatives of the main economic institutions of the Soviet Republic; they will provide the necessary guidance in various spheres of economic activity.

4. Food must be supplied to the hungry workers in Petrograd, Moscow, Ivanovo-Voznesensk, the Urals and all other industrial centres and areas. The main task of the **First Revolutionary Labour Army** is to collect systematically all surpluses of grain, meat, fats, and forage in the areas where such are to be found; to draw up an exact list of the food supplies which have been collected; to bring them together energetically and speedily for factories and railway stations; and to load them into goods wagons.

5. Industry needs fuel. A most important task of the **Revolutionary Labour Army** is to fell and saw up some of our forests, delivering the wood to factories and railway stations.

6. For lumbering and other works we need living quarters. The **Revolutionary Labour Army** will build communal living spaces where they are needed, thus assuring somewhere to live and a degree of comfort for themselves and for those workers who will later come to relieve them.

7. Spring is coming – time for work in the fields. Our run-down factories are still producing very few new agricultural implements, but against this the peasants hold quite a lot of old instruments needing to be repaired. The **Revolutionary Labour Army** offers its workshops, blacksmiths, metal workers and carpenters for repairing agricultural implements and machines. When work in the fields starts our Red Army sharpshooters and cavalrymen will show that they know how to plough and harrow our Soviet land.

8. Ural and Siberian proletarians and peasants live and work alongside the soldier-workers of the Third Army. The units of the Labour Army, its men, its commanders and commissars are in duty bound to establish friendly and harmonious relationships of comradeship and co-operation with all the toiling classes.

9. All members of the Army, from the lowest to the highest, must show brotherly care and consideration to unions, local soviets and executive committees, remembering that these are organisations of working people. Work on the spot must always be carried out in agreement with them, explaining the task which the Soviet Government has set for the Labour Army and calling on them to give active support to our great enterprise.

10. As its first priority the Red Army must take steps to ensure that in the area of its operations not a single factory suffers a lack of food. If an honest Red Army man is striving to rival the factory worker at his labour, at the same time, by making use of his own supply chain he must bring the worker's food supply up to match his own.

11. Inexhaustible energy at work, as on active service, as in battle.

12. All officials, technicians, specialists and craftsmen must be registered in lists and put in the right place, so that the whole Army machine starts up in its new career without delay and works in all matters swiftly and smoothly without hitches or over-heating.

13. An exact account must be kept of the resources expended and there must be a conscientious careful control of equipment and materials expended. Not a single pound of Soviet grain, not one log of the people's firewood must be omitted from our lists and wasted; everything must go into the foundations for our Socialist construction.

14. Commanders and commissars are responsible for their units at work as much as in battle. Discipline must not be relaxed in any way.

Communist cells must serve as models of perseverance and steady effort at work.
15. Communications in the Army must be strictly maintained, vigilance must not falter, enthusiasm must not slacken.
16. Commanders and commissars are to forward to their superiors precise operational labour reports, stating the quantity of grain collected, loaded and transported, the number of cubic metres of firewood felled and cut up, and all other work. These operational reports are to be published in the daily newspaper of the First Labour Army, naming exactly each separate labour unit, so that the most diligent and zealous regiments shall be accorded the respect which they have earned, while other more sloppy or lazy units may strive to catch up with the best ones.
17. The Political Section to carry out its work with redoubled energy, making every soldier a good workman, and preserving the martial virtues in every worker.
18. Tens of thousands and hundreds of thousands of printed appeals and speeches must explain to even the most backward Red Army men, and to all workers and peasants in the area, the sense of the great enterprise on which the Third Army is embarking.
19. The Army's Revolutionary Tribunal must punish scrimshankers, parasites, saboteurs or those who steal what belongs to the people.
20. Keep a close check on personnel so that there is no skiving off.
21. He who deserts from work is as contemptible and shameful as a deserter in battle. They both deserve stern punishment.
22. You soldiers with the highest social conscience, you, the leading workers and revolutionary peasant soldiers, we call on you to set an ideal for the others, inspiring them to march with us by your example and your boundless generosity of spirit.
23. Cut down manpower in the rear to the smallest possible numbers; anyone who can be spared must go into action on the work front.
24. When possible you should begin and end your work to the strains of socialist hymns and songs, for your work is no slavish toil, but a high form of service to our Socialist Fatherland.
25. Soldier of the Third Army, now of the First Labour Army, what you are starting on is a mighty cause! The whole of Russia will rise to respond to you. Soviet radio-telegraphy has already spread the tidings to the whole world that the Third Army, of its own free will has converted itself into the First Labour Army.

Soldier-workers, do not let down the good name of our Red Banner!

Chairman of the Revolutionary Military Council, Trotsky

DOCUMENT 4.15

When the commanders of the Third Army endorsed the official communication establishing the Third Labour Army, they were even keener than Trotsky to stress the element of socialist construction. As they made clear, their plan for economic recovery was to be socialist, not capitalist: 'We shall not restore the national economy by capitalist means', they proclaimed, and there is a utopian optimism in their statement that the country could quickly recover from destruction and then 'move over to the building of socialism'. Note also the stress in this document on the riches of Siberia and the need to transport it to the 'hungry provinces'.

RGVA, *f.* 164, *op.* 1, *ed. khr.* 7, *l.* 21

Order to troops of Third Army of Eastern Front

No.30, Talitsa, 18 January 1920

[extract]

I

[Trotsky's Order-memorandum No.313 of 15 January 1920 is reproduced, see document 4.14.]

II

The above Order-memorandum of Comrade Trotsky will serve as a general over-riding instruction. Every commissar, every commander, every Red soldier must learn this Instruction as thoroughly as he knows the Service Regulations. Every communist must have it on his person and keep it along with his Party card.

Herewith are laid out a series of practical Rules which every member of the First Labour Army must know and which he must follow honestly as a matter of conscience.

III

Comrade Red Army men, Commanders and Commissars!

The Civil War is drawing to its close. Home bred counter-revolution is laid low. Kolchak has been overthrown and arrested, General Denikin has been replaced and has fled. The Red Army is going from victory to victory and we are close to the time when the victorious arms of our Red heroes will show the whole imperialist world that we are unconquerable and will force them to conclude a long-overdue peace with us.

For two years the imperialist beasts have been trying to throttle the Soviet Republic and, as you can see, we are emerging as the victors from that unequal conflict. But we have paid a high price for the unequal struggle, being compelled to send our best forces of workers and peasants to the front, halting production in our factories and mills so as to throw all our workers into the front line for the defence of our proletarian Fatherland. Due to this our national economy and transport, already destroyed by the imperialist war and then by Kerensky's ruinous policy, has now been reduced to its most parlous condition.

The victories of the Red Armies on all fronts have now brought within our grasp areas rich in grain, meat, fats and other foodstuffs. There are millions of poods there, but because the transport system is not working we cannot bring this grain to the hungry provinces. We have no locomotives, not enough rolling stock, no fuel. During six years of war everything has been destroyed and little has been produced.

To restore our economy we must take heroic measures. All forces which are released from the front must be directed to restoring the economy, and first of all it is essential to provide fuel, to restore traffic on the railways and then give the workers bread, so that the workers who have enough to eat can get the factories and mills started.

Just as the war was won with the help of all honest working people, by the joint efforts of workers and peasants, so now we shall conquer destruction in our economy by the combined enthusiasm of all honest working people. We shall not restore the national economy by capitalist means. We can see that by the experience of the capitalist countries of Europe and America. Although the war caused less damage there, and although technology is much more advanced there, none the less we can see that there and everywhere else the economy is getting steadily worse and worse, bringing with it mass unemployment, cold and hunger.

From the capitalist way of running the economy we have got to move to socialism. We have already made a start on that process; now we have to take yet another step forward – we must move from uncontrolled ways of taking on labour to using our free armies to involve the mass of the population in the process of production. We shall be able to deal swiftly with the destruction and move over to the building of socialism only by mass action and introducing general mobilisation of labour. In our work the Soviet Government calls on you before all else to this task, brave soldiers of the Third Red Army.

We call on you as being the first large body of men to be released from the battlefield.

You have crushed Kolchak, you have thrown him back headlong out of the Urals. You have eliminated the remnants of his gangs in the lowlands of Western Siberia and it is to you first of all that the Soviet Government entrusts the Red Banner of Labour. You are called on to help to restore the economy in that very same area where every inch of ground has been watered with the hot, honest worker-peasant blood of Third Army soldiers – you must not betray their trust.

The Soviet Government must warn you as it places your hands on the plough instead of the sword: the enemy is still not utterly smashed, in his death throes he may still try to stab you in the back. Therefore as you take up the plough you must not let go of the rifle and at any moment at the first summons of your worker-peasant Fatherland you must be ready for battle to fell the foul, presumptuous enemy and wipe him off the face of the earth.

Our worker-peasant government hopes to find in you not only an actively working labour force, but also a means, a valuable centre round which can be grouped all the forces of the local population.

In your work on the labour front you must apply all the long months' experience of your hard time in battle. In this sphere also you must show the same firmness, courage, discipline and will to conquer destruction as you showed of these qualities in your battle with Kolchak's gangs.

Red eagles of the Third Army! You are the first men to have the chance of finding new ways to approach the restoration of the socialist economy. The workers and peasants of the whole world are looking to you. Do not let down our Red armed forces.

Henceforth the Third Red Army ceases to exist under that name and is renamed as the First Revolutionary Labour Army.

Long live the First Revolutionary Labour Army!

Long live the All-World Labour Army!

The Revolutionary Military Council of the Army:
Army Commander Matiyasevich
Members of The Revolutionary Military Council Lokatskov, Gaevskii
Head of Staff of the General Staff Sergeev

DOCUMENT 4.16

Like document 4.12, this telegram hints at tension between the Labour Army and other military units, and the wish of some commanders to move key personnel to active service units in other armies. It is also interesting to note that Politburo approval for the Labour Army came after government approval.

RGVA, f. 164, op. 1, ed. khr. 7, l. 28

Telegram from Trotsky to Council Member of The First Revolutionary Labour Army

No.366, 19 January 1920

First. Detaching units and institutions from personnel of Third Army to be carried out only on a limited scale which does not affect the Army's working capacity.

Second. Military institutions and units of the District Military Council for labour purposes will be subordinate to Council of Labour Army.

Third. Formation of Labour Army has been approved by Politburo of Central Committee.

Chairman of Revolutionary Military Council Trotsky

DOCUMENT 4.17

The more significant of the two government decisions given here is that to establish a Ukrainian Labour Army, thus extending what had begun as a particular experiment to a general policy. That Stalin should have been appointed to head such a body, in the border region with soon-to-be-hostile Poland, shows what a high profile was being given to the Labour Army concept soon after its establishment. Given Trotsky's enthusiasm for the idea, it was logical that he should be put in charge of the First Labour Army.

GARF, f. R-130, op. 4, ed. khr. 1, ll. 19-20

From Minutes of meeting of the Council of People's Commissars on forming Councils of Labour Armies

No.342, 20 January 1920

[*Heard*]:

4. On co-opting to Revolutionary Council of Labour Army the representative of the People' Commissariat of Internal Affairs (Vladimirskii).

[*Resolved*]:

4. To co-opt to Revolutionary Council of Labour Army the representative of the People' Commissariat of Internal Affairs, granting him the powers laid down in sections 9 and 12 of the Decree of the Defence Council of 15 January 1920 when deciding questions about organising cartage by requisitioning carts and mobilising the work force for mass construction work.

[*Heard*]:

7. Regulations on the Ukrainian Council of Labour Army (Stalin).

[*Resolved*]:

To confirm Regulations on the Ukrainian Council of Labour Army with the following amendments:

para.1 Omit First part up to words 'In the area of the South-Western Front'.

para.7 Edit as follows: 'All local institutions of departments listed in the said area (i.e., Council of the National Economy, Food Commissions, Land Departments, local sections, the People's Commissariat of Labour, People's Commissariat of Transport Communications) keep their linkage and subordination to their central institutions as laid down by the general laws of both Soviet Republics and are subject to particular orders and instructions of the Ukrainian Labour Army through its corresponding members.'

[*Heard*]:

8. Concerning the appointment of Comrade Trotsky, Chairman of RVS of the Soviet Republic as Chairman of Council of First Labour Army.

[*Resolved*]:

8. To confirm the appointment of Chairman of RVS of the Soviet Republic Comrade Trotsky as Chairman of Council of First Labour Army. To be published.

[*Heard*]:

9. Appointment of Comrade Stalin as Chairman of Ukrainian Council of Labour Army.

[*Resolved*]:

9. To appoint Comrade Stalin, member of RVS of Southern Front, as Chairman of Ukrainian Council of Labour Army (*Ukrsovtrudarm*). To be published.

DOCUMENT 4.18

From this telegram of Trotsky's it is clear that some of the organisational problems inherent in the Labour Army project were immediately apparent.

RGVA, *f.* 164, *op.* 1, *ed. khr.* 7, *l.* 36

Telegram from Trotsky to RVS of Council of First Revolutionary Labour Army

No.466, 23 January 1920

1. In military matters Labour Army is subject to RVS of Republic with the rights of a special army and reports directly to the Staff of the RVS of the Republic.
2. Operational labour reports are to be made to the Field Staff who will immediately pass them to me and the Defence Council.
3. Organisational changes in the institutions of the army in so far as they are essential in the course of its work are to be made on a temporary basis and reported to the Field Staff.
4. First priority: constantly to bear in mind that every step of practical work is more important than any organisational rearrangement or renaming.
5. I hope to visit you in February. At that time all essential questions will be resolved on the spot.

Chairman RVS Trotsky

DOCUMENT 4.19

As this telegram from the Red Army Commander in Chief S.S. Kamenev makes clear, there was immediate confusion concerning the question of whether the Labour Army remained a real military unit. For Kamenev the Labour Army was a reserve army to be called on at any time.

RGVA, f. 33987, op. 2, ed. khr. 89, l. 104

> Memorandum from C-in-C S.S. Kamenev to Chairman Republic RVS Trotsky on necessity for retaining military management of First Revolutionary Labour Army

No.376/operational, Moscow, 23 January 1920

On 20 January this year it was reported by the Revolutionary Council of First Labour Army that in view of the appointment of Commander of Third Army Matiyasevich as Army Commander, the Revolutionary Council of Fifth Army consider it unnecessary to appoint a Commander of Labour Army.

I assume that renaming an active service Army as a Labour Army does not entail the latter losing its designation as a military unit and that it is simply a reserve which must keep its essential fighting capacity and should be prepared to be transferred as soon as the tactical situation demands to one or other of the nearest fronts.

In view of this the Labour Army, while carrying out its new tasks, must keep the units it contains in a proper state of military readiness, i.e., must keep up their military preparation and training.

It follows that the Labour Army must have its command structure like the active service army with an Army Commander in charge, and this appointment I consider absolutely essential as demanded by the functions of the army and even more so by the circumstances in which we find ourselves.

C-in-C S.S. Kamenev
Member of RVS of the Republic Kurskii
Chief of Staff, RVS of the Republic Lebedev

DOCUMENT 4.20

In many ways this is the most interesting document in this chapter, for in his speech to army communists Zinoviev makes an overt link between the need to create Labour Armies and continue to mobilise the Russian population with the prospects for world revolution. In particular he links the continued fighting in the Caucasus mountains to the expectation of spreading communism to the peoples of the East, targeting the British Empire in particular. He also singles out Bessarabia; revolution there could easily spread westwards to Romania and beyond. In May 1920 the Soviet Republic of Gilan was established in Persia, and during the summer of 1920 the Red Army raced towards Warsaw in the confident expectation that revolution could be spread to Poland and thus to the West.

RGVA, f. 190, op. 2, ed. khr. 284, ll. 31–3

Speech by Comrade Zinoviev to Army Conference of Communists
26 January 1920

[extract]

[applause] Comrades, after our troubles in the autumn at our first meeting with representatives of communist soldiers from the front line I wish first of all to use this occasion to bring you warmest greetings from the Petrograd Soviet and all Petrograd workers for the excellent work done by our army, mainly with your help, in those days which were so difficult for Petrograd. Only after paying this tribute do I come to the main theme of my report [applause].

Comrades, the question of Labour Armies has only arisen quite recently. A couple of months ago we might say that no one had even dreamt of Labour Armies, whereas that question has now become a completely practical reality, and the Soviet Government has already decided to organise three Labour Armies. I will even detail which armies they are to be, but we must get a clear understanding what these Labour Armies will be, what part they will have to play – and especially why we have to go over now to a system of Labour Armies.

Everyone knows that the situation at the front could not be better. No one can doubt that we are close to seeing an end to the war, at least on most of the fronts which have given us so much trouble up to now. But at the same time everyone knows that in the near future we are carrying out one further mobilisation of the class of 1921, which had been deferred for a certain time. A peasant or a worker is perfectly entitled to ask: if you have trounced Kolchak and Denikin and defeated Yudenich why do we now need a fresh mobilisation? Why on the one hand are we preparing to transfer the army to peacetime duties, while at the same time we are carrying out another mobilisation? And after two years of war it would be perfectly natural if comrades raised the point:

perhaps we could simply disband the army, just keeping a small force on the frontiers.

These questions are being raised and front-line communist soldiers must above all come to a clear understanding on these questions, so that, as they lie in the firing line, in the trenches, in their barracks or in the rear, they can give clear answers to every rank and file peasant. Mobilisation is going ahead because, though our battle is three-quarters or maybe even nine-tenths won, we still have some fighting to deal with. We must finish off Denikin no matter what it costs. Up to date communiqués announce that he has still got about 40 000 troops and he is about to cross into Romania. But Denikin is still putting up a certain resistance on the Don. Besides that we have to liberate the Caucasus, and we must free Bessarabia in the near future. We have got to free the Caucasus above all because our oil is there, without which Russia's industry cannot be firmly re-established. If we don't get Baku with its huge reserves of oil we cannot assure proper supplies for our industry in Moscow, Petrograd or Ivanovo-Voznesensk.

Apart from that it is essential to free the Caucasus because millions of our brother peasants and workers are suffering there, not freed even now. [The Menshevik leaders of Georgia, I.G.] Tsereteli and [N.S.] Chkheidze are in power there. Having held power for two years they have contrived to keep the peasants from even having the slightest chance of getting land. The peasants there have received no land; it has remained in the hands of the former owners. Tsereteli and Chkheidze, as you may have read recently, have been in Paris asking the English and French gentlemen capitalists for help against us, which help they have been promised, as has Denikin. 'Just as we have helped Denikin, so we will help you too.' That must be said with quite a biting irony, for, as we know, Denikin's affairs have come to a sticky end. And when the French minister Clemenceau said with a smile, as it were: 'I'll help you just as I helped Denikin', he probably looked at them with pity and thought: 'You'll finish up the same way as Denikin has. You've just enough rope to hang yourself.' [applause].

There's no doubt about it, the Mensheviks will get short shrift from our Red Army. There's no escape for them. Nevertheless, according to radio-telegrams, the English and French have decided to send 200 000 troops. Probably 20 000 rather than 200 000 – they like to exaggerate a bit – but there is going to be a fight for the Caucasus, for Baku is a tasty morsel; even now they're probably thinking that they've got the oil in their pocket. Besides that the Caucasus and Bessarabia are tremendously important to us. Our Red Army men – and especially our communist Red Army men – need to study the geography of our country, and not only our country, but the whole world. They must know the configuration of the globe. The Caucasus is the gateway to a whole series of countries where we may expect to find hundreds of millions of potential allies. When we take the Caucasus we can move on further – just as when we take Bessarabia we shall come into contact with tens, or rather hundreds of millions of people who look to us for brotherly help.

When we take these places we shall be in touch with Asia Minor and Turkey; we shall help the mountain people against the Turks. When we have conquered the Caucasus mountains we shall join up with a whole series of peoples who are oppressed by the English. We are only at the start of the world revolution now. When we get through these gates we will see the flame of revolution spreading to India, Persia and a whole series of other countries, where hundreds of millions of people are under the heel of English capitalists and where they are waiting for the first Red Army regiment to appear in order to make their own revolutions.

That is why, comrades, the question of the Caucasus is not for us just about oil – although that is quite important – nor just about liberating several million peasants, who are still suffering under the capitalist yoke, but besides all that we have to think of the further development of our revolution, because our revolution will achieve its final victory only when we get new nations to join us. And in the east a hundred million oppressed peoples are waiting for us. They are so worked up there it is like a powder store just waiting for a match. There they pray to the Soviet Union; every word of the Soviet Government and the Communist International is received as gospel; in those places they are waiting for us to come to them. And now the time is near when we may not only dream of this but can actually go there, bearing in mind that we see in those areas the interests of our whole revolution and of all the world. Warfare along the old fronts is coming to an end, but, pushing towards the East, opening the way to those oppressed nationalities, one front will remain active in the near future – in the next few months or weeks.

Come what may, for weeks or months the struggle will be in the Caucasus, where the main conflict will be centred, because that is where the interests of the workers and peasants clash with the interests of English and French capitalists. Just as a short while ago Petrograd was the most important point and these two forces clashed round Petrograd, so we shall see the same happening in the Caucasus. The main forces will be concentrated there. And we shall need a definite army there. That is why we must conceive the war as having ended in such a way that we have got rid of a whole lot of fronts, but a few remain – and those are the fronts which will determine the fate of our revolution. Besides which, we know full well that victory in the present war does not always guarantee that you won't have another war on your hands tomorrow. We drove out Yudenich in the summer of 1919, but by the autumn he was back visiting us again. This time we have given him a good drubbing, but we can only hope that he will no longer be resurrected from the dead ...

DOCUMENT 4.21

This document, which refers to the foundation of the Military-Labour Revolutionary Committee, shows first of all the gradual evolution of the Labour Army concept towards planning and supply allocation, hallmarks of the five-year plans of the 1930s. The note is particularly significant: under war communism, as would be the case in the late 1920s, there was a deep suspicion of 'bourgeois' specialists; this, after all, was the start of a march towards socialism. The explanatory note refers to the bureaucratic dangers inherent in such a system of resource allocation, but offers little practical in suggesting how this can be avoided; indeed, it is even hinted that after economic recovery has begun the Military-Labour Revolutionary Committee might become a permanent feature of life.

However, there is a second element to this document worthy of comment. The explanatory note suddenly launches an attack on the peasantry, and suggests that the British and French were somehow trying to foster counter-revolution by making common cause with the 'petty-bourgeois' aspirations of peasant co-operatives; a revival of the SR Party is even envisaged as a possible danger. Such an attitude towards the peasantry was symptomatic of war communism, as it would be later of Collectivisation under Stalin; it was the very antithesis of the NEP introduced in 1921 and Lenin's last writings on the importance of co-operatives. It also shows how persistent Bolshevik hostility to the rural population was, even after the lesson of the Don rebellion.

RGAE, *f.* 3429, *op.* 1, *ed. khr.* 1527, *ll.* 23–5; *l.* 107

Draft Statute for Military-Labour Revolutionary Committee (*Voentrudrevkom*)

1. In order to give force to the introduction of labour mobilisation at revolutionary speed as agreed through the whole of Russia, and to make

use of the armed forces for organising labour, a Military-Labour Revolutionary Committee is hereby established as the military economic distributive organ of the worker-peasant government.

2. As the supreme manager of the country's personnel and the resources needed to ensure its intensive productivity, the Military-Labour Revolutionary Committee is instituting the dictatorship of labour.

3. The first task of the Military-Labour Revolutionary Committee is to create industrial (labour) fronts for the extraction and transport of material goods.

4. The functions of the Military-Labour Revolutionary Committee are:

(a) to make and evolve plans for the most vital work to be carried out for the Republic;
(b) together with specialists to examine in detail any limitations on these works occurring as a practical matter in certain areas, or in so far as they affect certain definite enterprises, and also to calculate their needs (for food supplies, fuel, work force, building materials, means for ensuring proper standards of hygiene, etc);
(c) to carry out such work with its own resources, or to entrust the responsibility for this to the appropriate commissariat, supplying all it needs for the task, while at the same time insisting on its being properly carried out;
(d) to organise the Army so that its active service and labour units can replace each other at intervals;
(e) to calculate the labour force and arrange for it to be mobilised, assigned to tasks, or transferred from one task to another.

5. The Military-Labour Revolutionary Committee will create disciplined fighting units, prepared to carry out any effective tasks as dictated by the demands of the current political situation (whether the tasks be military, agricultural, industrial or to ensure the supply of fuel and such like). The management structures will be organised not along bureaucratic lines, but flexible, ready for action, disciplined; in short, a military political model.

Note: Previous experience in establishing state management structures gives good cause for us to insist that only communists and workers should be brought into the managerial staff of the Revolutionary Committee, no one but communists and workers, supporting them with specialists acting purely as experts and technical executives in areas where specialised professional expertise is called for (this note not to form part of the statute, but put forward as a generalised proposition to be discussed, with a view to casting it into a definite shape and introducing it into the statute concerning the Military-Labour Revolutionary Committee).

6. The Chairman and five members of the Military-Labour Revolutionary Committee are elected by the All-Russian Central Executive Committee.

2 February 1920, Feinshtein

> Explanatory note to Draft Statute concerning Military-Labour Revolutionary Committee, 2 February 1920

Acute difficulties in the political and economic situation necessitate the creation of a specialised central apparatus to pursue unswervingly measures for restoring the ruined national economy at a revolutionary pace and on a labour basis which eliminates any remnants of exploitation. In order to achieve the stated aim this apparatus must be built on the following principles:

It must be competent to:

1. Define the points where forces are to be brought to bear (where special efforts are required, where the industrial fronts are), from which we must begin to resuscitate the national economy (Section 3 and Section 4, paragraph (a)). No matter how simple the question may seem to be at first glance, some central organ must be in overall control of defining the points where our forces are to be applied, in so far as we must select works which have the highest priority for the whole country, and must choose the area in which these works can be most easily and quickly be brought to fruition. Definite tasks must be assigned to each area of work in order to avoid squandering strength and resources, of which we have only a limited quantity.

2. Defining and putting into effect objectives for restoring the ruined economy step by step (Section 4, paragraphs (b) and (c)). In a situation in which both the organs and their sphere of activity exist only on paper, when the best intentions and words issuing from the centre may become buried in paper and lost therein, as rivers are swallowed up in the sands of the deserts of Central Asia, we need some organ which can push the economic apparatus along at points where it is weak and which may replace them with some temporary organisation, even by using army forces in places where there is essential work to do but actually no one to carry it out. But even in cases where efficient economic organisations are already in place or where they are being well

The Labour Armies of the Soviet Republic   163

and speedily organised, their planning entails raising the entire economic activity of the area, which under present circumstances can only proceed very slowly. The Military-Labour Revolutionary Committee, by singling out the works which are most essential for the state and equipping them more freely with all they actually need to do the job, can at the same time get the most essential work done in the shortest possible time (as, for example, in the Donbas by getting the coal which is best suited for locomotives, or in the forest areas singling out the work for pit props for mines, etc.).

3. It is essential that the committee should have the right to dispose of the labour force and productive resources in order to supply the shock points with real means of production and not simply ephemeral paper finance (Section 2 and Section 4, paragraphs (d) and (e)), since at the moment this paper money cannot secure what is necessary to sustain life and the workers' ability to produce goods. The committee must have these powers in order to ensure that the shock points are supplied with the necessities of life. The Military-Labour Revolutionary Committee must have the right to dispose of the available stocks of real resources and must be able to obtain those which are lacking with the help of the work force (deriving them from natural resources) or by military force (getting them from the proprietors). In so acting the Military-Labour Revolutionary Committee is not destroying its own commissariat's plans for procurement and output, but rather is rendering its task easier, either by aiding it with the supply of necessary resources or by achieving its objectives with its own resources, but within the overall limits of national regulations. (At a later stage, when the national economy is working in more normal conditions, this function of the Military-Labour Revolutionary Committee may be developed into a general national apparatus for controlling and supplying industry with its physical needs, while the actual procurement of these means will be transferred to the normal economic organisations.)

4. The fourth principle on which the statute is based is the revolutionary (military-political) nature of the committee (see Sections 1 and 5) as distinct from bureaucratic and economic normative administrative structures. This is required both by the immediate crisis conditions in the political and economic spheres and also by the Military-Labour Revolutionary Committee's intensive methods of grappling with problems.

What has brought about political and economic tension?

(a) It is essential to divert our victorious troops from aggressive tendencies (such as those displayed by Caesar) and by applying all the authority of a victor to direct their surplus energy to the spreading of communist culture. Demobilisation would be dangerous, both in view of possible changes in policy by the Entente powers, and also because of the destructive effect demobilisation would have, particularly on transport.

(b) The Entente have almost given up hope of smashing the revolution and installing a pliant dynasty with whose help, by preserving the remnants of the oppressive feudal regime, they might halt the development of Russia at the level of an underdeveloped economy and turn our country into a milch cow (on the model of India and China). Now they are trying to enter into an alliance with the Russian peasantry (as the victor class), and hope to bypass the proletariat by opening up relations with the co-operatives that unite the peasantry. The Entente powers are hoping to profit by the destruction of our industry by taking out our raw materials in exchange for manufactured goods, and by slaking the peasants' thirst for goods to seducing them with the advantages of petty proprietorship, thus bringing their interests into conflict with those of the proletariat. Hence the need arises to keep our minds firmly fixed on introducing general labour management and combating any relics of exploitation. This in its turn requires us to create a central apparatus which will act decisively in the spirit of our revolution.

(c) The ruined state of the economy and the prevailing slackness of labour discipline, with its threat of paralysing the labour force, make it essential to resort to exceptional measures such as can be carried out only by an apparatus equipped with exceptional powers, acting with one single tactic and not liable to be divided by inter-departmental squabbles.

We shall need revolutionary methods in the struggle to make general labour mobilisation effective, because, as petty proprietors see their last hopes disappear of having a quiet life dependent on profits and unearned income, so opportunities are again opened up for the SRs' frenzied propaganda and for the Mensheviks and the clever people inside our organisation who are controlled by them to undermine us in a stealthy way.

2 February 1920, Feinshtein (Pirogovskii)

DOCUMENT 4.22

In major industrial centres like Petrograd, the Labour Army was not to operate as a supply of unskilled labour for loading and unloading goods, but a mechanism for mobilising those with skills or the potential for skills. This proposal for the creation of 'Red technicians' shows how plans were developed to turn literate peasants into skilled workers through crash training programmes. 'Red technicians', unlike 'bourgeois specialists', would be politically reliable, or so it was assumed. The same desire to create loyal proletarian technicians would be characteristic of the 1930s.

RGVA, f. 227, op. 1, ed. khr. 14, l. 7

Memorandum to Chairman of the Petrograd Soviet Labour Army, G.E. Zinoviev, concerning the necessity to set up courses to prepare qualified specialists for the national economy

Petrograd, 9 February 1920

To Chairman of Petrograd Soviet Labour Army, G.E. Zinoviev

To restore our industry and transport we shall need thousands and hundreds of thousands of qualified workers, who are in short supply in Soviet Russia. We shall need particularly large numbers of skilled workers if we take into account future developments in the technology of agriculture. We need exceptional measures to swell the ranks of metal workers, engine drivers, electrical specialists, etc.

The Petrograd Labour Army contains several thousand young literate peasants who are only too eager to be taught, besides which by mobilising 17 and 18 year olds we could increase this total up to any figure.

Furthermore Petrograd with its factories and technical colleges affords every sort of technical opportunity for converting a large number of literate peasants into qualified workers.

We lost a great deal by not opening courses to train Red officers from the very first days after the October Revolution. The Labour Army must avoid this mistake. I consider that at the first session of the Labour Army the question must be raised about how to prepare several thousand 'Red technicians' in five or six months, who after a little practical work will be able to take on specialised work quite independently.

I suppose that only the military discipline and material resources which are at the disposal of the Labour Army will achieve quick results in this process, whereas similar attempts by the People's Commissariat of Education, Trades Unions and other civilian departments will be at only a comparatively primitive level. In addition, the military, i.e., the Labour Department, will find the easiest way is to make use of the great experience built up by those who organised the courses in the army which produced such remarkable results.

[Signature indecipherable. Annotations to the document make clear that Zinoviev read this document on 11 February and endorsed the comments that it had been a mistake not to train officers from the very first days of the revolution, and that it was therefore necessary to create 'Red technicians'.]

DOCUMENT 4.23

As this document clearly shows, once the Labour Armies were established the campaign for them became a mass movement, designed to harness popular enthusiasm for rapid economic change; here the dynamism of youth is being exploited and 'pen-pushers' identified as a target for anger. Again there are parallels with the popular movements launched in the 1930s to support Stalin's five-year plans. It is also noteworthy that the existing academic courses are deemed to include subject matter unrelated to the urgent task of building socialism.

RGVA, *f. 227, op. 1, ed. khr. 14, l. 96*

Minutes of meeting of members of Left Socialist Group of students of Petrograd Technical Institute re *necessity for accelerated output of engineers for needs of Labour Army*

No.6, 22 February 1920

Agenda

1. Report of comrade R. Gurvich on present situation.
2. [Report of comrade] L. Idson on measures of co-operation with Labour Army and necessity for accelerated output of engineers.

Resolution (agreed unanimously):

The time for words has passed, now is the time to act. To welcome the Labour Army not with resolutions but by the most urgent recruitment of engineers to its ranks. We have done enough sitting around on People's Commissariats of the Economy, scribbling on paper in the control organisations and ensconcing ourselves in water transport agencies as 'irreplaceable' draughtsmen and technicians. We must bend all our efforts to speeding up the output of engineers from among fourth and fifth year students and reinforcing the Labour Army with properly qualified specialist engineers.

To achieve this:

I. Fifth year students must complete their diploma papers by 1 May and fourth year students by 15 June.
II. Fourth year students to complete their examinations and projects by 1 May in groups – specialising in heating, bridge construction and building – in order that if necessary they can be used as engineers in separate specialisms (for restoring transport).
III. In furtherance of this aim to introduce a twelve-hour working day for students in the last year of their studies, to bring in compulsory mobilisation of students ensuring their food rations and hostels in which light is provided twenty-four hours per day.
IV. To put following proposals to [Petro]grad Lab[our] Army:

1. To declare that all fourth and fifth year students of Petrograd Technical Institute come under military discipline in the subject for which their accelerated course will qualify them, and to place them at the disposal of the Revolutionary Troika attached to their Institute irrespective of their place of work and present position.
2. To propose that all at work, wherever they may be serving, take secondment with their grant maintained if they are called for by the Revolutionary Troika.
3. To ensure that students completing the course receive the Labour Army ration (but to issue it only as training tasks are fulfilled), plus hostel accommodation in the Institute and lighting.
4. In order to implement the proposal for accelerating the output of engineers, to appoint a special Revolutionary Troika, consisting of one representative of the Soviet Labour Army and two representatives of the Left Socialist Group of Technical Students. To give this troika plenipotentiary powers in all matters concerned with accelerating the output [of engineers].
5. All technical students refusing to obey the present decree to be considered as deserters from the Labour Army with all the consequences which will ensue.

V. To put before the Council of Professors the proposal to make an urgent announcement about the accelerated output of engineers in order to:

1. Eliminate from the Institute's courses or to limit requirements in subjects which are outdated or have no direct bearing on the speciality selected by the student who is completing the course.
2. Allow projects to be completed in outline form.
3. Abolish unnecessary formalities and such requirements as are a

hangover from the old regime and are out of place in present conditions of intensive work.

VI. For reporting to the Chairman of Petrograd Soviet and supervisor of the affairs of the Labour Army as well as for relations with the Council of Professors to elect as delegates R. Gurvich, L. Idson, S. Pines.

Chairman L. Idson
Secretary Ruvim Gurvich

DOCUMENT 4.24

This simply reminds us that the Labour Armies were subject to military jurisdiction, and that failure to comply with the call-up would have serious consequences.

RGVA, *f.* 190, *op.* 3, *ed. khr.* 398, *l.* 31

Telegram from Chief of Staff of 7th Army Comrade Zarubayev to Commander of Shlisselburg Fortress on making workers subject to operational orders

No.01919, 4 March 1920

The Revolutionary Council of the Petrograd Labour Army has issued orders that the enlistment of workers shall be considered operational orders. Anyone who does nor carry them out shall be brought before a Revolutionary Tribunal, as they would be for failure to carry out a military order. Immediate effect must be given to 55th Division's Order 7 of 28 February placing workers at disposal of Khudokornov.

Report on fulfilment of order.

Chief of Staff Zarubayev
Military Commissar V. Antonichev

DOCUMENT 4.25

The relationship between the needs of Red Army active service units and Labour Armies was never satisfactorily resolved; here the shortage of specialists means that the Labour Army has been gradually poaching specialists from active service units.

RGVA, f. 190, op. 3, ed. khr. 400, l. 358

> Order of the Commander-in-Chief to Comrade Odintsov, Army Commander of Petrograd Labour Army on limiting the number of specialists to be withdrawn from the division

No.1244/operational, Moscow, 5 March 1920

With regard to former cases of significant numbers of specialists in various technical trades being withdrawn from units of a division, the C-in-C directed that this process should not take place, since it greatly reduces the combat readiness of divisions in the reserve. In particular those specialists withdrawn from 19th Division forming the subject of Divisional Commander's report in operational telegram No.698 must be gradually returned to the division.

Chief of Staff of RVS Lebedev
Military Commissar Vasilev

DOCUMENT 4.26

Stalin's Labour Army in the Ukraine was as prone as any other to criticism from the commanders of active service units. In this case M.V. Frunze, who later in the year would lead the Red Army against General Wrangel, argues that he who pays the piper calls the tune.

GARF, f. 486, op. 1, ed. khr. 25, ll. 18–19

> Memorandum to RVS of Republic from M.V. Frunze, Commander of Forces of Ukraine and Crimea, re keeping labour units under military discipline

No.1146/3674, Kharkov, 7 March 1920

In view of the fact that military units of the Labour Army transferred to the People's Commissariat for Labour will in all probability remain as a charge on the military department for all types of supply and maintenance and posting Red Army men to keep them up to establishment, with their command staff and their political sections also borne as a charge on the military, I consider that these units should remain directly subordinate to the military department. Otherwise without military control it will be difficult to keep the labour units up to a proper state of combat readiness or to ensure that they are able to give correct and timely service.

Commander of Forces of Ukraine M. Frunze
Chief of Staff of Forces of Ukraine Sologub

DOCUMENT 4.27

Here we learn more details about how the accelerated training of 'Red technicians' would be organised.

RGVA, *f.* 190, *op.* 2, *ed. khr.* 231

Memorandum from T.L. Zelikson, member of the Education Section of Petrograd Soviet, concerning the Technical College of the Petrograd Labour Army

10 March 1920

[Extract]

The aim of the Technical College is to train the lower ranks of the technical command staff for the Army.

Basic entry qualifications for the Technical College: reading, writing and the four rules of arithmetic.

Courses are to last $1^{1}/_{2}$ to 3 months, and must be extended for a further 2 to 3 weeks for backward groups.

In view of the short time span the curriculum is divided into narrow specialisms, which allows maximum simplification of the programme and makes it purely practical.

The best way to ensure that those on the course assimilate the material presented to them is to divide them into small groups of 10–15 students, combining 3 to 4 groups together to teach the social sciences.

It is essential that students should not be overladen with superfluous book learning. Instruction in the specialised subjects should above all be related to practice, for which reason teachers should be recruited from specialists in agriculture, engineers and practised technicians.

It is desirable that all the subjects in any one specialism should be taught by one lecturer – or at most two – which will allow the audience to concentrate better on the subject and the lecturer to keep an eye on how well his pupils are taking in what he has taught them.

The Technical College has three departments: (1) Agriculture, (2) Heating, (3) Building. These departments are sub-divided into sections . . .

L. Zelikson

DOCUMENT 4.28

This document chronicles the formation of another Labour Army in a diplomatically sensitive region, Archangel and the border area with Finland.

GARF, f. R-130, op. 4, ed. khr. 483, ll. 8-9

Telegram from RVS of 6th Army to Defence Council and Revolutionary Military Council re possibility of converting 6th Army into a Labour Army

Archangel, 11 March 1920

The mission entrusted to the 6th Army was completed on 9 March. The importance of our area, both for the Republic and internationally, makes it essential to install Soviet ideas and institutions and to affirm them speedily and unshakeably, to increase the production of timber, to conserve stocks already cut, and to make a prompt start on transforming the basis of our economy, which can be achieved only by military methods, making use of a Labour Army. The uncertain outlook of the international situation, the fact that it would be almost completely impossible with our few resources to offer any serious resistance to any large enemy units, the proximity of the Finnish frontier, and the question of Karelia and Finland do not allow us to transfer the whole army on to work as a labour force, and, in view of the run-down state of the army, almost two divisions must be kept in readiness to defend the coastal strip and the railway line to Murmansk.

The Council of the Labour Army, made up as the situation demands, must accept as its mission:

1. Acting on instructions from the centre and from provincial organisations, to work out a general labour plan for the whole area, for construction purposes making use of the technical services of the army and the broad mass of Red Army men who have been released from military duties;
2. to allocate the labour force necessary for the requirements of local economic organs.

We request that the new Labour Army shall be named the Northern Labour Army.

Samoylo, Luganovskii, Kuzmin, Orekhov, Eyduk

DOCUMENT 4.29

It is clear from this document that just before the start of the war with Poland, which put most Labour Armies back on a war footing – and raised the prospect of world revolution – the Labour Army experiment was heading towards problems stemming from what, for the Bolsheviks, were unexpected sources; enthusiastic communist cadres were no longer displaying much enthusiasm for the Labour Armies, leaving them short of reliable cadres. Those cadres which remained were of low quality and their behaviour was already causing problems. The author of the document hopes that an answer could be found in better Party training of the young, but as events later in the year would show it was not as easy as that.

Once the war with Poland was over, Trotsky was eager to repeat the experiment with labour mobilisation; but in the autumn of 1920 Lenin was no longer willing to support him, and so began the great trade union controversy in the Bolshevik Party in which the so-called Worker's Opposition campaigned vigorously against the idea of labour mobilisation and the Bolshevik Party itself seemed on the point of collapse. It was working-class communists who led that opposition, and there is more than a hint in this document that working-class communists, or at least communists in the Labour Armies, were less than happy with the concept. At the very least this document shows the paucity of communist cadres through which the great experiment in socialist construction was to be achieved.

RGVA, *f.* 190, *op.* 1, *ed. khr.* 15, *ll.* 248–9

Report by V. Volodin, Chief of Political Section of 7th Army

15 March 1920 [dated by note on document]

As the position at the front has improved and the Army has gone over to labour duties, the flow of communists into the Army has completely dried up. In order to get economic, soviet and Party organisations going in the rear we have had to transfer some of our activists from the Army – and the best among them at that. The Central Committee in its latest directives to Party cadres in the army makes it clear that we cannot now look on rear organisations as a source from which to recruit Party workers for the army.

All this and the great losses of our finest Party officials in battle has led to a severe shortage of the best Party comrades in the army. At the same time, over the last few months the number of communists has doubled or even increased threefold. Alongside this mass of young

Party members there are only a tiny proportion of men who have seen long service in Party work; the very concept of 'old Party member' has completely changed. Party membership of 1½ or 2 years' standing now serves to denote an 'old Party member'. The mass of recently joined members is still too inexperienced. It has brought into our ranks a great amount of revolutionary fervour and healthy idealism, but at the same time this mass of new men has come to us with all the prejudices and faults of that worker-peasant stock which is closest to their heart. Among this sort of people in our Party it is very easy to become a leader by playing on their weaknesses. They have a very poor grasp of political tactics, and at any time they may be knocked off the course which has been firmly laid down for us to follow, when they attach a disproportionate importance to questions which come to the fore in Party business at any particular moment. That is why the Party's 'Old Guard' finds itself faced with unusually difficult conditions at work.

On the one hand we are compelled to contain a huge torrent of fresh energy and to direct it into normal channels, while on the other hand we have to meet the tremendous need for Party activists which is demanded by the development of the Revolution. We can find these extra hands only among the young Party members. We have to bring them on and prepare them for their work – that is the basic question now facing the Party. The coming 9th Party Congress is also bound to be concerned with this problem.

The problem is even more acute in the army because so many Party men have gone out of it. At the same time our Party's ranks contain tremendous creative forces. During the last few months we have seen an influx of the best type of people, tempered in the fire of the Civil War. We must make the widest possible use of their creative talent and draw them into practical work for the soviets, the army, and the Party. We must set about this now with boldness and in the true spirit of the revolution, just we did at the beginning, when we brought thousands of the best workers and peasants into our work, from whom were developed the best military, soviet and Party cadres.

How are we to do this? We can get quite a lot of guidance from our experience over more than two years. We have now got to release quite a lot of our best officials for the rear, and their places must be taken by comrades from the lower rungs of the service and Party ladder. In their turn these must be replaced by comrades who are still lower down the scale, while these latter posts shall be filled by young rank and file members of the Party.

This is the most attested method for involving broad Party circles in practical work. We must apply this method now, with daring, decisiveness and on a wide scale.

We must be bolder in appointing rank and file Party members to higher posts, include them in various commissions, draw particularly large numbers of them into cultural-educational work, etc.

Of course in the early stages there will be definite risks attached to this policy, plus a lot of inconvenience and rough edges. Quite a few mistakes are bound to be made by the young Party members; they will often get into a wrong course of action by giving rein to their prejudices and the illusions to which they still cling. But, employed in this way, they will be all the quicker to shed their prejudices and illusions, get their communist beliefs straightened out and develop further along proper lines.

Party members in post have a rich store of experience in these matters. We must spread this experience, in order to make our Party into a powerful mechanism for involving the broad proletarian masses in our movement to administer the country and to build communism. Communists now serving are invited to forward their practical reactions to this idea and to share the benefit of their experience.

V. Volodin

5 The Final Curtain

Conventionally histories of the Civil War finish in late 1920 or early 1921; by the end of 1920 the military victory of the Bolsheviks was assured, but most historians take the story to the spring of 1921 to show how bitter the fruits of that victory were, with the strikes in Petrograd in February, the mutiny in Kronshtadt in March, and the peasant rebellion in Tambov province which lasted throughout the spring. However, the conventional approach is a simplification; it would be more accurate to date the end of the Civil War to 1922.

As made clear in Chapter 1, the Civil War began as a war between the Bolsheviks and the SRs, between different tendencies of socialism, the urban and the rural; that Civil War only ended with the trial of surviving members of the SR Party in June 1922. Russia's other Civil War, that between the Bolsheviks and White Generals such as Denikin, also continued into 1922; and it is to that last campaign that the following documents relate.

The Civil War began in Siberia and Chapter 1 was concerned with the situation there until Admiral Kolchak seized power from the SR Directory in November 1918. Kolchak's tenure of power was to last little more than a year. The high spot of that year was the summer of 1919 when the Bolsheviks were driven to the point of defeat; Kolchak's troops seemed on the verge of making contact with Denikin's forces on the Don, as considered in Chapter 2. However, by the autumn of 1919 the military situation had worsened, and in November 1919 Kolchak was forced to evacuate his capital at Omsk. By then, the SRs were in a position to take revenge for their overthrow a year earlier. By the end of 1919 peasant insurrections were taking place all over Kolchak's territory and he clung to power only by the most brutal use of terror. Finally, an insurrection took place during the first week of January 1920 which toppled Kolchak's government and the SRs then assumed power: the Czechoslovak Legion, which had been neutral in November 1918, when it allowed Kolchak to seize power, was not so on this occasion; it detained Kolchak and handed him over for trial.

After Kolchak's downfall events moved quickly. The Bolsheviks soon extended their authority over the SR administration which had replaced that of Kolchak, while the British, the French and the Americans decided to end their intervention and withdraw their missions from Siberia; at the same time the Czechoslovak Legion was evacuated. But that did not remove all foreign forces from Russian soil. The Japanese had landed in Vladivostok in August 1918, and still controlled the Maritime Province. So, in the first half of 1920, the Bolshevik forces re-occupying Siberia were in danger of coming face to face with the Japanese and becoming involved in a new conflict.

It was against this background that in May 1920 the Bolsheviks accepted what was initially an SR proposal to form a Far Eastern Republic, to be administered by a coalition socialist government comprising both Bolsheviks and peasant socialists. Although the Japanese agreed to the creation of this buffer state in July 1920, it soon became clear to them that it was a sham and the Bolsheviks had *de facto* control of both the supposed coalition government and the Far Eastern Republic's army. So the Japanese decided to intervene once more. The White Government in Vladivostok had voted in November 1920 to join the Far Eastern Republic and the region had participated fully in the elections to its Constituent Assembly in Janaury 1921, despite the continued presence of Japanese troops. However, in May 1921 the Japanese encouraged a group of Rightwing Whites to stage a coup and establish a government in the Maritime Province which would have nothing to do with the Far Eastern Republic, and would even be prepared to go to war with it. That new government banned all communist activity, introduced press censorship, and gave the Popular Assembly it summoned only the sort of limited rights the Tsar had once granted the State Duma (Assembly).

In autumn 1921 this government's leading generals, General Verzhbitskii and General Molchanov, launched an offensive against Bolshevik-controlled pockets within the Maritime Province. At first it went well, but by the spring of 1922 the offensive had failed and the generals and the government were at loggerheads. By May 1922 the government was in crisis and tried to dismiss Verzhbitskii and dissolve the Popular Assembly. This political crisis was only resolved by asking Lieutenant-General M.K. Diterikhs to leave his base in Harbin and form a new government. But Diterikh's government soon found itself working in a very hostile climate.

Over the summer of 1921 the Far Eastern Republic and Japan had seemed to be on the point of war. To avoid this the USA decided to persuade the two sides to attend a conference in the Manchurian city of Dairen; the conference lasted until April 1922 and at first seemed to have made no progress other than preventing the outbreak of hostilities. However, under further US pressure, in July 1922 the Japanese announced that they would evacuate all Russian territory including the Maritime Province by November 1922; they also agreed to open talks not only with the Far Eastern Republic but with the Soviet Government as well. By September

The Final Curtain 177

1922 Moscow's diplomats were holding talks in the Manchurian town of Ch'angch'un with Japanese representatives; although these talks did little to improve Soviet–Japanese relations, the Japanese did confirm the commitment to evacuate Russian territory.

So Diterikhs took over the government of the Maritime Province at the most inauspicious moment imaginable, when the Japanese were already deciding to withdraw. Diterikhs had fought the Bolsheviks longer than anyone else. He had been appointed before the October Revolution to head the Czechoslovak Legion, and although deprived of that post by the Bolsheviks, travelled with the Legion on its long journey through Siberia; when it mutinied in June 1918 and took up arms against the Bolsheviks, he rallied to the cause; as one of the Legion's leaders he was among the first to arrive in Vladivostok and helped the Czechoslovaks there overthrow the Bolshevik administration. During Kolchak's administration, he was the man appointed to oversee the investigation into the execution of the Tsar and his family. After Kolchak's fall, Diterikhs moved to Harbin.

As these documents show, he was a complex figure. Clearly a committed Orthodox Christian, he had a mystical commitment to the old autocracy and the Tsar as the little father of the people. The regime he established was replete with linguistic allusions to Russia's folk traditions and history. Thus his army was not called *armiya*, an army, but a *rat*; this archaic word is difficult to translate but conjures up images of a troop of knights in medieval armour rather than a modern army: he describes himself as *voevoda* of that army; again, this is an old word for 'leader' most frequently used to describe knights of old leading troops against the infidel: and the army is called the Zemskaya army; again, this is an old term for land or nation, echoing the Zemskii *sobor* or Assembly of the Land summoned by the early Romanov Tsars to advise them on how to rule Russia. In Vladivostok Diterikhs summoned his own *Zemskii sobor* on 23 July 1922 which voted overwhelmingly on 6 August to make him *Pravitel* (Ruler); his power would be checked only by an advisory *Zemskaya Duma*. In an essentially romantic way Diterikhs was committed to an idea of the autocracy as the representative of a truly loyal and Christian Russian people.

Once it became clear the Japanese were leaving and the forces of the Army of the Far Eastern Republic could not be resisted, Diterikhs had no choice but to flee. The army of the Far Eastern Republic entered Vladivostok on 25 October, the same day as the Japanese left. Some units of Diterikhs' army were directly evacuated from Vladivostok by boat, but the bulk retreated to Posyet, a town about 150 miles further south; from here some escaped to Korea, again by boat, but Diterikhs took the core of his forces to the border with Chinese Manchuria. From the border town of Hanch'un it would be a difficult journey to Chilin (Kirin), but thereafter there was a rail link to Ch'angch'un and a further rail link to Harbin. Both towns were within the Russian security zone which ran either side of the Chinese Eastern Railway. This railway, which cut directly across Chinese Manchuria from Chita to Vladivostok, was the first route taken by the Trans-Siberian Railway and under international agreement Russia had been allowed to establish a security zone around the railway; this became a centre for Russian businessmen and administrators and turned Harbin into a Russian city within China. Harbin was clearly Diterikhs' preferred destination.

The problem was the status of the Chinese Eastern Railway and its security zone. On assuming power in 1917 the Bolshevik Government made many propaganda announcements to the effect that it intended to transfer this zone and the railway to the Chinese authorities; the Japanese and the various White governments in Siberia, on the other hand, had seen no need to do so and had continued to control it under an agreement signed by Kolchak. However, when the Japanese announced they were evacuating Siberia, including the railway, the Bolsheviks made clear that they were, after all, interested in asserting control over the railway. Soon it had become a bargaining chip between the Soviet Government and the Manchurian war-lord, Chang Tso-lin, with the Bolsheviks hinting in November 1922 that the Manchurians might yet be granted control of the railway if they took a firm line with White Russian refugees. And so Diterikhs had nowhere else to turn; not even the Russian community of the Chinese Eastern Railway would be open to him. Diterikhs crossed the border and threw himself on the mercy of Chang Tso-lin. On 10 November 1922 the Far Eastern Assembly voted in favour of incorporation into Soviet Russia, and the Civil War was over.

DOCUMENT 5.1

The most striking thing about this document is Diterikhs' confident belief that he would be able to retain some form of military organisation once inside China. The whole atmosphere is one of military discipline and order, despite the fact that this is the Whites' final retreat. Point 7 makes particularly clear Diterikhs' wish to appear as an army, not a rabble. In point 10 the concern for the proper use of horses also reflects the need for discipline in a retreating army.

RGVA, f. 40189, op. 1, ed. khr. 7, ll. 4–5

Order to the Zemskaya Army concerning the organisation of troops when on the move inside China

No.1, the port of Posyet, 23 October 1922

From this 24 October I am establishing the following organisation of the Zemskaya Army for movements inside China:

1. Infantry – Major-General Molchanov.
Two regiments: Major-General Sakharov and Colonel Yefimov. Railway Police – Colonel Rostovtsev.

Note:
(a) Units of the Frontier Guard, separate commands of the Siberian Group, the militia and various rear echelons and directorates are disbanded and included in regimental strengths at the disposition of General Molchanov.
(b) Those who do not wish to join the ranks of the Army are disarmed and included in the refugee colonies.
(c) For mounted infantry on horseback retain only teams of mounted orderlies attached to commanding personnel.

2. Cossacks Major-General Borodin.
Organisation of the cossack troops in squads.

Note:
(a) On horse retain only teams of mounted orderlies attached to commanding personnel. Harness all remaining horses to civilian carts for family use.

3. Artillery – Colonel Bek-Mamedov.

The Regiment of Artillery contains the artillery of the whole Zemskaya Army.

Note:
(a) All gun crews on foot. Horses harnessed to civilian carts for family use.

4. Mounted squad of Major-General Khrushchev in the meantime to form rearguard of Zemskaya Army.
5. Medical transport.

To be formed from all the infantry's medical personnel and resources.

6. 23, 24, 25 October for General Molchanov to assemble all personnel in area Posyet–Novo-Kievsk [today Kraskino], to assign them to units and include them in unit strengths.

7. I insist that all military ranks in the Zemskaya Army should wear shoulder straps and in general have the appearance of military ranks and units, not comrades in a herd of refugees.

8. I appoint Major-General Semenov as officer-in-charge of the Army. I am subordinating all command staff to my aide Lieutenant-General Verzhbitskii. In addition he is in command of Major-General Puchkov and the Spasskaya and Nikolsk-Ussuriyskaya Militia.

Duties:

(a) In Novo-Kievsk prepare transport for families and separately for refugees.
(b) Supervise carrying out of general garrison duties in garrison points.
(c) Supervise choice of bivouac sites for Zemskaya Army in movement through China.
(d) Make arrangements for establishing internal order and guarding of bivouac or lodging sites.

Note:

General Molchanov to transfer to General Verzhbitskii 10 horses out of those received from Yankovsky and 10 saddles from cavalry now dismounted as infantry; remaining 10 horses received from Yankovsky to be handed over to staff of the Army.

9. By morning of 25 October through General Semenov 100 wagons should come hired by me in Hanch'un to be at the disposal of General Verzhbitskii. Also all groups, units and any echelons arriving separately should by the evening of the 24th, under General Verzhbitskii's command, leave Novo-Kievsk to the north-west [in the direction of Hanch'un] with all Army carts and those belonging to the local population, no matter how laden, plus all horses, dismounted cavalrymen and cossacks.

All local carts are bought up by me and are the property of the Army. The horses of the locals, and the drivers, are to be released; harness the carts with our horses from dismounted cavalry and cossacks.

10. The commander to ensure that no one shall have horses except those authorised by me. Any person on horseback not in accordance with the regulations to be dismounted and the horses taken for the general wagon train.

11. Army will move in three columns: (a) column of families, (b) military

column and (c) column of refugees. In overnight quarters the columns (a) and (b) will be placed together, column (c) separately.

12. Order and time of movement I shall indicate in a supplementary instruction.

Lieutenant-General Diterikhs

Chief of Staff Major-General Petrov

DOCUMENT 5.2

This document brings the first warning that Diterikh's initial aspirations might be different from the reality of what Chang Tso-lin would agree to. Diterikhs' representative, sent ahead into China, has succeeded in preparing some of the practical ground for the border crossing, but can only hope that the Army is allowed to enter China with its guns; whatever happened, those guns would have to be hidden and the troops would have to behave impeccably so as not to frighten an already nervous population. The author knows that Chang Tso-lin himself had a long record of anti-Bolshevik activity, but is equally aware that the international situation had dramatically changed.

RGVA, f. 40189, op. 1, ed. khr. 7, ll. 2–3

Report of Colonel Lovtsevich, representative of the Zemskaya Army staff with the Chinese leadership and the possible plans of [the Manchurian war-lord] Chang Tso-lin

To the Army Chief, Hanch'un, 24 October 1922

On 22 October I sent a telegram to the marshal in the afternoon, and in the evening I sent an orderly to you with a report. Until now, 8 a.m. on 24 October, I have received no news from either you or the marshal. The three orderlies I asked for – to scout out the local villages, the telegraph network and supply dumps – have not arrived, and without them there is little preparatory work I can do. I know nothing of your situation, and I fear that time is passing. I enclose a map of the region, made by the garrison commander and not checked by me; as to the number of farmsteads, my questioning has not even given the most approximate answer.

I have come to the following conclusions.

Our best hope is that the marshal, shunning publicity, will risk instructing Colonel Yan to let us across the border with our arms hidden in the carts, and then provide us with every possible help once we are across the border (of course, the question of the carts still has to be resolved). On the other hand, the worst case for us would be if the marshal is afraid of falling into a difficult international situation and, entrusting the secret telegrams and their fulfilment to the colonel (a provincial, not sharing the same ideas as the marshal), tells him 'to act as agreed, making no distinction between Reds and Whites'; in my heart of hearts I hope things work out as suggested above. I presume that the marshal's representatives sent to us with personal instructions will be able to inform General Diterikhs of the true decision of the marshal.

From what I have said, and from my own experience crossing the border near the Manchuria railway station, I think the following points are essential:

1. Send the families at once to Hanch'un town, using the carts I was given by the garrison commander to carry shells and some of those used for troops; the families must be counted and listed in groups with a leader – this helps both the removal and the Chinese officials. These lists I will give to the garrison commander and the regional authorities.
2. Once the carts have been freed of the families and their belongings, the transfer of military units and equipment can begin, to villages in the surrounding area as marked on the enclosed map; it is essential that arms are kept in the carts, and hidden in the most careful and convincing way; the troops too will then be seen as refugees: no soldier or officer should appear in the town, which is at present seized with panic at the prospect of 'some sort of Russian Army arriving'. Looting or coarse behaviour towards the local population could ruin everything.

Once we are on Chinese territory, people's attitudes will be different – we need to have talks aimed at moving us as quickly as possible to Chilin [Kirin].
3. For the days when we cross the frontier and for the first days in Hanch'un we must avoid any misunderstanding by living off our own supplies, even if this means reducing rations.
4. The Army Staff should not be housed in the town, but in the countryside close by.
5. The artillery should be stationed, I suggest, in the villages to the north of the town.
6. The crossing should be made without noise or confusion, and I should be informed in advance to warn the garrison chief.
7. I will take measures to ensure that nothing is confiscated at the Chinese (English) customs post.

Keep me informed by coded telegram of the decision of the Ruler.

DOCUMENT 5.3

This document shows how Diterikhs followed the suggestions of his representative to the letter. He was clearly still hoping to retain a military organisation in China, surrendering only a token number of weapons and hiding the rest.

RGVA, f. 40189, op. 1, ed. khr. 6, l. 17

Telegram from the Ruler [Pravitel] of the Amur River Region and Commander of Zemskaya Army Lieutenant-General Diterikhs to Colonel Lovtsevich on preparation of troops for crossing frontier and on projected routes for movement of military columns in area of Chinese frontier

To Colonel Lovtsevich

24 October 1922

For your information:

1. Families and refugees will be moved to Hanch'un in the course of 25 and 26 October and should be quartered in the town of Hanch'un.
2. Military column will leave Novo-Kievsk on 27 October and will spend night in Russian part of Hanch'un. Column will cross frontier on 28 October, having loaded equipment on to carts. Vanguard will go in front with 200 infantry, one machine gun and one field gun (out of action), which we will make a show of disarming (if we have to pretend to do that). Military column (main body) not to be brought through town but across river near Hanch'un. Essential to prepare guides to bring units round through villages, bypassing the town.

I assign following areas to troops:

Infantry (Major-General Molchanov): villages Yan-Mu-Lin-Zy, Khua-Shi-Di-Sua, Lo-To-Khe-Zy and the settlement outside east gate of town.

Artillery (Colonel Bek-Mamedov): village Che-Da-Zhen-Gau.

Cossacks (Major-General Borodin): villages Guan-Me-Tszua-Tszy, In-An-Khe, Khuy-Yuan'-Yun, Dun-Chan-Tszy.

Headquarters and cavalry: settlement outside south gate of town.

Command staff (Lieutenant-General Verzhbitskii): in the town with the refugees, to preserve order and prevent any violence.

As rearguard: cavalry ready for action, to cross frontier 30 October.

Until 30 October I shall be at the Russian customs post and will cross frontier with rearguard, to see what Reds will do.

Absolutely essential that rearguard should not put down arms (even as a pretence), since the Reds might make a scene.

No.129/operational

Lieutenant-General Diterikhs

DOCUMENT 5.4

These extracts once again show that Diterikhs planned to retain a military organisation and thus followed closely the advice given to him in document 5.2. The command post referred to here would be responsible for civil order among the refugees, while the Army Staff would be based outside the town. The threat to execute on the spot those involved in incidents against the local population shows how important Diterikhs felt it was not to alienate the Chinese population. Despite his fundamentalist Christian beliefs, he was ready to respect Chinese religious practices.

RGVA, f. 40189, op. 1, ed. khr. 7, l. 6 [extracts]

Order of the Zemskaya Army for the regrouping of troops for the border crossing and behaviour on Chinese territory

During 25, 26, and 27 October the families and refugees, led by General Verzhbitskii, will concentrate in the town of Chinese Hanch'un. The command post will also be established in Hanch'un, and will oversee order in the town, not allowing any soldiers or male refugees into the town, unless carrying a pass from the Army Staff, or group commander, or the commandant. When crossing the frontier and while in the town, command post staff will hide their rifles in the carts.

On 27 October the military column under my command will concentrate in the following regions . . . The vanguard will have one cart with a small supply of arms, artillery shells and hand grenades. If circumstances dictate, this vanguard will be disarmed by the Chinese. All other military columns will hide their arms in their carriages and cross the border, then get themselves across the river without going into the town of Chinese Hanch'un . . .

In those villages where troops are stationed, the strictest measures should be taken to prevent looting, drunkenness and violence against the local population. Commanders should not hold back from shooting culprits on the spot. All ranks of the Army should be aware that the kinder we are to the Chinese, the kinder they will be to the troops.

Special attention must be paid to preventing the destruction of wood and other fuel stores. Respect must be shown to Chinese temples and shrines.

I demand of all commanders that order and discipline be kept to the highest order.

Lieutenant-General Diterikhs
Chief of Staff Major General Petrov

DOCUMENT 5.5

This document shows Diterikhs' first realisation that his army faced being disarmed. Although Diterikhs felt he was not responsible for the acts of violence carried out by some cossacks, violence did occur in Posyet, where he had recently been based and General Glebov was under his command until his departure from Posyet. (This telegram is sent from Novo-Kievsk, today Kraskino, a town between Posyet and the Chinese border.) The incident clearly made disarmament more likely, but Diterikhs was firmly against this; however, his hope that the international situation might improve if he waited a few more days at the border was quite unfounded.

RGVA, f. 40189, op. 1, ed. khr. 6, l. 8

Telegram from M.K. Diterikhs to Colonel Lovtsevich about exceptional nature of incident of violence to Chinese population by cossacks of Zemskaya Army in Posyet, and about not allowing troops to be disarmed except in the most extreme cases

To Colonel Lovtsevich, copy to General Verzhbitskii.

Acts of violence in Posyet were carried out by Glebov's cossacks who are proceeding to Genzan [in Korea]. Reassure head of garrison that in other units of Army there has not been a single instance of violence, as all local population can testify. Tell head of garrison from me that I come as a friend bringing men to serve the marshal, so that actual disarming will create a terrible impression on the troops. I understand the international position, but can agree to actual disarming only in extreme cases and that is why I ordered troop movements to stop at the frontier awaiting more favourable conditions for crossing frontier. Families will be in Hanch'un 27 October. I await further decisions.

26 October 1922, Novo-Kievsk, No.443
Diterikhs

DOCUMENT 5.6

This document shows the financial crisis which lay at the heart of all Diterikhs' problems; he had run out of money. Clearly if Chang Tso-lin was going to have to pay 4900 roubles per day to Diterikhs' forces from the very moment they crossed into China, they would have to do exactly what he told them. While 7650 armed men and 3000 horses was nothing when compared to the Red Army, it was still a force of some potential, even though encumbered by 2000 women and children.

RGVA, f. 40189, op. 1, ed. khr. 6, l. 9

Telegram from M.K. Diterikhs to Colonel Lovtsevich concerning numbers of troops of Zemskaya Army, sent to Korea and emigrating to China, and concerning daily quantity of produce necessary to sustain them

To Colonel Lovtsevich

For lack of financial and transport resources I have sent Far Eastern Cossack Group of General Glebov (1500 cossacks, 2200 women and children) on ships to Korean ports. Main forces of Zemskaya Army (4500 infantry, 600 artillery, 750 cavalry, 1800 cossacks, 2000 women and children, 3000 horses) I am sending to Hanch'un. Figures approximate, changing from day to day. If Chinese provide 500 wagons in Hanch'un I shall be able to embark infantry, allowing us to transfer the whole body of troops to Chilin [Kirin] in ten days. Essential from 1 November to charge food supplies to Chang Tso-lin. Approximately 40 kopecks per man per day and per horse 30 kopecks, amounting to approximate daily sum of 4900 roubles for the total strength.

26 October 1922, No.492 operational

Diterikhs

DOCUMENT 5.7

This document shows how Diterikhs continued to be optimistic about being able to cross the border with arms, and preferred to sit on the border and wait for things to improve rather than get involved with the marshal's representatives in Mukden, his seat of power.

RGVA, f. 40189, op. 1, ed. khr. 6, l. 16

Telegram from M.K. Diterikhs to Colonel Lovtsevich concerning probable failure of talks with Chinese military command on keeping arms

To Colonel Lovtsevich

In reply to your No.2327.

I consider it completely useless to send a military representative to Mukden now to resolve the arms question: first, he will disappear without trace and without result as did Nikolai; second, time at my disposal depends on the enemy. At the moment I am not under pressure, I can stand and wait here; from past experience I am convinced that representatives in Mukden get nothing but polite flummery. You see to getting the Chinese to take in and provide with food the families and horses who will come into Hanch'un by this evening. I can put into store and conserve field guns, shells, spare rifles and cartridges. But to protect us from local trickery [the term used is *Khunkhuzichestva*], only as an extreme measure will I agree to put away all our arms.

27 October 1922, Novo-Kievsk, No.499

Diterikhs

DOCUMENT 5.8

Two points are made in this document. First, Diterikhs acknowledges for the first time that his troops might have to disarm, and second that the families, which had already crossed the border, were finding it very difficult to adjust to Chinese style rations.

RGVA, f. 40189, op. 1, ed. khr. 7, l. 7

Zemskaya Army Order on necessity of accepting severe material privations and difficulties with food supply arising from plight of refugees and relying on Chinese military command for our food supply

No.4, Novo-Kievsk

From reports reaching me I see that neither troops, nor families, nor supply institutions consider it necessary to take into account the circumstances in which we are living, and in spite of my warnings that I have no resources they are trying to continue to live, feed, and supply themselves at a normal level.

To avoid reprimands and misunderstandings I absolutely insist that all those in charge or responsible for families should inform all ranks of the Zemskaya Army as follows:

1. When we have crossed the frontier soldiers of all ranks in the Zemskaya Army are subject to the rules of general international law on troops of a foreign power subject to internment. That is to say: if ordered by me troops must disarm and become refugees, whom I am asking the Chinese Marshal Chang Tso-lin to take under his protection.
2. Since my own resources are extremely limited I am making every effort to have us taken on as soon as possible to be supplied by Chang Tso-lin and of course these supplies cannot be as they were in our Army.
3. In order to live more economically on our territory while the details of our placing and our fate in China are being clarified I command that from now we should give up our rations as they have been hither to and go over to consuming such food as exists in China and which will be our diet after we cross the frontier, namely: potatoes, cabbage, rice, Chinese millet, bean oil for people and oil cake or rice and straw for horses.
4. Anyone who is not agreeable to taking on our future status as refugees living in China I suggest should take thought now and leave the ranks of the Army, since it will be too late to think of this after we have given up our arms. I shall share the common lot of the soldiers in the Army and of course will do all in my power to improve our general position.
5. The families now living in Chinese Hanch'un must accept the supplies made available for them from the inhabitants by order of the Chinese authorities. Only for the first few days can I allow them to supplement in some measure the children's food by giving them tinned milk, so that the change-over to more difficult conditions shall not have a sharp effect on their health.
6. I must remind all ranks of the Zemskaya Army that compared to our nearest and dearest, acquaintances and friends who have remained against their will in Soviet Russia all these years, we have here not experienced or suffered any real needs. The time of need is coming for us also when we must bear our privations courageously without losing our organisation or *esprit de corps*. We must show that we are strong

not only as warriors against the Soviets but also as brother warriors sharing our common lot.

The weak must leave the ranks now.

Lieutenant-General Diterikhs
Major-General Petrov, Chief of Staff

DOCUMENT 5.9

By the end of October Diterikhs had realised that the international situation was not going to improve and the Chinese authorities were never going to agree to him crossing the border in military formation. So he proposed to cross the border, surrendering his arms not to the customs authorities but to Marshal Chang Tso-lin's own representatives, a small face-saving gesture.

It is worth noting that Diterikhs had already reduced his expenditure from 40 kopecks a day to 20 kopecks a day.

RGVA, f. 40189, op. 1, ed. khr. 6, l. 11

Telegram from M.K. Diterikhs to Colonel Lovtsevich on the need for the Zemskaya Army to cross the frontier and head for Chilin [Kirin] without the permission of the Chinese military leadership

To Colonel Lovtsevich

Copy to General Verzhbitskii.

If I receive no answer from Mukden by 1 November, then I will be forced to cross into China on my own say so. My destination is Chilin [Kirin]. Warn the garrison commander so that the customs officials do not ask the columns to surrender their arms. This would, in any case, be impossible. As I said: I will surrender the weapons myself when and where the marshal decrees. Since there is nowhere to settle in Hanch'un, the army will pass through it and, without delay, march for Chilin [Kirin]. Families will leave from 1 November. We are being supplied for now on local resources at 20 kopecks for a human and 15 kopecks for a horse. We must hurry to Chilin [Kirin], before the frosts come. Prepare information about villages on route.

30 October 1922, no.534, Novo-Kievsk

Ruler Diterikhs

DOCUMENT 5.10

This document is self-explanatory. Clearly not all Diterikhs' troops were as disciplined as he hoped.

RGVA, *f.* 40189, *op.* 1, *ed. khr.* 6, *ll.* 52–3

Operational order to troops of Zemskaya Army on necessity for troops to observe precisely demands made by the command staff to avoid conflicts with Chinese authorities

No.542/operational, Customs post, 1 November 1922

To all:

In my operational order No.195 for wagon trains to cross into Chinese territory on 1 November it was laid down that there should be as few men as possible with the wagons and absolutely no arms or cartridges. It has nevertheless occurred that the Chinese customs, examining one group of Siberian cossacks, counted more than 300 infantry, which makes up a quarter of the entire complement of the group, and many rifles, cartridges and grenades were taken from them. This indicates to me that either the command staff exercise no supervision over their subordinates, or those in charge do not realise how essential it is to carry out my demands to the letter.

To avoid me being placed in a false and complicated international situation and being exposed as a trickster in front of the Chinese authorities, I warn you that even more complicated international circumstances may await us in the future and if, thanks to my orders not being carried out, I am to be shown up as a deceiver to the Chinese authorities, they will cease to trust me and they will then have perfect grounds for any arbitrary actions they may wish to take.

Ruler Diterikhs
Chief of Staff Petrov

DOCUMENT 5.11

By 2 November it was clear to Diterikhs that his forces were to be disarmed. Even this final plea for the most modest of forces was rejected.

RGVA, f. 40189, op. 1, ed. khr. 6, l. 13

Telegram from M.K. Diterikhs to Colonel Lovtsevich

To Colonel Lovtsevich

Tomorrow on 2 November the troops cross over into China and will surrender for safe-keeping their arms to representatives of Marshal Chang Tso-lin's military command.
I would like to retain the arms of officers and an escort of 20 men. This is covered by the international agreements. The front of the column will arrive at the Chinese customs post at 8 a.m. My staff will be at its head. I await your reply.

1 November 1922, No.1355

Diterikhs

DOCUMENT 5.12

In this document Diterikhs first addresses the problem of how to retain some degree of organisation among what had become simply a group of refugees. At this stage he was clearly thinking in para-military terms, with regiments and commands being retained.

RGVA, f. 40189, op. 1, ed. khr. 7, l. 8

Order of Zemskaya Army *re* personnel of units changing to refugee status and receiving political asylum in territory of foreign State and for the preservation of the Army's military structure under these conditions

No.5, Chinese Hanch'un, 3 November 1922

Under international law the Zemskaya Army, once it has surrendered its arms, ceases to be a military organisation and becomes a group of refugees receiving asylum on the territory of a foreign state.

In order to preserve our internal organisation and make for an easy solution of supply problems and other practical details I order:

1. General Molchanov's groups of refugees from the Volga to make up 4 regiments: (a) Railway, (b) of the Kama River, (c) of the Volga and (d) Moscow.

2. General Borodin's group of Siberian cossacks – 2 regiments: (a) Orenburg and Uralsk, (b) Siberia and Trans-Baikalia.
3. Establish units of supply for the regiments – a common fund for all squads forming part of each regiment; names of those in charge of each supply unit to be communicated to the Army staff.
4. Artillery Regiment to be disbanded and men reassigned to appropriate regiments.
5. Families of present groups and regiments to be assigned to regiments, while families of the Spassk, Yegersko-Uralsk Regiment and Ussuri Cossack Squad remain as hitherto with families of Siberian Cossack Group.
6. Under the care of General Zoshchenko leave only the families of the Siberian Rifle Group, whose leaders are interned in Pogranichnaya [the town where the Chinese Eastern Railway crossed from Vladivostok into Manchuria *en route* for Harbin and Chita].
7. Keep the command post for the time being in the town of Hanch'un, but reduce its strength to 50 men and 10 horses, since it is now carrying out only general police duties. Send all spare men to their own units and hand over 46 horses to General Zoshchenko to carry the families of the Siberian Rifle Group.
8. All local carts bought by me to be placed at the disposal of the Army staff for their reassignment should the need arise to families of the Siberian Rifle Group. General Zoshchenko to collect information on these carts in the command post and present reports to me.

Lieutenant-General Diterikhs
Chief of Staff Major-General Petrov

DOCUMENT 5.13

In this, the first of two addresses to his followers, Diterikhs outlines the state of affairs after the Army's disarming. Several things strike the contemporary reader. First, we learn a lot about Diterikhs's world view. His anti-semitism was unabashed; he was firmly convinced that the Bolsheviks were Jews. But this was a religious anti-semitism; Jews were the killers of Christ and so their rule was by definition the rule of the anti-Christ.

We also learn that Diterikhs clearly still had hopes of Chang Tso-lin. He believed that Chang's attitude towards the Zemskaya Army was simply a result of the current international circumstances, which might change in 'the next few months'. As was noted in the introduction to this section, the key issue here was the future of the Chinese Eastern Railway and its security zone; unless this was 'neutralised' by Chang Tso-lin's administration, barred to both Reds and Whites, the Bolsheviks were determined to establish Soviet control over it. Two other small points need to be noted: first, spending per day was likely to be reduced still further, from 40 kopecks to 20 kopecks and finally 8 kopecks; and second, final agreement on what sort of organisation could exist in China had not been reached.

RGVA, f. 40189, op. 1, ed. khr. 6, II. 62–3

Address by the Leader [voevoda] *to the Zemskaya Army*

No.1, Chinese Hanch'un, 4 November 1922

The Soviets' occupation of the Maritime Province region has made the political situation very unfavourable to us, irreconcilably opposed as we are to the anti-Christian tyranny and socialist communism of that regime. Other states in the world, out of fear for their own peace, had already reached various compromises with those fanatics of the Jewish tribe who now actually control power in Soviet Russia. These other states are now finally shaken in their political and national firmness of purpose and are forced at the official level to distance themselves from us in every possible way, so as not to risk being thought of as defending those who have clearly demonstrated by their four-year battle their hostility to the followers of the anti-Christ regime.

Our position will also be difficult in this province of China under the sway of the Chinese Marshal by the name of Chang Tso-lin. It will be difficult for two reasons: first because I do not have the resources to sustain the whole mass of men with their wives and children who have left the Maritime Province. You will all in the near future have to make do with what the Chinese give us for nourishment. Second because, at any rate for the next few months, Chang Tso-lin, perhaps against his own wishes, cannot show us as much kindness and goodwill as we might have previously expected, knowing as we do that he himself is definitely an irreconcilable opponent of the Soviet regime. He is, however, too weak physically to have openly hostile relations with the new masters of the Maritime Province. It is partly the Japanese who force his hand in many aspects of policy as they do with us. Therefore he will be able to look on us purely as refugees until there is a change in his own political fortunes, which have been generally weakened by taking us in to shelter in his territory.

We cannot but be grateful to him for the shelter he has given us, and we cannot shirk trying to help him out of the difficult political circumstances which have been created, for how far we succeed in this governs the fate of the whole mass of people who have been faithfully answering the call of duty in the ranks of the Zemskaya Army.

From information which I have received during the last few days I am forming a clearer picture of the difficulties which we shall have to face in the near future. In the first place, in order to prevent Soviet power being established in disputed Russian-Chinese territory (the so-called security zone), Chang Tso-lin, evidently by agreement with Soviet representatives, has had to neutralise this zone on condition that access to it will be barred for both Reds and Whites entering from the Amur River Territory. Therefore any former military personnel trying to reach Harbin from Vladivostok through Korea are not allowed further than Ch'angch'un.

In the second place I expect that it will be demanded of me as Ruler to re-organise the Zemskaya Army in such a way that seen from outside it should not resemble a military organisation, but officially can be seen only as a refugee organisation. The basis for this has already been established with the unconditional surrender of all our arms. To agree further conditions General Din has been ordered to come to me for talks and he should arrive in Hanch'un on 6 or 7 November. When he arrives we should see clarified the conditions under which all the Chinese authorities will hold us. I learned today how much the Chinese in charge spend per day on feeding their soldiers (apparently 8 kopecks), whereas we at the moment, even after reducing our ration, are spending 21–5 kopecks a head. Accordingly, in the not too distant future we shall have to get used to a completely new kind of diet, since it is hardly likely that the Chinese will spend more on us than on their own men, for that would be unjust towards the mass of the nation who have taken us into shelter. We must be prepared for this modest level of food and be prepared to bear with courage any limitations decreed from on high.

In my decrees and orders I have never concealed the truth and I have called each fact and circumstance by its proper name, defining it as my conscience told me to and as my faith in Christ prompted me. I am doing the same now in the harsh circumstances in which God has punished us.

Why has this punishment from God been visited upon us – why must we too suffer the poverty, the privations and the sad fate of our brothers, dear ones, children, mothers and fathers who have remained during these years in Russia under the monstrous Soviet regime?

Many people are probably exercised by this question and each one of us tries to find his own answer as things appear to him, as each according to his capacity meditates on events, circumstances and causes.

I too will give you my answer, my brave fighters, so dear to me and close to my heart, as to what I think about this question, in which I can clearly discern the causes and reasons God has sent us this punishment.

I shall reply in my next messages to you.

Lieutenant-General M. Diterikhs, 4 November 1922

DOCUMENT 5.14

In this second address to his followers, Diterikhs asks who is to blame for their defeat, and in so doing reveals much about himself and his ideas. Some of the culprits he seizes on are fairly obvious, such as disagreement and squabbling among the various White forces, and between army commanders and politicians. But the striking feature of the address is Diterikhs' argument that these occurrences were simply reflections of a much deeper malaise; everyone was to blame, because the army had been inspired simply by hatred of the Bolsheviks rather than the Christian love of mankind.

The other striking feature of the address is his profound misconception of the nature of the Soviet regime: 'Soviet power relies not on the feeling of people's love for one another, not on the basis of voluntary help and people giving service to one another, not on that devoted form of brotherly love which Christ preached to his disciples as he built the Christian unity of people on earth, but is based on violence, despotism, coercion, and bending the will of the majority to the evil will of a minority'. Of course, the Soviet regime was despotic, as many documents in this collection show, but equally most idealistic young communists were motivated by ideas of brotherly love and self-help.

Only at one point, then, when he talks of the White forces paying insufficient heed to being creative, does Diterikhs come close to explaining the defeat. If the White armies had addressed the social problems of Russia by advancing some sort of Christian socialist programme, it is just possible they might have competed with the idealism which inspired so many young communists and retained popular support; but for that to happen, the Orthodox Church would have had to have been a very different organisation from that which existed in 1917.

RGVA, f. 40189, op. 1, ed. khr. 6, ll. 65–6

Address by the Leader to the Zemskaya Army

No.2, Chinese Hanch'un, 5 November 1922

Who is to blame?

All Russians who the last four years have been in the anti-Soviet camp are divided into two basic categories: first those with arms to hand, who are actually fighting and dying at the front in White military formations, and second the unarmed population in the rear areas, who by what they hold dear count themselves, as is commonly said, among the enemies of Soviet power and the Soviet regime. There have always been ten times more of this second category than of the first. Those in the first category have always demanded that the second category should support their forces, while the second category have considered themselves as being at the core of anti-Soviet state organisations; they have done much preaching and propaganda work and think that they are duty bound to defend those in the first category to their last breath and the last drop of their blood. When hard times came for the insurgent White state organisations, those at the front accused those in the rear of not supporting them and failing to lend them strength at the critical moments, while the second category accused the first of insufficient firmness, of quarrels between the units and their commanders, of the commanders being incompetent, of the unreliability of some persons in the military formations and so on.

Indulging in these mutual recriminations both the first and second category were rolled back as a close entity, rolled back to the ocean, could not make a stand and, now thrown right out of their country, they have fetched up in foreign lands and in the unbelievably difficult circumstances of being refugees abroad. In the terrible desperation of their existence they are faced with the questions: 'Who is to blame?', 'Why has God visited such a punishment upon us?', 'Is everything finished for us?' – or if it is not, then 'Where does our salvation lie and how do we revive our mighty beloved Mother and Fatherland?'

My dear comrades-in-arms, it is on these questions that I wish to share with you my thoughts and feelings.

Who is to blame?

When Christ's disciples, meeting those blind from birth, asked their teacher 'Who is to blame that these people were born blind – they or their parents?', Christ replied 'No one is to blame, but it is so that God's glory should be manifested in them. I am telling you the truth, the very truth, if you do not believe me you will all perish also.'

As members of both the insurgent White camps I have mentioned above, we too must be blind, as those others were blind from birth, if we believe firmly – have faith at this very moment in the strength and might of God's work and His almighty will that we shall be saved through His glory, by the glory of God and not by any human agency, such as that which has blinded us all throughout the whole four years of our fight against the Satanic power of the Soviet monsters.

If we are blinded by that human glory there is the answer to the question: 'Who is guilty?' Everyone was blinded by it, both those who died at the front and those who perhaps did nothing and in no wise helped in the rear.

How was that glory manifested? Insomuch as I affirm that we were blinded by human glory thus far were we all guilty, every single one of us, notwithstanding the fact that thousands of our soldiers sacrificed their lives honourably in the struggle, while thousands of others valiantly spilt their blood for the cause they believed in and to which they had dedicated their lives. None of you doubted for a minute, nor do you doubt now, that Soviet power is founded mainly on denying that Divine Force has any meaning in this world as a Higher Ruler over all earthly phenomena and the conditions of our life, that it denies the significance of religion, faith and Church. None of us is in any doubt that, as a social regime instituted under the conditions of our earthly life, Soviet power relies not on the feeling of people's love for one another, not on the basis of voluntary help and people giving service to one another, not on that devoted form of brotherly love which Christ preached to his disciples as he built the Christian unity of people on earth, but is based on violence, despotism, coercion, and bending the will of the majority to the evil will of a minority. It follows therefore that Soviet power for all of us Christians is a power of anti-Christ, and the fight against it is a religious fight, a fight for our faith, and our Church.

If this fight is a religious one then we must base it on lofty principles, on morality, on religious uplift: not only of us all collectively, but also of each separate man out of the general mass of White insurgent organs of state.

Now let each one of you lay his hand on his heart and looking back over the past answer sincerely and faithfully whether throughout the whole four-year struggle you were inspired by a strong religious feeling; did you acknowledge with your whole being and your whole soul that you were fighting for the Faith, for Christ, for love of those closest to you? That you were consecrating your life and spilling your blood for a conscious, lofty, holy ideal, for the idea of pure moral motives and bright, clear heartfelt feelings?

No, it was not so. Remember the Urals, Omsk, Chita, the Pacific Far East. Were there then ideals of a Christian struggle? Were there ideals of sacrificing oneself in the name of others, in the name of brotherhood through all our body of men, in the name of 'laying down his life for his friends'?

There was no such consciousness, no such faith, no such love. We fought inspired not by any feeling of love for one another, not with any consciousness that the Lord's cross was raised over us, but with a deep terrible feeling of savage irreconcilable hatred against Soviet power. Our soldiers died not with a consciousness of dying for boundless love of their neighbour, but with a feeling of relentless hatred for their enemy, and it was from that hatred and not from love that they drew strength for the fight, for martyrdom, for suffering and death. This main feeling of hate stifled all other feelings and if at times we turned to God, turned towards the Holy Writ which he gave to mankind, we did that in words, but not with our hearts and passionate burning faith. We consecrated ourselves to Christ's service with words, but not with feeling, not with all our being.

And in this mistaken emotion which overrode our other feelings we became blind men, for we went about in the battle just feeling our way, but not consciously, in the name of some great idea. We were possessed only by a burning desire to wipe out the enemy, to expunge him from the face of Russia. We paid little heed to being creative or to conducting our struggle for our friends and brothers relying only on our Christian faith; we did not feel that nor think of it, since hatred of the enemy was blinding us.

We were all guilty of being thus blind, both those who fought at the front under arms and those who created the White insurgent organs of state. People argued and quarrelled among themselves, accused each other of being at fault for secondary causes, caught each other out in little human foibles, competed with each other in the activities of this world, sought honours and heroic deeds, and vied with each other in the pursuit of glory – glory to distinguish one man from another, purely human, earthly glory.

We all went blind and forgot that the only man who can count himself a believer and follower of Christ, a fighter for ideals and the holy basis of man's existence on earth, is he who seeks glory from God and not glory from men, as they strive to gain glory one from the other. 'How can you have firm faith when you take glory from one another and do not seek the glory which comes from God alone', says Christ. We thought ourselves Christians in the fight against the anti-Christ force of Soviet teaching; we thought we were sons of Christ's teaching and followers of his precepts on love, but we were blind in our hatred for the enemy, hatred which obscured the deep roots of our Christianity, thus making us all blind men.

In just such an unprincipled, soulless blind struggle we went through the grievous events of the Urals, Omsk, Chita and Vladivostok. Towards the end of our time in the Amur River Region the bright star of Christ's mighty resurrection in us tried to enlighten us in the idea of a struggle for Faith, Tsar and Country, but it was already too late to grow into the bright flame of the all-conquering purifying fire of our spiritual potency. The four preceding years of grievous struggle pursued only in hate, blinded by our spiritual darkness, in spite of many glorious pages of human warfare in our past, overlaid the hearts of all the White insurgent soldiers and servants of the word with too thick a cover of coarseness, callousness, egoism and envy. The little star shone with its bright and majestic radiance and left only its unfading traces and memories in the history of two camps of blind people fighting each other. Then it swept away into the infinite space of the Almighty Creator, and will reappear over the Russian land when we are purified from our blindness by suffering need, hunger and poverty, when we shall realise and be aware that we are blind through our own fault. Then we shall see our way clear to taking on the only true glory in our earthly struggle with anti-Christ – the glory of the Only God.

Who is guilty in the Lord's punishment that has been visited upon us?

All of us! We are all guilty, for we were all blind and have been blind from the outset of our struggle with Christ's enemy.

M. Diterikhs

DOCUMENT 5.15

After Diterikhs' talks with Chang Tso-lin's representatives on 6–7 November it became clear that the Chinese would not tolerate even a paramilitary style of organisation for the refugees, and so Diterikhs issued this order transforming the Zemskaya Army into a new, but very ill-defined organisation. There were not to be officers, but the 'conscious' would know who the officers were.

Diterikhs still clung desperately to the belief that the international situation might change, making it essential to preserve some sort of organisation; thus he was determined not to embarrass the Chinese with any premature operation into Soviet territory. Ironically, much of his insistence on 'consciousness' and elders having the confidence of the masses parodied Bolshevik practice.

RGVA, f. 40189, op. 1, ed. khr. 6, ll. 67–8 [extracts]

Directive of Ruler Diterikhs

To General Lokhvitskii; copy to General Smolin

With the transfer of the Zemskaya Army across the border and the surrendering of our arms to the Chinese military authorities, the Army ceases to be a military organisation and its main internal task becomes simply to preserve as far as possible the existing internal cohesion of the units, since, on the one hand, amongst those soldiers who trust us the idea must not develop that in these difficult circumstances the officers are abandoning their men, and on the other hand, a degree of organisation is desirable among the refugees so as to ease the problems of dislocation, supply and undertaking various jobs.

To this end it is most important to keep in the organisation only those officers and rank and file soldiers who:

1. in the sphere of ideology will never surrender to Soviet power;
2. want to remain in a group, not because they always have been, because they want to do nothing and receive a ration, but who are fully conscious of the fact that the time has come when starvation and cold face us, and that without work we will have nothing;
3. sincerely abandon, albeit temporarily until the international situation changes, all attempts to continue secret political work among the refugee organisations, except work emanating from the command staff.

To achieve this I categorically prohibit the retention of any kind of military unit or the struggle to form units.

Today that simply does not respond to the circumstances, for in the coming months life in China will be so hard that we will survive it without grumbles, agitation and internal unrest only if we consciously address ourselves to the problem now, and, in the realm of ideology, search for solutions which will preserve the ranks of our organisation.

For the sake of the distant future, our organisation must purge itself, **throughout** its ranks, of everything that is the least bit lacking in consciousness, unideological, and therefore of no use to us in the future.

I will allow no adventurist plans or undertakings.

Facts are facts: we lost the 1918–22 stage of the struggle and are interned in a foreign country as refugees. That is the starting point for our future struggle – the liberation and restoration of a Great Autocratic Russia . . .

No one in China can consider us a military organisation and it is in our interests to help them out of their difficult situation as soon as is possible, helping them by organising the refugees (from the Army). This must be understood from the very beginning, and we should ourselves create the new forms of organisation which will allow the Chinese to say that it is an organisation of refugees and not an army. Thus there can be no place for ranks, and officially everyone will simply be a refugee, not a general, officer or soldier. Officially there can be no question of separating officers and soldiers. But internally, amongst the ideologically conscious elements, there are officers and generals and that will remain the case. I will be the only exception, since I was and will remain the Ruler, but will no longer be the Leader.

We have no resources, and have to base ourselves exclusively on what the Chinese can supply . . .

In the immediate future I give all local leaders the following task: to care for people and to seek work.

So, at the head of each group of refugees all local leaders should appoint an elder, someone who is popular among the mass of people and is capable of organising their work and relaxation. Groups are to include officers, soldiers, women and children. Those senior local leaders who are not elders should assign themselves to a suitable group.

Those people who do not wish to submit to this decree are excluded from our organisation and will have to organise their own fate.

All horses and all material, once our state property or the property of individual military units and administrative organisations, are to be sold on my order to provide for the needs of the organisation.

I have got rid of my own horses.

Reports and telegrams should not be sent to me, but to Colonel Baftolovskii.

14 November 1922, Chinese Hanch'un, No.663

DOCUMENT 5.16

This document is reproduced as evidence of the gradual dislocation of the Zemskaya Army in its new guise, as Diterikhs had to cope with those who preferred to go home. No doubt there were incidents of this type, and no doubt this specific incident was inspired by Soviet black propaganda; but the most significant thing about this document is its date, for by the end of December 1922, far from travelling on to Chilin [Kirin] or Harbin, the Zemskaya Army refugees were still holed up in the provincial backwater of Hanch'un.

RGVA, f. 40189, op. 1, ed. khr. 7, ll. 26–7

Order of the Zemskaya Army replying to a letter from a group of officers who have deserted from the Army accusing the Force Commander of peculation and calling for our return to Soviet Russia

No.21, Chinese Hanch'un, 25 December 1922

The Commander of the Volga Group has handed to me an anonymous letter inscribed by its authors: 'Please distribute amongst soldiers and officers'.

In any sound and honest organisation of honest men the correct method for informing all ranks of news and communications is by a Notice in Orders. This was the way we were instructed in the pre-Revolutionary period and this is the way I have proceeded and intend also to proceed now. I am therefore promulgating herewith the contents of the letter which has been brought to my attention.

If its authors really were honest men they would have given me earlier their accusations against Colonel Sotnikov, before their secret flight, to have these accusations cleared up publicly in an honest way, by an open enquiry and an open Order of the Day. However, they did not do that, but had recourse to a stratagem favoured by thieves, scoundrels and Bolsheviks, namely to slander, spread foul underhand rumours and hide themselves away.

Dear Fellow Sufferers

We are leaving the Army today and I will say our last word to you in this letter. No matter how much I wanted to say this to you earlier it was completely impossible because otherwise they would have killed me straight out and you would still have been none the wiser. You probably still think that we are going away to Chilin [Kirin] and Harbin. Some of you may even think that apparently we have been

The Final Curtain

robbing the Quartermaster and now we are leaving. No, brothers. We are going away, not to Harbin, but to where we are summoned by our duty and our conscience, to Novo-Kievsk and on into Russia. The mighty Russian people have spoken: they will not seek revenge for what is past, they call us to come back and to work for the restoration of our country, laid waste by the Civil War. And now we are going where everyone must return if he has even the slightest trace of conscience, if he has not yet forgotten that he is a son of the great revolutionary people.

Now I shall tell you who has led you here and who is leading you now. All these men with their shoulder straps of generals and colonels are rogues, political adventurers and criminals who are building their good fortune on your blood. One person of this type is your commander Colonel Sotnikov, whom many of you may trust even to this day. I'll tell you what I know about him as former Quartermaster of part of the Kama Regiment:

1. During the campaign in Khabarovsk, Sotnikov did not account for 1540 gold roubles. He got through this money for his own drink and his own pleasure, and to cover up the shortfall it was said that this sum had remained with Colonel Turkov who was killed. That is not true. Turkov died with nothing in his pocket.
2. When Sotnikov went away to Vladivostok after he was wounded you were soon all informed that the regimental Paymaster Lieutenant Nazarov had lost public funds at cards. That is also not true: the money was lost not by Nazarov, but here too by that very same Sotnikov. He lost 1780 roubles, but to save the honour of the colonel of the General Staff, Nazarov for a certain pay-off took the blame on himself. How much he was paid off I don't know.
3. Junior Ensign Smirnov was appointed Paymaster to succeed Nazarov, from whom Sotnikov managed to take and lose another 500 roubles. When I got back from the front and found all this out I put an end to all this gambling, threatening otherwise to reveal all his crimes. From that time there began;
4. Small robberies of 10–15 roubles which Sotnikov took from me against his signature. These small sums built up again to a sum of 1448 roubles, but that is still not all; there were sums which he was receiving without letting me know. In this fashion Sotnikov stole 1540 + 1780 + 1448 = 4760 roubles.

Now inevitably the questions arise, how could such sums pass unnoticed and where in general did such money come from?

When the regiment was in Novo-Kievsk in the autumn of 1921:

Galvanised iron sold for	600 roubles
For demolishing a building	200 roubles
For hay sold in Razdol'ny	800 roubles
Total	1600 roubles

In the daily log Sotnikov did not show this sum as income and it was as though it had never been. As I have already said, during the Khabarovsk campaign out of the sums allowed for operational and quartermaster's requirements Sotnikov spent 1540 roubles on his own pleasures, pretending that this sum had been lost with Turkov. The rest of the money which was short was written off against officers' and soldiers' pay, which Sotnikov got as a total for all those who were killed, taken prisoner, went missing or deserted, and against the money allowed for soldiers washing in the bath house, for stores and equipment and other regimental necessities.

If it were not for the retreat from the Maritime Province region Sotnikov would be in prison now for robbery and other crimes on duty, and would not take you all in with his honeyed tongue as he has done hitherto. Just think what is going to happen to you with leaders such as Sotnikov – for most of them are like that. You will go on starving and shedding your blood, while behind your back the parasites and criminals will still be fed. Don't believe all their promises about work, that's just eyewash. The criminal generals are preparing the ground for other adventures in which your blood will be spilt again and once more the scoundrels will start their drunken debauchery to your misfortune.

Think about what I have said to you, and if you yourselves can do nothing with criminals such as Sotnikov then come to where we are going. But the criminals will not escape the people's justice; sooner or later they will be brought to book for their misdeeds.

Fare you well, Grenadon. Smirnov. Arnol'd.

God will be a judge on your foul slander. The loss of money has been investigated in good time and the officer in charge of the Volga Group will make an announcement about this in his Order of the Day. Soldiers and officers of the Zemskaya Army, now that you know the contents of the letter, I just want to say to you:

The authors of the letter, appealing to your 'conscience' for you to return to Soviet Russia, remind you that you are 'sons of the great revolutionary people'. Neither in the past, nor now, nor in the future have

I, your senior commander, ever belonged, do belong or ever shall belong to a 'revolutionary people' and for five years I have been battling with the monsters of the Soviet regime in Russia for the very reason that I consider myself not as a son of a revolutionary people, but a son of the mighty Russian Christian people who, due to our sinful ways, have fallen temporarily under the rule of those monsters of the human race, the Bolsheviks and those sons of the monstrous anti-Christ religion of **LIES**. I have never concealed this from you and in the cathedral before all the people of Vladivostok I have publicly affirmed my Faith in Christ by swearing to remain faithful to the Christian nation of Russia as it has made its history.

I reject the vile naming of the Russian people as a 'revolutionary people'. The nation to which God gave me the great fortune to belong, has been, is, and will remain solely a Christian people. If the monster leaders and supervisors have exploited it as a mass which had little understanding of politics for their malicious, cruel revolutionary aims, ruining and destroying the wonderful, mighty structure of the Russian State, then they have in no wise prevailed over its Christian principles.

I know of only one revolutionary people: that is the people of Israel, who in punishment for their abnegation of Christ God scattered thus depriving that revolutionary Jewish people of their state, for a 'revolutionary people' cannot form and hold together any sort of unitary state. Therefore, as I publish this letter, I am repeating to you now also, soldiers and officers: any of you who are not agreed with my opinion that the Russian Christian people at present find themselves enslaved by the Soviets, anyone who supposes that he belongs to some sort of Russian 'revolutionary people' – let him depart from me, depart into the Amur River Region away from your leaders, who have been fighting the Bolsheviks for five years solely with the hope and faith of helping the Christian Russian people to free themselves from the monsters of the anti-Christ tribe.

I have given you no promises for your future, as I give none now, and I have not tempted you by any promises of work to remain with me and your leaders. Work can only be promised by someone who proposes to open and set up some sort of enterprises, mills or factories. But I could not promise you that, if only for the reason that we are in a foreign land and I am the same type of humble refugee as you are.

I have only one care about organisation and only one enterprise to set up, namely to form and preserve a group of people tightly knit by pure, old Russian Christian faith. For a Christian believer work is something which lives within him: if he wants to work he will find work, but he never counts on someone else being bound to provide work for him. If he has a worthy faith that everything proceeds from God then work will appear also. It is only the godless Bolsheviks who have promised the Russian people that they will provide them peace, work and riches. But in place of work what have they provided? Slavery, persecution, ruin, hunger and cannibalism . . .

I will avail myself of the present invitation from the Bolsheviks to say to you once more, soldiers and officers, while we are still close to the frontier: think well, search your hearts – and let those who do not feel able to proceed by faith alone, simply by the faith of finding comfort in any trials we may face, any hunger and cold, let them turn back and depart from us: you are not our brothers, you are not the sons of Christ's Russia; as the authors of the letter say, you are the sons of some sort of 'revolutionary people' – but a people I do not recognise.

This Order to be made known to all soldiers and officers.

Lieutenant-General Diterikhs
Provisional Chief of Staff Lieutenant-Colonel Baftalovskii

Index

agrarian policy: of Bolsheviks, ix, xiii, 45, 47–51, 53–4, 56–7, 67, 83–4, 99, 108, 113, 127–32, 139, 148, 160–1, 165, 170, 175 (*see also* Labour Armies; peasants); of Directory, 28–31, 175; of Komuch, 21
All-Russian Council of National Economy, 131, 138, 142
All-Russian Executive Committee of the Soviets, 56, 91, 162
All-Russian Provisional Government (appointed by Directory), 11, 13–18, 34; Council of Executive Ministers of, 16
Allied Armies, Higher Supply Council for the, 25–6, 36
Allied Czechoslovak Legion, *see* Czechoslovak Legion
Allied interventionist forces, x, 1, 3, 18, 33, 42–5, 134; impact on Russian Civil War, 43; ships arrive (November 1918), 43; support for Denikin, 45, 47; withdrawn (1919–20), xii, 175, 193
Allies: commitment to restoring united Russia, 43; relations with Directory, 25, 35; relations with Komuch, 4–5, 8–9, 11, 17; relations with Siberian Government, 9, 11; relations with Urals Government, 9; relations with URR, 9, 11; *see also* British; French; USA
Altay Province, 31–2
Amur River Region, 183, 194, 199, 205
anarchists, 82–3, 85–6, 89; *see also* Greens; Makhno; Revolutionary Partisan Army
Anglo-Russian alliance, proposed (1918), 2–3, 5, 8

anti-semitism, 82–3, 87, 192–3, 205; *see also* pogroms
Antonov-Ovseenko, Commander V.A. (Red Army), 80–9
Archangel: and British Military Mission, 2, 5, 9, 23, 42; and Allied landings, 45, 147, 171; insurrection (1918), 23
Argunov (URR), 9–10
Astrakhan, 92–4, 96, 110–11; inter-ethnic tension in, 92, 110
Austria, *see* Germany

Baftolovskii, Colonel (Zemskaya Army), 201, 206
Balashov, 78, 102
banks, 35; and Bolsheviks, 22; and Directory, 27; and Komuch, 22–3
Bek-Mamedov, Colonel (Zemskaya Army), 179, 184
Beloborodov (Bolshevik), 69–70, 100–2; organises Tsar's execution, 100
Bessarabia, 85, 157–9
Bogaevskii, A.P. (Don cossack leader), 46, 74–5
Bogolyubov (SR), 9–10
Boldyrev, General (Directory), 13–15, 25
Bolshevik Government, 38, 126, 143–4, 159, 178, 193–4; *see also* Bolsheviks; Bolshevik regime
Bolshevik Party (Communist), vii–viii, 47, 93, 97–8, 144, 150, 158, 161, 164, 174
Bolshevik Party Central Committee, 2, 45, 49–52, 55, 57–9, 71–3, 75–6, 92, 98–9, 108, 110, 153, 172
Bolshevik Party Organisational Bureau, 47, 49–50

207

Index

Bolshevik regime (Soviet Russia), xi, 36, Ch. 4, 193–9, 202, 204–6
Bolsheviks, vii–xi, xiii–xiv, 1, 5, 7, 21, 23, 32, 39, 41–2, 54, 172–4; and Bessarabia, 157–9; and British Empire, 157, 159; and capitalist countries, 151; and Chang Tso-lin, 178, 193–4; and cossacks, Ch. 2, 89, 91–2, 99, 110 (*see also* decossackisation); and Diterikhs, 192; and disagreements within leadership, 125, 141; and Don Rebellion, Ch. 2; and Greens, xiii, 82–92; and Left SRs, ix, 176; and Mensheviks, 164; and October Revolution (1917), ix, 1, 20, 102, 165, 177–8; and Poland, 157; and political work, *see* commissar system; and Romania, 157; and rural population, ix, 45 (*see also* agrarian policy of Bolsheviks; peasantry); and socialism, *see* socialism, Bolshevik construction of; and SR Party, 160, 164; and terror, *see* Terror, Red; and trade unions, 125–6; Army, *see* Red Army; dissolve SR and Menshevik soviets (1918), 2; economic policy, *see* economic policy of Soviet regime; fuel policy, grain requisitioning, industry, NEP, oil; relations with Britain, 1–2, 8, 158, 160; relations with Czechoslovak Legion, 15; relations with France, 1–2, 80, 158–60; relations with Germany, x, 1–2, 38, 47 (*see also* Lenin; Treaty of Brest-Litovsk; (Trade) Treaty); relations with Japan, xii (*see also* Far Eastern Republic; Maritime Province); urban policy of, ix; war against SRs, ix–x, xiii, 1–3, 20, 175
Bolshevik Revolutionary Military Council (oversaw Bolshevik war effort), Ch. 2, 83

Bolshevism, ix, xiv, 45, 48, 50, 72, 89
Bonch-Bruevich, General M.D. (Red Army), 131–2
Borisoglebsk, 73, 100
Borodin, Major-General (Zemskaya Army), 179, 183, 192
Breshkovskaya, Granny (URR), 9–10
Brest-Litovsk Treaty (March 1918; Bolsheviks and Germany), x, 1–3, 5, 8, 45, 85
Britain, relations with anti-Bolshevik forces, 158, 160
British Cabinet: and proposed Anglo–Russian alliance, 2–3; breaks links with Bolshevik Party and supports anti-Bolshevik forces (May 1918), 8; supports democrats (post-First World War), 42–3
British interventionist forces, xii, 44–5, 158, 175
British Military Mission, 23–5, 39, 175; to support Bolsheviks against Germans, 2; *see also* Poole, General
Brushvit, I.M. (Komuch), 6–7, 22

Cadet Party, 8, 89
capitalism, Bolshevik views on, 150–1
Caucasus, 65, 125–6, 147, 156, 158–9
Chang Tso-lin (Manchurian war-lord) and Zemskaya Army evacuation, 178, 181–2, 185–6, 188–9, 191–4, 199; and Bolshevik talks over Russo–Chinese territory dispute, 194
Ch'angch'un, 177–8, 194
Chechens, 66, 110
Cheka (Extraordinary Commission for Combatting Counter-revolution, Sabotage and Speculation), Bolshevik secret police, 37–40, 42, 54, 84, 103–6, 112–13, 121–3
Chelyabinsk, 4–6, 9–11, 19, 31, 34, 134–5; talks between Komuch

Index

Chelyabinsk – *continued*
  and Siberian Government
  (15 July 1918), 6–8
Chelyabinsk State Conference (1918),
  11, 25
Chilin [Kirin], 178, 182, 186, 189, 202
China, 164; and evacuation of Zemskaya
  Army, 178–94, 199–201
Chinese Eastern Railway, 178, 192–3
Chinese regiments (supporting
  Bolsheviks), 38
Chita, 178, 192, 198–9
Chkheidze, N.S. (Menshevik), 158
'class war in the countryside',
  Bolshevik policy of, in Ukraine,
  83, 86; *see also* decossackisation;
  agrarian policy of Bolsheviks
commissar system (Bolshevik political
  education), viiii, 36, 48, 54,
  56–8, 71–3, 75–8, 82, 84–5,
  87–8, 90–101, 103–4, 106–7,
  122, 129, 134, 136, 138, 140,
  142, 148–50, 173
Commissariat of Labour, 21, 126
Committees of the Poor, 50, 56, 80,
  83, 85–6, 89
communes, agricultural, 129
Communist Party, *see* Bolshevik Party
Comrades Courts, 72, 95–6
Congress, Third, of Peasants, Workers
  and Partisans, 86–7
conscription of labour, Bolshevik
  policy of, 131–6, 138–40, 142,
  152, 154, 156–8, 160–1, 164–5,
  167–8, 172
Constituent Assembly, x, 3, 14, 44,
  117; and All-Russian Provisional
  Government, 16–17; and
  Directory, 11; and Komuch, 4–7;
  armed units, 18; Battalion, 14;
  Bolsheviks close down (January
  1918), x, 1; Congress of
  Members, 10–11, 14, 18–19;
  elections permitted by Lenin
  (November 1917), ix, 1, 3;
  forces loyal to, 42–3
co-operative movement and
  co-operatives, 13, 26–7, 29–32,
  34–5, 117–18, 129, 160, 164

cossacks, 18, 91–2, 110–11; Don,
  xiii, Ch. 2; forces, committed to
  democracy, 20, 41–2, 45–6; in
  Krasnov's forces go over to Red
  Army, 46–7, 53; in Zemskaya
  Army, 179–80, 185–6, 190, 192;
  loyalty to Russian autocracy, 51;
  proposed Bolshevik mobilisation
  of, 64; soviets, Bolshevik
  establishment of, 50, 56
Council of People's Commissars, 137
Councils of People's Deputies, 38
credit unions, 31–2
Crimea, xi, xii, 44, 124–5, 169
Cunningham (British consul, Samara),
  23–5
Czechoslovak Legion, 3, 9–10, 17,
  25, 104–5, 124; and Diterikhs,
  177; and Komuch, 18; joins with
  SRs against Bolsheviks, 3,
  14–15; turns against Bolsheviks
  (1918), x; withdrawn (end 1919),
  175
Czechoslovak mutiny (June 1918),
  3–4, 177
Czechoslovak National Council, 17–20
Czechoslovak Republic, impact of
  creation on Czech involvement in
  Russian Civil War, 17–20

decossackisation, Bolshevik policy of,
  47–53, 58–9, 66–7, 75
Denikin, General (White), x–xi, 87,
  89–90, 93, 100, 117, 158, 175;
  and Don Rebellion, xiii, 45–7,
  49, 54, 59, 63, 65–6, 71, 75, 77,
  80; and advance from Don,
  86–7, 89–90, 93, 100; Bolshevik
  defeat of (1920), xi, xiii, 86,
  112, 124, 150, 151, 157–8;
  see also Don Rebellion
Denikin's Army, Ch. 2, 86, 89–90,
  100–2, 124, 158, 175; *see also*
  Don Rebellion
Desertion of soldiers, xiii, 37; Red
  Army, 69–71, 94–7, 108–13,
  149, 167; Revolutionary Partisan
  Army, 88–9; Zemskaya Army,
  202–4

Directory, xii–xiii, Ch. 1, 68, 117, 175; formation of (1918), 11–13, 15; relations with Administrative Council of Siberian Government, 12–13; deposed by Kolchak (1918), 17, 36, 43
Diterikhs, General M.K. (White administrator of Maritime Province; leader of Zemskaya Army), xii, 194; analyses own defeat, 195–9; and Chang Tso-lin, 178; and difficulties of financing Zemskaya Army, 186, 193; and disarmament of Zemskaya Army, 187–93; and disbanding of Zemskaya Army, 192–3, 200–6; and evacuation of Zemskaya Army to China, 179–86, 188–93; and Japan, 193; and Maritime Province, xiv, 176–8; *see also* Zemskaya Army
Don (river and region), ix, xi, 4, 9, 45–7, 49, Ch. 2, 82, 89, 113, 120, 158, 175
Don government (White; headed by Denikin), 118
Don rebellion (led by Denikin – Spring 1919), xiii, Ch. 2, 99, 160, 175; *see also* Denikin; Denikin's Army
Donbas, 125, 163
Donburo (underground Bolshevik organisation), 47, 49–53, 55–6, 58–9, 68, 72
Donets Basin, 62, 81
Donets (river), xi, 47, 58, 61–2, 68, 71, 73, 76, 80
drug abuse 121–3
Dutov, General (Siberian cossack leader), 18–19
Dybenko, P.I. (Bolshevik), 85–6, 88
Dzerzhinskii (Chairman of All-Russian Cheka), 40, 42, 137
dzhigits: and Bolsheviks, 94–6; and inter-ethnic tension, 95

economic policy: of Directory, 26–36, 133; of Komuch, 21–3; of Soviet regime, 21–2, 67, 116, 124–32, Ch. 4; *see also* Five Year Plans; NEP
Ekaterinburg, 9–10, 14, 16, 30, 100, 134–5, 142–3, 146; liberated by Czechoslovak Legion (1918), 9
Ekaterinoslav Province, 86, 90
engineers, Bolshevik need for, 166–8, 170
Entente Powers (Britain, France, Russia, USA), 147, 164

Far Eastern Republic (established by Bolsheviks to assuage Japan; nominally independent), xii, 176; Army, 176–7; Constituent Assembly elections (January 1921), 176; government, 176; votes to be incorporated into Soviet Russia (November 1922), 178
Filippovskii (Komuch), 12–14
First World War, impact of on Russian Civil War, x, 151; impact of armistice (11 November 1918) on Russian Civil War, 17, 42, 45–6, 82, 102, 151
Five Year Plans, Soviet economic strategy of, 160, 166
food and supply shortages amongst general population, 37–38, 78–9, 127–9, 188, 194, Ch. 4
French interventionist forces, xii, 43, 158; Red Army defeat of, in Ukraine (March 1919), 80, 82; withdrawal (end 1919), 175
French Military Mission, 25, 43–4, 175
Frunze, Commander M.V. (Red Army), 169–70
fuel policy of Bolsheviks, 135–6, 142–3, 147–9, 151, 161

Gaevskii (Labour Army), 133–6, 138–43, 145–6, 150–2
Galkin, General (Bolshevik), 13, 137
German Army, occupation of Ukraine, 2, 85; *see also* Treaty of Brest-Litovsk

Index

German embassy, evacuates Moscow (1918), 37–8
Germany: evacuates Don region (November 1918), 45, 80; possible overthrow of Bolshevik regime, x
Gilan, Soviet Republic of (established Northern Persia, May 1920), 126, 157
grain requisitioning, Bolshevik policy of, 38, 80, 83–4, 124, 126, 145–9, 151
Green Army, 89–90; *see also* Revolutionary Partisan Army
Greens, xiii, 82–92; *see also* anarchists; Makhno
Grigoriev, Major N. (established Soviet but not Bolshevik Ukraine, May 1919), 80, 82–5; Bolshevik relations with, 82
Guinet, Colonel (French Military representative), 4, 6
Gulyai-Pole, 86–8

Hanch'un, 178, 180–9, 191–4, 196, 201–2
Harbin, 34, 176–8, 192, 194, 202–3

Imperial Army, *see* Tsarist Army
industry, Bolshevik policy on, 127–31, 133–4, 143, 147–8, 151, 158, 161–5
informants, Bolshevik, 107; *see also* Cheka; Special Section
Irkutsk, 28–9, 32, 34–5; SRs and Mensheviks seize power (January 1920), 124; Red Army secures (March 1920), 124
Iudenich, General (White), xi
Ivanovo-Voznesensk, 147, 158

Janneau (French consul, Samara), 4–6
Japan: and Far Eastern Republic, 176; controls Maritime Province, xii, 176; evacuates Maritime Province (October 1922), xii, 176–8; relations with Bolsheviks, xii, 176–8; relations with China, 193; and Far Eastern Republic, 176; relations with USA, xii, 176
Japanese troops, 176
Jews, *see* anti-semitism; pogroms

Kalmyks, 66, 73–4
Kamenev, Commander-in-Chief S. (Red Army), 155–6
Kazan, 38, 42, 125; falls to People's Army (August 1918), x, 39; Red Army recaptures (September 1918), 39, 41, 68
Kerensky (Prime Minister of Provisional Government), ix, 151
Kerensky's Provisional Government (1917), ix, 4, 7, 151
Khabarovsk, 203–4
Kharkov, xi, 90
Kherson province, pogroms in, 82
Khodorovskii, T. (Bolshevik), and the Red Army, 58–68
Khoperskii, 51, 54, 67; insurrection, 55
Kiev, 81; pogroms in, 82
Kirghiz, 94–5
Klimushkin, I. (Komuch), 12, 22
Knox, General (British Military Mission), 25
Kolchak, Admiral (White), x, 13, 19, 25, 71; advances from Siberia (1919), xi, 122; arrested and executed (February 1920), xii, 124, 175; defeat of (1920), xi–xii, 112, 124, 150, 152, 157, 175, 177
Kolchak's Coup (seizes power from SR democratic administration in Siberia and establishes military dictatorship, November 1918), x, xii, 17–20, 25–6, 36, 41–3, 175, 178
Kolchak's forces, 73–4, 80–1, 124, 152, 175
Kolchak's government, 177; toppled (January 1920), 175
Kolegaev, A. (Bolshevik), 52, 68–71, 77
Komuch (Committee of Members of the Constituent Assembly), xii,

Komuch – *continued*
  3–5, 10, 16, 20–1, 23, 25, 41; administration for Ufa and Urals, 11–12; and British Military Mission, 23; and Bolsheviks, 7–8, 20; and Germany, 5, 8; and Left SRs, 7–8; and proposals for All-Russian Government, 6–8; and Whites, 5; commitment to democracy, 5–6, 8, 19–20; commitment to United Russia, 4–8, 16–18; Council of Departmental Administration, 18–19; Council of Departmental Directors, 12–18, 20; dissolution of (1918), 11; Financial Council, 22; Labour Office, 21; plans for army to fight Bolsheviks, 5, 8 (*see also* SR Party); relations with Allies, 5, 8; relations with Britain, 23–5; relations with Czechoslovaks, 17–20; relations with France, 4–5; relations with Siberian Government, 4–8, 11; relations with Urals Government, 5; relations with URR, 9–10
Korea, 177, 185–6, 194
Kornilov, General L. (White), ix, 45; attempts to seize power from Kerensky (August 1917), ix
Kozlov, 47, 56–7, 62
Kozlovskii (Bolshevik), 109, 137–8
Krasin, L. (Bolshevik), 77, 79, 127–32, 137
Krasnov, General P. (Don cossack leader or ataman, pro-German), 4–5, 45–7, 50, 59, 63
Krol, L. (URR), 9–10
Kronshtadt, 38; rebellion (March 1921), xiv, 175
Kuban, ix, xi, 43–6, 66, 73–4, 89, 124–5
Kuban Regional Parliament, committed to All-Russia, 44

Labour Armies (formed 1920), xiv, Ch. 4; to control all aspects of economic and social life, 125, 133, 136, 138, 140–2; Labour Councils of, 144, 153, 155; Technical Councils of, 144
labour mobilisation, Bolshevik policy of, *see* conscription of labour
Lebedev (Bolshevik), 156, 169
Left SR Party, 7, 68; and anarchists, 86; ends alliance with Bolsheviks, 39; in Ukraine, 83–7, 89; Lenin promises to form coalition government with (1917), ix
Lenin (Bolshevik leader), vii, ix, 68–9, 77, 80, 85, 89, 103; and Anglo-Russian alliance, 2; and Constituent Assembly, ix, 1; and co-operatives, 160; and cossacks, 48, 59; and Labour Armies, 125, 137–8, 143; and labour mobilisation, 172; and NEP, xiii–xiv, 124; and peasantry, xiii, 49; and Red Terror, 102; and relations with Germany, x, 2, 39; and Soviet regime, xi, 2; and Trade Treaty with Germany, 39
Lockhart, Bruce (British agent), 8–9
Lokatskov (Bolshevik), 133, 145–6, 150–2
Lomov (Bolshevik), 127–32, 137–8
Lovtsevich, Colonel (Zemskaya Army), 181–3, 185–6, 189

Maiskii, I. (Menshevik; Departmental Director for Labour, Komuch), 7
Makhno, N.I. (anarchist; leader of Revolutionary Partisan Army), 82–3, 85–8, 90; *see also* anarchists; Greens; Revolutionary Partisan Army
Manchuria, 178, 182, 192; Soviet–Japanese talks (organised by USA), 176–7
Maritime Province, 177; Japanese control of, xii, 176; Soviet occupation of, 193; White campaign, led by General Diterikhs (October 1922), xiv; White government established (May 1921), xii, 176–7; White retreat (1922), 204

Index

Markovna, Paulina (Cheka), 121-3
Matiyasevich (Red Army; creator of First Labour Army), 133-6, 138-41, 145-6, 150-2, 156
Mensheviks, 1-2; 158, 164; and soviet elections (1918), 2; with SRs arrest Kolchak (1920), 124
Mikhailov, I.A. (SR economic adviser to Kerensky; Minister of Finance in Siberian Government), 7, 9, 11-12, 14-15
Military-Labour Revolutionary Committee (Bolshevik), 160-3
Millerovo, 47, 57, 63
Milyutin (Bolshevik), 127-32, 137
Mironov, F.K. (Red Army), 67, 72-3
Molchanov, General (Zemskaya Army; White government, Maritime Province), 176, 179-80, 183, 191
Morozovskaya, 52, 63, 67
Moscow, xi, 2-3, 35, 45, 47, 49, 79, 84, 92, 122, 125, 134, 141, 147, 158, 169; failed Left SR uprising (1918), 39; food shortages, 37-8
Mukden, 186-7, 189
Murmansk, 2, 171
Muslim population, relations with Bolsheviks, 92-3, 96; *see also* dzhigits

Nakhichevan, 116-18
Nesterov, I. (Komuch), 12, 22
New Economic Policy (NEP), adopted by Lenin (March 1921), xiii, xiv, 124-6, 160
Novo-Kievsk (Krasino), 180, 183, 185, 187, 189, 203-4
Novocherkassk, 45, 65, 74, 114, 120

Odessa, 38, 84
Omsk, 3-4, 6, 9, 15-17, 20, 25-8, 30-4, 37-8, 135, 198-9; taken by Bolsheviks (November 1919), xi, 124, 175; *see also* Siberian Government
Operations Section (Cheka), 104-5, 122
Orenburg, 13, 31, 37

Orenburg Government (democratic, anti-Bolshevik, 1918), 6

Pares, Sir Bernard (British, author of *My Russian Memoirs*), 26
partisan warfare, 90-1; *see also* anarchists; Greens; Makhno; Revolutionary Partisan Army
peasant anarchist groups, 82-3, 89
peasant disturbances, xii-xiii, 3, 175
peasant rebellions (Spring 1921), xii, xiv, 124, 175
peasant resettlement, Bolshevik policy of, 49, 53, 56-7; *see also* decossackisation
peasant socialist groups, 82
peasantry, 159, 173; and Bolshevik mobilisation of (non-Cossacks), 63-4, 66-7; and Labour Armies, 139, 144, 146, 148-9, 151-2, 157-8; and Left SRs attempt insurrection, Ukraine (1918), 83-4; and Red Terror, 80; and relations with Bolsheviks, 63-4, 66-7; 85, 98, 126, 160, 164
People's Army (SR; Komuch), ix-x, 10, 14, 18, 20, 39, 68; Ufa Accord proposes merger of with Siberian Army, 12, 25
People's Commissariat of Agriculture (Bolshevik), 131, 138
People's Commissariat of Economic Affairs (Bolshevik), 130, 166
People's Commissariat of Education (Bolshevik), 165
People's Commissariat of Internal Affairs (Bolshevik), 132, 154
People's Commissariat of Labour, 132, 137-8, 142, 154, 169
People's Commissariat of Supply (Bolshevik), 137-8
People's Commissariat of Transport Communications (Bolshevik), 131, 142, 154
Penza, 3, 38
Perm, 10, 30, 79
Persia, 159; *see also* Gilan
Petlyura, Commander S.V. (Ukrainian Nationalist forces), 80-1, 90

Petlyura's forces, 90
Petrograd, ix, xi, 2, 38, 125, 147, 157-9, 164-5, 169
Petrograd Soviet, 2, 157, 165, 168, 170
Petrograd strikes (February 1921), xiv, 175; (1918), 2
Petrograd Technical Institute, 166-7, 170
Petrov, Major-General (Zemskaya Army), 181, 185, 189-90, 192
pogroms (Grigoriev unleashes against 'Jew-Communists'), 82-4, 87; see also anti-semitism
Poland, 153, 157
Polish War (Polish Army invades Russia, April 1920; armistice signed October 1920), xi-xii, xiv, 124-6, 153, 172
Politburo, 48, 125, 153
political crimes, xiii; see also Terror
Poltava Province, 90; pogroms in, 82
Poole, General (British Military Mission), 2-3, 5, 9, 23, 39; see also British Military Mission
Popov (Bolshevik), 127-32
Popov, Lieutenant-Colonel (White), 119-20
Popular Socialist Party, 8, 10
Posyet, 177, 179-80, 185
propaganda: Bolshevik, viii-ix, xiii, 26, 72, 74, 91-93, 102, 108, 178, 202; cossack, 52; Left SR, 84; SR, 164; White, 74, 196

railway construction and restoration: Bolshevik policy on, 135, 142-3, 151, 165, 167; Directory's policy on, 28
Rakovskii (Bolshevik), 83, 87
Red Army (Bolshevik), viii-xiii, 37-8, 42, 46-7, 50-1, 58-70, 82, 89-90, 92-112, 122, 136, 159, 161, 165-6, 168, 173, 175, 205; and agricultural labour, 126-32; and Bolshevik propaganda, xiii; and Don rebellion, Ch. 2; and Labour Army, 137, 140, 146-53, 155-6, 162-3, 169-72; and Ukraine, 85-6; and Whites, 134, 157-8; defeat of Diterikhs, 183-4, 186-7, 189; demobilisation of, 130, 164; hold Irkutsk (March 1920), 124; Party cadres, 172-4; Political Department, 72; Revolutionary Tribunal, 23, 149, 168; supply shortages, 74, 76-9, 87, 89, 92, 96-100, 108, 113, Ch. 4
Red Cavalry, xi, 61, 63, 94, 99-100, 124, 146, 148
'Red technicians', 165-6, 170
Revolution, October (Bolsheviks seize power, October 1917), ix, 1, 20, 102, 165, 177-8
Revolution, Russian (February 1917), ix, 20
revolution, world, belief in imminence of, ix, 112, 126, 156-7, 159
Revolutionary Military Council of the Republic, 125, 131, 133-4, 142, 153, 171
Revolutionary Partisan Army (Green; led by Makhno), 85-8, 90; see also anarchists; Green Army; Makhno
Rostov, 37, 45, 65, 74, 113-18; Red Army take (January 1920), 124

Samara, 3-6, 8, 13, 23-4, 29, 31; fall of, to Bolsheviks (October 1918), 15, 41; housing crisis (1918), 23-5; uprising, SR led (June 1918), 39, 41
Samara Committee of Representatives of Commercial Banks, 22-3
Saratov, 51, 95, 97
Sereda (Bolshevik), 127-32, 137
Serpukhov, 80, 103, 106
Sevastapol, xii, 43-4
Shmidt (Bolshevik), 127-32, 137-8
Shmidt O. Yu. (Bolshevik), 127-32, 137-8
Siberia, x-xi, 3-4, 29, 31-5, 147-8, 150, 152, 175, 177; Bolshevik control of, xii, 176; Bolshevik economic policy in, 127, 133-4,

Siberia – *continued*
136; events of 1918, 1, 118;
Kolchak's military dictatorship
in, x (*see also* Kolchak); White
governments of, 178
Siberian Army, 20; Ufa Accord
proposes merger with People's
Army, 12, 25
Siberian Government (formed 1918;
anti-Bolshevik; refused to
combine with Komuch), 4, 9,
14–15, 25, 33, 36; relations with
Allies, 4; relations with Komuch,
4, 6, 11; relations with Urals
Government, 9, 16; dissolution of
(1918), 12
Siberian Government Administrative
Council, 11
Sklanskii (Bolshevik), 59, 137–8
Skorapadskii (White; head of
pro-German government in
Ukraine), 4–5
socialism, construction of under Soviet
regime, xiv, 124, 126, 138, 141,
145, 147–52, 160, 166, 172, 193
socialist planning, xiv, 160; *see also*
Five Year Plans
Sokolnikov, G. Ya. (Bolshevik),
49–51, 55, 58, 63, 68–70
soviets, 37, 52, 83, 89, 113, 148,
172–3; Bolsheviks to dissolve
those in SR and Menshevik
control (1918), 2; elections to,
2–3
Soviets, Congress of Peasant, Makhno
attempts to organise, Ukraine, 86
Soviets, Fourth Congress of, 1
Soviets, Seventh All-Russian
Congress of, 91–2
Special Section, The (Red Army
equivalent of Cheka), 39–41, 93,
106–12
SR Party (Socialist Revolutionaries;
peasant socialists), ix–x, xii,
1–2, 4, 7–10, 20, 39, 50, 83,
160; alliance with Czechoslovak
forces against Bolsheviks (1918),
3–4; alliance with Mensheviks,
1–2; and Brest-Litovsk Treaty,
1–2; arrest of Kolchak, 124;
commitment to Constituent
Assembly and democracy, x, xiii,
1–3, 16; relations with Directory,
11; relations with Lenin, 1–2;
relations with URR, 9; right
wing of, 8; working class and
peasant support for, 1–2
SR Party Central Committee, 15
SR Party leadership, 3; arrest and trial
of (1922), xii, 175
SR Volunteer units, 14–16; 20
SR war against Bolsheviks, ix–x, xiii,
1–3, 20, 175
Stalin (Bolshevik), viii; and
collectivisation, 160; and Five
Year Plans, 166; and Labour
Armies, 153–5, 169; and NEP,
125; and relations with Germany,
2; and period of his rule, viii;
and strikes: Petrograd, (1918), 2;
(February 1921), xiv, 175;
railway, possibility of (1918),
13–14, 20
Suglitskii, N. (Bolshevik), 71–5
Syrovoy, General (Czechoslovak
forces), 13, 19
Syrtsov, S.I. (Bolshevik; head of
Donburo), 49–52, 55–6

Tambov, 51; peasant insurrection
(Spring 1921), xii, xiv, 175
Teodori (Bolshevik), 44, 103–5
Terror, Red (Bolshevik), ix, xiii,
36–42, 102–8; and cossacks,
49–50, 52, 55, 67, 75; and
Ukrainian peasants, 80; within
Red Army, 101; *see also*
decossackisation
Tkhorzhevskaya, Lidiya, 118–21
Tomsky (Bolshevik), 127–32, 138
Treaty of Brest Litovsk (Lenin and
Germany; March 1918), x, 1–3,
5, 8, 45, 85
Treaty, Trade (Lenin and Germany;
August 1918), x, 39
Trotsky (Bolshevik Minister of War),
viii, xi, 3, 42–3, 59, 80; and
desertion, 112; and Don

Trotsky – *continued*
  rebellion, 64, 70; and Labour Armies, 125–33, 136–8, 141–50, 153–6; and mobilisation of labour, 172; and proposed alliance with Britain and France (1918), 1–2; and terror, 39
Tsar's execution (July 1918; Ekaterinburg), 9, 100, 177
Tsar's monarchy, ix, 53, 176–7; White support for, 199
Tsarist Army (Imperial Army), 83, 103–4
Tsaritsyn, 46, 49, 56–7; falls to Denikin (June 1919), xi, xiii, 45, 77, 107; State of Emergency (1918), 37
Tsaritsyn province, 56
Tsereteli, I.G. (Menshevik leader, Georgia), 158

Ufa, xi, 13–17, 25, 31; Kolchak's offensive against (1919), 80
Ufa Accord (1918), 11–12, 16
Ufa State Bank, 13
Ufa State Conference (September 1918), 11, 14, 17, 25
Ukraine, 4, 71, 80–92, 125; and Labour Army, 153–5, 169–70; conscription into Kolchak's army, 74; German/Austrian occupation of, and imposition of reactionary dictatorship, under terms of Brest-Litovsk Treaty (1918), 2, 38–9, 80, 82–3, 85; Left SRs attempt to organise peasant insurrection (March 1918), 83; Red Army defeat in (1919), 65; 'Soviet' not Bolshevik regime established by Major Grigoriev (May 1919), 80, 82–3
United States, interventionist forces, xii; withdrawn (end 1919), 175; *see also* Allied forces
United States, relations with Japan and Far Eastern Republic (1922), 176
Upper Don District, 46, 65, 89
Urals, 31–2, 105, 152, 198–9; and Bolshevik economic policy, 133–6, 140, 142–3, 147–8; and events of 1918, 1, 16
Urals Government (democratic; anti-Bolshevik), 5–6, 9–10, 13, 33
Uralsk, 130, 135, 140, 142
URR (Union for the Regeneration of Russia), 8–11; and British Military Mission, 23; relations with Komuch, 9–11

Vatsetis, Supreme Commander-in-Chief I.I. (Red Army), 77–81, 102–6, 131
Vedenyapin, M.A. (Departmental Director for Foreign Affairs, Komuch), 9, 12, 14–16
Verzhbitskii, General (Zemskaya Army; Maritime Province Government), 176, 180, 183–5, 189
Veshenskaya uprising (1919), 50, 52
Vladimirskii (Bolshevik), 127–32, 137, 154
Vladivostok, 3, 27, 35, 176, 178, 192, 194, 199, 203, 205; Allied interventionist forces route, 42, 45; Czechoslovak forces overthrow Bolsheviks (1918), 42, 45; White government (1920), 176, 178
Voitsekhovskii, General (Czechoslovak forces), 10, 19
Volga, x–xi, 23, 38–9, 45, 81, 105, 108, 118; and events of 1918, 1, 3–4, 9
Vologodskii (leader in Kolchak's coup), 17–18
Volskii, V. (Komuch president), 9, 14, 22
Volunteer Army (White; pro-Allies), 37, 45–6

'war communism', Bolshevik policy of, 124–5, 147, 160
White: armies, vii–viii, 37, 90, 108–9, 114–16, 124, 147, 195–6; collection of levy from local capitalists, 116–18;

Index 217

White – *continued*
generals, viii–x, xiii, 1, 42, 175; officer brigades, 9, 19; refugees (Zemskaya Army and their families), 178–81, 183–4, 187–9, 191, 193–4, 196, 199–202, 205; supply problems, 113–16; *see also* Denikin; Diterikhs; Don rebellion; Kolchak; Kornilov; Krasnov; Skorapadskii; Volunteer Army; Wrangel; Zemskaya Army
Whites, ix, 91, 94, 178, 195–6; and Bolsheviks, 175, 195; and democracy, ix
'Workers' Opposition' (to labour mobilisation), 172
workers' rebellions (Spring 1921), 124
workers, skilled (specialists): Soviet need for, 127–30, 132, 134, 141–2, 148, 161, 168–70; Bolsheviks suspicious of, 160, 165
world revolution, Bolshevik belief in imminence of, ix, 112, 126, 156–7, 159, 172

Wrangel, General P.N. (White), launched attack on Bolsheviks, during Polish War, xi–xii, 86, 124–5, 169; exiled (November 1920), xii
Wrangel Campaign (1918), xi, xiv, 86

Yudenich (White), Bolshevik defeat of (1919), 157, 160

Zazupsbyt, 31–3, 36
Zemskaya Army (led by General Diterikhs), 177; cavalry, 179–80, 183, 186; lack of supplies, 182, 186–9, 191–4, 200–1, 204; final retreat, 178–84; evacuation to Manchuria, 185–99; disarmament, 185, 188–99; disbandment, 191, 194, 200–4
Zenzinov (Directory), 12–13, 15–16
Zinoviev (Bolshevik leader) 126, 156–60, 165–6
Znamenskii (SR), 12–13, 15